Faith and Meaning in the Southern Uplands

LOYAL JONES

UNIVERSITY OF

ILLINOIS PRESS

Urbana and

Chicago

Unless otherwise noted, the photographs
in this book were taken by the author.

Library of Congress Cataloging-in-Publication Data
Jones, Loyal, 1928–
Faith and meaning in the southern uplands / Loyal Jones.
p.   cm.
Includes bibliographical references and index.
ISBN 0-252-02431-1
ISBN 0-252-06759-2 (pbk. : alk. paper)
1. Appalachian Region—Religion. 2. Ozark Mountains—Religion.
3. Piedmont (U.S. : Region)—Religion. 4. Christian sects—
Appalachian Region—History. I. Title.
BR535.J66   1999
277.69—ddc21   98-25359
CIP

For my parents, George Alec Jones and Cora Morgan Jones,

my brothers and sisters, living and dead, Troy, Vertie, Elmer, Garnett, Wilma, Willis, and Nina,

and for all those who contributed to this book

Contents

Preface

This book has grown out of my unhappiness with the many articles and books that have been critical of Upland people and their religious beliefs and practices. For many years I have gathered materials that I believe give a different picture of Upland people and their faith. I have had a lot of help in this endeavor.

First of all I want to thank the ministers and lay Christians who granted interviews or allowed me to record church services and gave me permission to use their words in this book.

At Berea College I encouraged my students to interview individuals in their home communities for research papers on various topics, including religion, and I also found money to hire students to interview people during one summer. Among those who contributed invaluable interviews and other material were Garner Hargis, Kathie Bell Kiser, Gary King, Stephen Burgess, Bill Richardson, and Layna Cheeseman, plus one student who recorded Primitive Baptists but did not identify herself on the tapes and whose name has been lost.

Since colleagues knew what I was doing, some offered interviews they had done. I thank Jeff Todd Titon, John Wallhausser, Herb E. Smith, Mike Yarrow, and the late Joyce Ann Hancock for such material. Several other people gave me books, articles, recordings, and other important items. I thank Elder W. J. Berry and Mrs. Mabel Berry, Elder John Sparks, the Reverend Fred Lunsford, Jess D. Wilson, Brother Alfred Carrier, Virginia Hall, Sister Sue Cox Cole, Mrs. Henkle Little, and the folks at the Church of God Mountain Assembly.

I appreciate the help of the staff of Special Collections in the Hutchins Library at Berea College—Gerald Roberts, Shannon Wilson, Sidney Farr, and the student workers. I also appreciate help from Katherine R. Martin in getting copies of interviews from the Oral History Project of Alice Lloyd College, and permission from Dean Wallace Campbell of Alice Loyd for permission to quote from them.

Finally, I am grateful to Judith McCulloh, assistant director of the University of Illinois Press, who encouraged me to do this book and Bruce Bethell, who did a great editing job.

In doing this book, I have come to accept Thomas Carlyle's statement, "It is well said, in every sense, that a man's religion is the chief fact with regard to him."

Faith and Meaning in the Southern Uplands

Introduction

> Jesus saith unto him, Thomas, because thou hast
> seen me, thou hast believed: blessed are they that
> have not seen, and yet have believed.
>
> —John 20:29

On Monday morning, May 19, 1902, at 7:30 A.M., just after the area's miners had gone to work, an explosion ripped through the Fraterville Mine at Coal Creek, Tennessee, killing 184 men. Most of the miners died instantly, but some survived into the afternoon hours, when they ran out of oxygen. Several of the latter wrote notes to their families or to the families of those who died with them. Their thoughts were on loved ones and the hereafter.

From Powell Harmon:

Dear Wife and Children:
My time is come to die. I trust in Jesus. Teach the children to trust in Jesus. May God bless you all is my prayer. Bless Jesus it is now 10 minutes till 10 and we are almost smothered. Don't know how long we will live but it is our time to go. I hope to meet you all in heaven. May God bless you all wife and children for Jesus sake good bye until we meet to part no more.

From Jacob L. Vowell:

We are shut up in the head of the entry with a little air and the bad air is closing in on us fast and it is about 12: o'clock. Dear Ellen, I have to leave you in a bad condition. But dear wife set your trust in the lord to help you raise my children. Ellen, take care of my little darling Lily. Ellen, little Elbert said that he had trusted in the Lord. Chas. Wood says that he was safe if he never lives to see the outside again he would meet his mother in heaven. If we never live to get out we are not hurt but only perished for air. There is but few of us here and I don't know where the other men is. Elbert said for you all to meet him in heaven. All the children meet with us both.

My Boys, never work in the coal mines. Henry and Condy be good boys and stay with your mother and trust for Jesus sake.

From John Hendren:

Dear Darling Mother, Brothers and Sister:

I have gone to heaven I want you all to meet me in heaven. Tell all your friends to meet me there and tell the Church I have gone to heaven. Oh dear friends don't grieve over me because I am in sight of heaven. Oh dear stay at fathers or your fathers and pay all I owe if possible. Bury me at Pleasant Hill if it Suits you all. . . . This about 1 1/2 o'clock. So Good bye dear loving father, mother, Brother and friends. I have not suffered much yet, your boy, brother.

For Henry Beach:

Alice, do the best you can. I am going to rest. Good bye Alice. Elen, darling Good Bye for us both, Elbert said the Lord had saved him. Do the best you can with the children. We are all praying for air to support us but it is getting so bad without any air. Horace, Elbert said for you to wear his shoes and clothing. It is now 1/2 past 1.

Powell Harmon's watch is in Andy Woods hand. Ellen I want you to live right and come to heaven Raise the children the best you can. Oh! how I wish to be with you. Good bye all of you. Good bye. Bury me and Elbert in the same grave by Little Eddy. Good Bye Elen Good Bye Lily, Good Bye Jimmie Good Bye Horace. We are together. Is 25 minutes after Two. There is a few of us alive yet JAKE & ALBERT.

Oh God for one more breath. Ellen remember me as long as you live. Good Bye Darling.

From Scott Chapman:

I have found the Lord. Do change your way of living. God be with you Good Bye

From James A. Brooks:

My Dear Wife and Baby
    I want you to go back home and take the baby so Good Bye. I am going to heaven. I want you to meet me there.

From Geo. Hutson:

To Geo. Hutson's wife—If I don't see you no more bury me in the clothing I have. I want you to meet me in heaven Good Bye. Do as you wish.[1]

These letters were written at a time when most American mainline denominations were in the process of sending hundreds of missionaries into the Southern Uplands to save people who were seen as lost to mainline religion and perhaps to God also. Many of these missionaries were unimpressed with our religious life and sometimes even appalled by it. Their purpose was to change us through a better religion. In the process, to raise money and to get denominational support, missionary entrepreneurs produced many tracts, articles, books, and fervent speeches about the inadequacies of mountain religion and of mountain people themselves. Although there was truth in many of their assertions, they usually presented a worst-case scenario and thus created and perpetuated negative stereotypes.

Most of the missionaries whom I have met, and probably those who went before them, were fine people who truly wanted to give mountain people a choice in their religious lives and to provide schools, clinics, and social services, which were sorely needed. I feel, though, that some of these workers never really understood or liked the people they described and to whom they tried to minister. Their attitudes sprang from both cultural and class differences. These same attitudes were held toward other lower- and working-class rural people, foreigners, blacks, and Native Americans. Yet there was something about Appalachia that caught the attention of more people, so that stereotypes about mountain people became prominent.

For many years American Christians have perceived this region in dual ways: as an unchurched area with people who have little religion or an inadequate faith or as part of Mencken's Bible Belt, with many small unacceptable fundamentalist churches and fervent believers. Upland Christians have usually been seen as having little similarity to mainline Christians. Perhaps this is partially because mountain people have persisted in their Calvinism, with its dim view of the human condition. Most Americans, imbued with a more optimistic faith, have little patience with religion that does not herald a movement toward improvement in the human condition.

The stereotypes about mountain people had taken a strong hold by the first decade of the twentieth century. Early missionaries and other travelers had reported a strange and peculiar people. Few of the later observers had the ability to observe another culture with any sense of objectivity, and religious people were particularly intolerant of religious beliefs and practices that were markedly different from their own. Henry Shapiro, in his book *Appalachia on Our Mind* (1978), suggested that missionaries created a public image of Appalachia that never corresponded to reality so as to justify and obtain support for the work they proposed to do in the region. At the time, few people questioned the work of missions to "underdeveloped people," whether they were seeking to save lost souls, to turn professing Christians from an odious fundamentalism, to educate the ignorant, or to minister to the sick.

In my view, no group in the country has aroused more suspicion and alarm among mainstream Christians than have Upland Christians, and never have so many missionaries been sent to save so many Christians as has been the case in this region. Mainline Christians believed strongly that Appalachian people had to be saved from themselves—not only from their ignorance of standard educational matters but especially from their cultural values and native religion. Hundreds of mission churches, schools, clinics, and social work programs were set up in the mountains. The educational institutions were badly needed and readily accepted because most mountain counties had only one-room schools before World War I. Clinics, hospitals, and social programs were also needed and used. I must point out, too, that many Upland Christians accepted the religious messages of the missionaries and joined their churches. I have no problem with this, because I believe people in a decent society ought to have choices in all things.

It was in religious matters, however, that tensions grew. Representatives of mainline churches were mostly unable to understand or accept much of mountain religion because it was so different in theology and in practice from that to which they had committed their lives. They had little tolerance for difference in something as important as the spiritual realm, and most of them spent scant time studying the historical and religious background of those they sought to save.

Growing up in the mountains of western North Carolina as a rural Southern Baptist and near a school that people from elsewhere had built to improve life in the community, I saw at a young age differences in attitudes about how life should be lived and how worship services ought to be conducted. The school had teachers and workers from "off" and visiting students from progressive colleges who were not shy in expressing opinions about worship and other local practices.

As a boy, eager to learn about new things yet respectful of traditional practices, I was often caught between the two camps—for example, regarding things that my culture and religion discouraged but that the newcomers promoted, such as folk dancing. I dimly remember a visit from Frank Smith, later to be my friend and teacher at Berea College, who announced at a meeting in my community that he wanted to organize and teach courses in folk dancing. I remember—or picture it in my mind as related by my father—the grim-faced Baptist deacons sitting through his presentation and my father rising to say that such a class would not be welcome. Later the school succeeded in promoting folk dancing by the device of calling it "folk games." Even Baptists had participated in children's games, such as "Ring around the Rosie" and "Way down Yonder in the Paw Paw Patch." If the music came from singing, then the activity was acceptable. If the fiddle and banjo were the source, then it was dancing, and good Christians didn't participate.

Later, after I had professed faith and was baptized into the church, I found myself in a serious bind when the annual revival coincided with special courses at the school where interesting outlanders merrily danced away the evening hours. I confess that I sometimes showed up at church to be seen and noted and then slipped away through the woods to dance a few rounds before stealing back for the windup of the revival service, sometimes troubled in mind.

This conflict between the appeal of the local with that of the "fotched-on" culture affected me in many ways, most importantly with my choice of a college. Although no one in the community had ever suggested that I go to college, when I expressed interest in attending the nearby state college, the school's director told me forcefully that if I were going to continue my education, I should go to Berea, and she then helped me to apply and administered entrance exams.

It was the best advice I ever got. My Berea education affected my life in many positive ways. The great legacy of Berea was the sense of tolerance for and acceptance of people who are different in some way. Berea's mission included the cause of black people in a hostile society, growing out of Berea's abolitionist roots, and of disadvantaged people from the southern Appalachians. At Berea I first learned about the work of anthropologists, folklorists, novelists, and others who have accepted the cultural expressions of any group of people as legitimate and important just because they are human expressions.

However, Berea also heightened my awareness of the strength of the missionary imperative, because in a fundamental sense, Berea at the time was essentially a missionary enterprise, promoting liberal Christianity linked to a strong liberal arts program. In those days Berea's radical history attracted teachers and administrators who were mostly products of liberal Christianity, a goodly number of whom were former foreign missionaries. Most had attended the best universities. They were, for the most part, from more privileged classes. We students, on the other hand, came from the working class, primarily from Appalachia, and we had to show financial need to be accepted. The educational mission, however the philosophy was expressed, was to uplift us students and to make us more like other Americans, both in values and in religion.

Later, as a graduate student at the state university, I also got an education in superior attitudes, including that institution's pride in being the oldest state university in the country and in being located in the most enlightened part of the state. On learning that my foreign language was Spanish, a department chairman who knew of my mountain origins said, "It figures," thus dismissing me, hillbillies, and the Spanish-speaking world in one fell swoop. In a similar vein, a local story was told about a classics scholar meeting a student from the mountains who was carrying a lamp. The classicist inquired, "Are you Diogenes?" "No," replied the student (in a caricature of a mountain accent), "M' name's Johnson."

We mountain people are usually modest and retiring and are hesitant to confront those with whom we disagree. Instead we may keep our own counsel and resist in other ways. There is a whole cycle of stories relating to religious differences or to the conflict between the native believer and the outside missionary. This humor allows the mountaineers to resist what they do not agree with, avoid direct conflict, keep their dignity and self-respect, and have a little fun, too:

> A missionary from up North arrived in the mountains eager to save souls. He drove up a back road and saw a mountaineer sitting on his front porch. He jumped out of his car and without saying hello said, "Brother, are you lost?"
>
> "Why, no," said the mountain man. "I've lived here all my life."

"I mean, have you found Jesus?" the preacher asked.

"Well, I live so far back up this holler that I don't hardly ever get any news. I didn't know He was lost. You know, the Bible says He's up in heaven till the Second Coming."

The exasperated evangelist said, "Are you a member of the Christian Band?"

"No, I'm not, but there is a Bill Christian lives about three miles on up the road."

"What I'm trying to find out is, are you ready for the Judgment Day?"

"Well, when is it?"

"We don't know about such matters. It might be next week or it might be next month. We just don't know."

So the mountaineer said, "Well, when you find out, you let me know, 'cause the old woman will probably want to go both days."

This book has grown out of my uneasiness in encounters I have had with missionaries (and other agents of uplift) and with the many articles and books that are critical of Upland people and their religious beliefs and practices. The people among whom I grew up in the mountains of North Carolina were devoted to and thoughtful about their religion and were profoundly influenced by it. Through religion they found meaning in their lives and hope for something beyond. Religious salvation changed people; it made them want to do better, gave them purpose, insight, and resolve, and made them more caring. It was a light in their sometimes bleak lives. For the most part, they worshiped modestly and discreetly, but at times they were overcome with joy and excitement in their faith. As much as anyone, they were aware of the deep mysteries in their lives and had many unanswered questions. Yet their faith made them largely a contented people.

I have noted too the movement toward the secular in mainstream life, with sophisticated people becoming more reticent to discuss religious matters. In contrast, many people in the Uplands are still faithful churchgoers, and they talk freely about their religious lives. Thus it appears to me that instead of being a problem, religiously speaking, Uplanders are in many ways an asset and a resource.

So a good many years ago, I began talking with a wide variety of ordinary people in the region about their faith and their ideas about God, the world, and the devil and about themselves as struggling human beings in a sometimes baffling existence. Some with whom I talked were mainline denominational people, but I concentrated on those within the small churches:

several kinds of Baptists—Southern, Primitive, Old Regular, Freewill, United—a few nonstandard Methodists, Christian Church groups, a variety of Holiness-Pentecostals, and some freethinkers not bound by any particular doctrine. I attended and sometimes recorded church services, and I also carried a radio recorder as I drove through the region and recorded religious radio broadcasts.

I pored over Baptist and Holiness-Pentecostal publications that contained articles of faith, circular letters, and sermons and testimonies that laid bare the basics of faith. I found a rich source of personal statements in the sermons, lay comment, and group discussions of sixty-four churches in seven Appalachian states recorded by the late Earl D. C. Brewer, professor of sociology of religion at Emory University's Candler School of Theology, and others as a part of the Southern Appalachian Studies of 1958–60. This study was conceived and administered by W. D. Weatherford Sr., at Berea College; financed by the Ford Foundation; and directed by Thomas R. Ford, of the University of Kentucky. The results were published as *The Southern Appalachian Region: A Survey.* I also went through interviews that the Glenmary Sisters conducted with Appalachian people to help in their study of mountain religion and studied interviews with mountain people conducted by the late Joyce Ann Hancock for the Berea College Museum. From these collections I copied excerpts of statements by mountain Christians that contained their convictions on religious subjects. The Glenmary papers, the Southern Appalachian Studies materials, and the Appalachian Museum papers are in the Weatherford-Hammond Mountain Collection and Southern Appalachian Archives of the Hutchins Library, Berea College. (Incidentally, the tape recordings and other material that I have collected for this book will be deposited in the Special Collections Department of the Hutchins Library at Berea College.)

My collection has grown over the years, and during this time I have patiently listened to a half-bushel or so of cassette tapes of interviews and church services and transcribed statements that I thought communicated ideas clearly and sometimes dramatically. This book, then, is mostly the voices of Upland Christians. I have used the real names of everyone involved, if known, except for one person who did not wish to be identified publicly with the project. I have commented on the speakers and their statements, but I have tried not to intrude in interpreting what is already abundantly clear. I have arranged the material in a way that allows the informants to comment on specific topics in chapters. The topics are as follows: the human condition, God, the world and the devil, the Word, salvation, and praise in Zion. I conclude with some additional observations.

Many of the books about Upland religion are based on written sources. This one depends primarily on oral tradition, although sources other than the spoken word were used, such as letters, written testimonies, minute books, and other materials that were locally published. Although the statements of the miners quoted in the beginning are not strictly in the oral tradition, they are in the vernacular. I believe that truly to understand Upland religion, one has to get out among the people and into their churches, where the oral tradition is of primary importance.

Religious practices in the churches with which I am concerned here are to a great extent in the oral tradition. Upland Christians listen to oral sermons, quote the Scriptures from memory, and engage in endless discussions of religion with family and neighbors. Preachers study the Scriptures, but in many of these churches they do not prepare sermons in the usual way. Rather, they expect inspiration from God to direct them to the message for the day. Biblical texts are often quoted from memory in the midst of the inspired sermons. Religion, like the folk traditions of singing ballads and songs and relating traditional tales, relies heavily on the memory and oral rather than written expression.

When quoting from the Bible, I have used the King James translation throughout because it is the one used by most of the Christians quoted in this book.

I have chosen to talk about "Upland" people rather than "Appalachians" or Southerners in general. In my study I have ranged through most of the Appalachians, but I have also visited and interviewed in the Ozarks and the Piedmont. I have thus enlarged the region with which I have been most identified—Appalachia—to include some interesting people who are a part of the groups I have studied. The term *Southern Uplands* is not a new one in Southern literature. It caught my fancy, and I decided it was a good designation for the people I quote. There is, I believe, a similarity of beliefs among the people throughout this region.

Perhaps I need to explain my frequent use of the term *mainline* in relation to churches. I mean primarily the mostly urban churches of the best-known denominations of Protestantism. I refer the reader to the bibliographic essay at the end of the book and especially to Deborah McCauley's *Appalachian Mountain Religion: A History* for the historical development of the indigenous churches of Appalachia in contrast with American mainline Christianity. This essay mentions other books that I have found useful in the study of Upland religion.

In *All the King's Men* Robert Penn Warren has Governor Willie Stark comment on the law. He says, "It's like a single-bed blanket on a double bed and three folks in the bed and a cold night. There ain't ever enough blanket to cover the case, no matter how much pulling and hauling, and somebody is always going to nigh catch pneumonia."[2] The Christian Gospel, on the other hand, is an ample blanket that covers the multitudes who tug at it, and for the most part it covers them all, of high and low estate. The Bible is an all-purpose book. It reveals some of the nature of God and the history of people on the earth, their endless journeys to find some modicum of security, and more important, their search for meaning and for God. It helps folks make sense of a puzzling, inconsistent, and cruel world, and it gives hope for a life beyond this sometimes disappointing one.

To some extent we are all egocentric and believe, like my Baptist grandmother did, that what we believe and what we do is entirely logical and supportable and ought to be practiced by others as well. On religious matters people tend to be at their most dogmatic, because religion is important to them. We all have the missionary urge to correct those whom we perceive to be straying from what makes sense to us. Some fundamentalists and some educated Christians are particularly prone to assume that those who deviate from their beliefs are lost to God and to common sense until they are converted to their way of thinking. But whether practitioners err in interpreting Scriptures, their beliefs sustain them and help them to find meaning in baffling lives, and generally Upland Christians are humble and use restraint in telling others what their religious lives ought to be.

The sociology of the thing dictates different needs and emphases for different people. Successful, tenured, insured, financially secure persons have needs different from those of marginal people who have little in their earthly existence to bring reassurance of their worth. Religion serves a need for each but in different ways and with differing intensity. The blanket of religion serves its purpose and thus can be effective in the lives of all.

Because we Christians do find comfort under the same theological blanket, we are more alike than we are different. We read the same passages from the Bible. We sing some of the same traditional hymns. We worship the same God and are influenced by the same teachings of Jesus. Each of us would find familiar words and practices in each other's churches.

We are not alike in our needs, however, whether spiritual or temporal. Our religious needs and perceptions vary according to our circumstances and our yearning to feel worthy in the sight of God, our neighbors, and ourselves. Upland Christians have struggled with faith and meaning as assiduously as any people in the country. We have sometimes wrought beliefs, or emphases on beliefs, different from those of more mainline Christians, but we are fervent believers nevertheless, and our beliefs profoundly influence our lives. Because of our differing needs, we all should become more tolerant and more accepting of one another. As Elder Frank Fugate, an Old Regular Baptist, said: "We need more tenderness now. We need people with more [for]bearance, more endurance. The weapon of God is prayer and [for]bearance with other's weakness and it's forgiveness and it is respect and honor for others and not being eager to condemn others and to always take time, because everybody's entitled to be heard."[3]

The miners at Coal Creek were simple people by the definition of some with better education and prospects. They lived relatively isolated lives. They toiled long hours in darkness with little time to "improve" themselves, but they had a faith in God, in family, in the church, and in a sense of what is right and wrong. When their day came to die, they had time to reflect, and their final thoughts were on God, their families and friends, the church, and heaven. They helped one another to communicate with their loved ones about the principles they held dear. They behaved as honorably as any other people I know about. I think of them as I think about Upland religion.

In the rest of this book, beginning with the view of the human condition, we shall hear statements of faith and belief from Christians in many kinds of Upland religious groups. They speak from the heart. Listen. Everyone, as Elder Fugate says, is entitled to be heard.

1 *The Human Condition*

And God said, Let us make man in our image,
after our likeness: and let them have dominion over
the fish of the sea, and over the fowl of the air, and
over the cattle, and over all the earth, and over every
creeping thing that creepeth upon the earth.
 So God created man in his own image, in the
image of God created he him; male and female
created he them.   —Genesis 1:26–27

For I delight in the law of God after the inward
man:
 But I see another law in my members, warring
against the law of my mind, and bringing me into
captivity to the law of sin which is in my members.
 O wretched man that I am! who shall deliver me
from the body of this death?
                              —Romans 7:22–24

We Upland people, like those in the processions before us,
wonder about our nature, purpose, and eventual destiny. We
observe others and ourselves to try to understand our erratic nature. We in
this particular place hold a view close to Reinhold Neibuhr's that the essential human tragedy is that we see clearly what we should be and do and yet
we fail consistently to bring that about. Many of us are heirs to Calvin's belief,
supported by Scripture, that we are limited creatures, and this brings a
modest view of ourselves.

 We divide our existence into two spheres, the natural and the spiritual, or as Paul and the Old-Time Baptists say, the inward person and the

outward one. Many of the religious groups in the Uplands see the natural world and our natural state regressing rather than progressing. This contrasts starkly with the mainstream educated world's usual belief that each generation is improving through religion, education, counseling, or whatever (ignoring the probability that this has been the bloodiest century). In many Upland churches there is a latter-day mentality, and evidence is always at hand to support the view that we may be regressing toward the imminent end of the world. But whatever their view of the world and the human condition, Upland people see themselves and their lives here through the lens of their religious beliefs. God is in the picture. Why did He make us, what is our purpose here, and will we exist in another form at some other time and place?

Purpose in Life

We Upland people are not reticent about the meaning of our lives here on earth, although we may not always be certain about our place in the scheme of things. Audrey Wiley, from Estill, Kentucky, is one woman with a fine certitude about our purpose and the continuing importance of the Creator in making things work:

> The purpose of life is to fulfill the plan of God. To start with, He created the heavens and the earth, and He created Adam and Eve to replenish the earth. That is the sole purpose, for God to get glory out of man. He put us on earth to get glory out of us. He's getting it in some ways. He's got some people on this earth who's going to be obedient to Him as long as the earth stands.
>
> We need more love. People don't love one another. They don't need each other anymore. You can teach a man to love, but first he has to seek after it. He must seek the Lord first, and all the other things will be added. It comes from God. I know that there are people in this world that you can't love without a greater power to make you love them. It's hard to love a person who hates you and says all manner of evil against you. It's hard, but you're looking on them with the carnal mind when you feel that way, but when you become a Christian, you're no longer speaking with a carnal mind. You see things different. God said he has created a new creature, created in you a new heart. So there is your answer. God has to be in the arrangement of everything for it to turn out right. Without Him we can't do anything.[1]

I met Herbert Barker in 1986 through his daughter Gina, who had attended a workshop in Appalachian studies that I directed. He grew up as a Presbyterian in Hazard, Kentucky, but had lived in Point Pleasant, West Virginia, for many years before his death in 1995. He was deeply religious but viewed himself as a freethinker with many questions about organized Christianity. He commented on God's purpose for us: "I think it is for us to glorify God, His intended purpose for us from the beginning. But since the time of the Fall, man has certainly gone by the wayside, and nothing short of rebirth—regeneration by the Holy Spirit—can fix a person where he can truly worship God. People say that they worship God, but Jesus said that those that worship Him must worship Him in spirit and truth, and the truth means the Word of God, the Bible."[2]

Pansy McCay was a Mt. Vernon, Kentucky, evangelist who worked in several counties, preaching and distributing clothing and food to needy people. Once a Baptist, she later embraced Pentecostalism. She had a simple statement of God's purpose for us and a belief that Christian people make the world a better place: "God's purpose for people is for us to follow Him, and read the Bible and keep His Commandments. He wants parents to bring up their children in fear and admonition of Him. 'Seek ye first the kingdom of God.' We do have Christians who are true to the Lord, or this world wouldn't be standing."[3]

Human Nature

Garfield Sloan, eighty-four years old at the time of the interview, had a pessimistic view of humankind and little affection for the world:

> Worry, worry, worry, worry. A man who is born of woman is but a few days and full of trouble. . . . Vanity, vanity, and vexation of the spirit. That's what it is. . . . You know, man's about the weakest thing that I ever read after in my whole lifetime. . . . The righteous man is tempted on every side. . . . We fight awful hard to get born into this world, but I wouldn't give a nickel to stay. . . . The Lord said that man loved darkness better than he loved light. He also said it would wax worse and worse. Well, we couldn't have hopes of it getting better and better if it waxes worse and worse.[4]

Southern Baptist minister Buell Kazee was one of the most remarkable people I ever knew. He recorded and performed Appalachian folksongs and banjo tunes in the 1920s but left show business to preach the Gospel for fifty-seven years, although he returned to folk music after he retired from preaching in the 1960s. He held to a simplicity of faith usually identified with the Old-Time Baptists, especially in regard to the fallen nature of humankind and our propensity to sin:

> Oh yes, man is a sinner. He's born that way, though. Man is born in sin, and anything he'll do is wrong. Oh, not [necessarily] morally wrong, but he's a sinner against God, because he refuses to let God do what He pleases with His own—His highest creation. . . . A man is, we say, a free moral agent, and he is a *free moral agent*, but he is not a *free spiritual agent*. Spiritually, he's bound by sin in his heart. Morality has to do with whether he obeys the laws of man—and they're made for people instead of God, you know—whether he's living according to the customs of life. Your relationship to man is *moral*. Your relationship to God is *spiritual*, and that takes a new, a re-creation.[5]

I have noticed that the perfectionism of the Methodists and Holiness-Pentecostals has permeated most churches today, even the traditionally Calvinist churches, so that a great deal of emphasis is on improving the nature of humankind and also on how religion can empower us to do better in the world. The idea of sanctification has laid a charge on people to rise above sin and improve themselves. If they can improve themselves, then they can improve human institutions and the world. Even Southern Baptists, nominally Calvinistic, have been affected by this longing for perfection (although the conservative wing now in power is working to return the church to its Calvinistic roots). Billy Graham preaches that if we would only turn to God, many of our social problems would be solved. Some so-called fundamentalists such as Jerry Falwell and Pat Robertson suggest that if people would embrace religion in the appropriate way and support the right politics, the world would be a better place. Many Presbyterians have also moved away from Calvin and Knox to preach a gospel of social uplift.

Rev. Buell Kazee believed, on the other hand, that we are doomed to sin and failure as long as we inhabit the flesh and that the main point in living is to accept a relationship with God; nevertheless, this relationship will necessarily cause us to be better and to be concerned about our fellow creatures in the world. Kazee, who was a college graduate but had no seminary training, explained:

> The Social Gospel . . . came out of Germany; it came through the seminaries, and that's where it's being preached. And now today, reli-

gion is a *thing* . . . to solve the ills of the country. I was under the impression that now that I am "saved" I must "do better." [Even though] I had a genuine spiritual experience with Christ, of course, I was failing because I still had all the weaknesses of the flesh that I ever did, and that put me in bondage. . . .

The emphasis now is on *conduct*. . . . Yes, certainly your conduct will improve if you're taught right. . . . It's humbling to a man to have to confess, "I'm a sinner and the only hope I have is in Jesus Christ"—for there's where the hope is. It's not here . . . in the world . . . , and it never will be here . . . , but men don't want to believe that. They want to say, "I'm going to *do it myself*. I'm going to improve!"

Well, when you preach the Gospel, you take away all the *pride* of man. Man can't improve himself. He'll always be a sinner, but if he's saved, the fact that he's in Christ and knows his salvation's in Christ and he has the spirit of God in his heart which sets him against sin, he'll be against his sin against God. And then he changes his objective in life. Instead of getting things here in the world, he'll give himself to Christ and find a life which takes him out of himself to something else.

There's no doubt that we're leaving *regeneration*. We're on the religion of *reform*. If a fellow can live morally better than he did, he thinks he's converted. Well, the fact is, the holier you become, the more you'll see the sin in you that you never saw before. If you have the spirit of the Lord in you, you'll condemn it, even though it may get out of hand, even though it may rise up and have its way—condemn it, and by God's grace, overcome it. It's a question of where you are with respect to sin, on God's side or your side. The Lord took care of the *sin* question, as far as the judicial part is concerned. I've never been charged with a sin since 1914 [when he was converted] in God's book. But I can see more of it now than I ever saw before. My salvation is in Christ, and that is settled. . . . One of these days He'll help me get rid of the whole thing, but that is what death is for.[6]

Primitive and Old Regular Baptists view human nature somewhat differently than do most Christians. They believe there are two parts to a person, the spiritual and the natural. Elder Mike Smith, of the Blackberry Primitive Baptist Church in Pike County, Kentucky, had a dim view of humankind when it is separated from the empowerment of God: "The

Bible says we are nothing, less than nothing. Man in his best state is nothing. We've got nothing to plead. We've got no righteousness to plead. The only righteousness you and me have is the imputed righteousness of Jesus Christ. I believe that God, when he pulled man out of the dust of the ground, He gave him a commandment to keep, and man broke the commandment."[7]

I admire the spirit of Elder Frank Fugate, who is featured in the Appalachia Film Workshop's film *In the Good Old Fashioned Way,* which is about Old Regular Baptists. I knew his grandson when he was a student at Berea College. In the film Mr. Fugate spoke of the importance of overcoming nature's control: "I try not to forget the most important thing, the only security you have in this life and the life to come. Life is not going to be worth nothing to you here if nature, which sin controls, controls your life. You'll never be able to lay down and feel, 'Lord, I feel comfortable today. I feel that you have blessed me to live in obedience to your will.' [If you control nature] you can lay down and relax and take a sweet rest, and give God the glory for that day that He has give you, guided you in the way of the right path."[8]

Elder John Hinkle, a Primitive Baptist, believed that the Gospel makes no sense whatever to the natural man, basing his opinion on 1 Corinthians 2:14, "But the natural man receiveth not the things of the Spirit of God; for they are foolishness unto him: neither can he know them, because they are spiritually discerned." He explained how one is transformed from the natural to the spiritual state:

> The natural man can read the Scriptures all the days of his life and he will not know any more about the things of God, in the divine sense, than he did when he first began. For he is not in the kingdom, he is dead, and he must be born again out from under the law of sin and death, made alive, translated into the kingdom of His dear Son by the washing and renewing of the Holy Ghost. We can understand the things of man. Why? Because we all have the spirit of man. Even so, the things of God knoweth no man save the Spirit of God, and when the individual is born of the Spirit of God, then he can understand the things of God, and not before.[9]

Whereas Elder Hinkle skirted predestination in the previous statement, Elder Teddy Ball of Coon Creek Primitive Baptist Church in Pike County, Kentucky, did not. He talked of the two distinct human states but concentrated on the elect. Note his belief that the elect can be everywhere, in all kinds of churches, but perhaps are in none of them:

I'll tell you what, the Bible teaches the sheep and the goats, and you might take a goat out yonder and duck [baptize] him forty-hundred times, if you wanted to, and he'll come out a goat every time you ducked him. A sheep is a sheep, and you can't make nothing out of him but a sheep. Though he may be a lamb, he's still a sheep. That's all you can make out of him. Jesus said I'll give unto the sheep eternal life, no end to it, and they shall *never* perish. I'm glad he knows every one of the sheep, ain't you? He said none is able to pluck them out of his Father's hands. Boy, I'll tell you right now, you're in safe hands . . . and in spite of the devil and all his hosts, the sheep is going to be carried home to glory when Jesus comes again. It's not just us Old Baptists either. It's not just one certain denomination, but they're scattered over every tongue and nation of this earth, and many of them sheep don't have their names on no book down here on earth, but their name is written in heaven. If they are written there, nobody can rub them out. . . . The righteous are all right. They are on safe ground.[10]

Elder Elwood Cornett, moderator of the Indian Bottom Association of Old Regular Baptists, discussed the influence of nature as opposed to the Holy Spirit. He used the biblical terms *inner man* and *outward man* to reflect the conflicts that Christians have in this world:

There's a part of nature that is directly the handiwork of God. So there is that element in nature . . . that is a very positive thing. On the other hand, there was a man and a woman in a garden who had a nature . . . of transgressing God's law. And there's a nature in me that says, "Don't be subservient to anything, the Spirit or anything." And that gets in my way. I think that's the same thing that Paul was talking about with the thorn in the flesh. That nature is the nature that we're going to leave in the grave. That's the nature that makes it difficult for us to get up into the stand and try to preach. And that's the nature that causes us all the trouble that we have. . . .

This warfare is going on between the inner man and outward man, and it makes me feel good if the inner man controlled the outward man all of the time, but he doesn't. . . . God could have made everybody so that they would have been His obedient child forever, but what glory would He have gotten from that? You could say to your child, "In a few days it's my birthday. Go down here and buy me a birthday present. You wrap it up real pretty and bring it back here." But what good would that do? But if that child does something real special for your birthday because of love, then that can be compared to the glory that God could get from his children. It may be that your child forgets your birthday sometimes. It may be that I'm influenced by vanity as we all are—I forget to pray like I should, or . . . I fly mad and lose my temper and so forth. I think this means that this outward man has manifested himself. I think also that God has a way of working with us . . . , lets us understand that we have displeased him.[11]

Herbert Barker, quoted previously, believed that people need to grow in faith, whether or not we grow in our worldly state:

As long as we live in this life, I don't think our condition and our position in the Family of God will totally merge because we are told to grow in grace and in the knowledge of our Lord and Savior, Jesus Christ. If we've already arrived, there wouldn't be any room for growth. Paul told Peter to grow, and he doesn't leave us without means to grow. When I became a Christian, I wanted to go to bed at night a spiritual pauper and wake up in the morning a spiritual giant, but that's not the way you grow, physically or spiritually. You grow by means. In 1 Peter 2:2, Paul said—and he's speaking to Christians—"Desire the sincere milk of the word, that ye may grow thereby." You grow by means. The Word of God becomes part and parcel of us. It has a transforming effect in our lives, and that is why we are told to study it. A lot of people would like to grow but are too lazy to utilize the means to grow. . . .

I think it is good to feel inadequate. Then you rely on the power you have within. The believer has the Holy Spirit. If I am efficient and I can do the work without the Holy Spirit, then it would be the work of man. God couldn't claim anything from that, but it is only the work that the Holy Spirit does through me that has lasting and eternal benefit.

Paul says to work out your own salvation with fear and trembling. Now he's speaking to *Christians*. He's not telling sinners to work for salvation. He's telling the Christian to work out, or work at his own salvation. The Holy Spirit does not work apart from the person, but It uses the person. We are co-laborers with God, Paul says. It is not something you strain at—arrive at some state of perfection—because that won't happen.[12]

Perfectionism and Human Progress

Associated with Arminian beliefs is the doctrine of perfection, that salvation brings a new life free from the old sinful one. Some Protestants, such as Methodists and Holiness-Pentecostals, believe in sanctification that they believe can come after the act of salvation. This means that Christians are sanctified against sin. This is in opposition to the Calvinist belief that we all sin, that as long as we are in the flesh, we are sinners, but that God can forgive our sins. Sybil Mallard, a member of a Dekalb County, Alabama, Church of God congregation, commented on sanctification: "Sanctifying will take away the desires of the world and the habits. . . . It will take away the old man, so to speak, and get us ready for where we're going."[13] Delwayne Maggard, a member of an Independent Baptist church in Charleston, West Virginia, added: "That's purely rebirth and regeneration from sinful ways to godly ways, and you are washed and cleansed in the blood of the Lamb. . . . Jesus come into your heart, and you are born again—from a sinner to a godly person."[14]

Tennessee Church of Christ pastor Tom Smith spoke of sanctification as a process and some of the problems that may arise from this belief:

> Most see sanctification as a process. You receive the Holy Spirit when you are baptized. Then you go through the process of growth. It is a maturation process. I don't think anyone would say that you ever become perfect. Some get closer to it through the process.
>
> There are problems in the Arminian system. Do I ever know that I am saved? If I sin does that mean I'm not? People go back and question their salvation. I have them coming who have been saved for twenty-five years, and they want to be baptized again, and I say, "Why?" Invariably they say, "I've sinned in this way. I've sinned in that way, and I know God can never forgive me for it." You have a lot of emotional distress. I deal with this teaching-wise by calling them back to what happened when they were converted. There you have become a child of God, and that puts you in a father-child relationship. I find myself using the term "walking-worthy," [meaning] that you walk in a manner worthy, or appropriate to, that relationship. What happens when you are a child? Sometimes you disobey, but you are forgiven. You are still a part of the family. You are not ostracized.[15]

Rev. Fred Lunsford, a Southern Baptist, my parents' pastor in their late years and a regional missionary for the North Carolina Baptist Convention, spoke of the human condition and problems it brings to the doctrine of perfection:

> I'm a strong scriptural believer, and of course man has fallen into a sinful state, and he is by nature a sinner. His inclination is in that direction. When a man trusts the Lord and becomes a Christian, he still has fleshly inclinations. This is his nature. However, when he becomes a Christian he takes on a new nature, and there comes a constant warfare in his life. This takes him back to priorities, and he must decide which he must put first. . . . Man is a sinful creature, but there is something else I'm convinced of, and it is that God never placed in a person an appetite or hunger that he couldn't satisfy, if we look to Him.
>
> Now there are groups who believe in perfectionism—that we can live above sin—but there is a peculiarity here. Also, along with it is the idea that a person does not have eternal security. He can be saved today and lost tomorrow. Not all people who believe in falling from grace are perfectionists, but the groups I know about who believe in perfection believe in falling from grace. This creates disillusionment and anxiety, because when they come to the point where they have sinned and failed, then they may feel that they are not saved any more. Therefore, some may feel that since they have failed, they might as well go ahead and do anything. This does create a problem.[16]

I have talked with many who became disillusioned when their religious experience did not bring the transformation in their lives that they had heard or read about. Many people struggle daily with temptations and decisions about how a Christian should live. Nonetheless, I didn't expect to hear reservations about sanctification from Dr. Donald Bowdle, a church history scholar at Lee College, Cleveland, Tennessee, and an ordained minister in the Church of God, Cleveland. He holds two doctorates, has studied at several universities and seminaries, and is an articulate spokesperson for Pentecostalism. But he also saw problems in the idea of perfection. He speculated on its emphasis in his own church and some of its pitfalls: "I think one of the greatest motivations for perfectionist teaching may have been the premillennial return-of-Christ doctrine . . . at the turn of the century. If the Lord's return is imminent, then one would want to be without spot and without wrinkle. And if the Lord's return is tomorrow, then maybe one can 'hold out' for a while, but the perfectionist teaching is so inconsistent with experience, and more importantly with Scripture, I'm just not sure it is a viable spiritual option."

When asked whether there is a problem when salvation does not solve people's personal problems, Dr. Bowdle replied: "When their problems are not solved, disillusionment sets in. I think I am in a position to know, working with young people for twenty-four years, to see a great deal of that. I think that not only does disillusionment set in, but sometimes the denial of what really is spiritual settles in as well, because if a person is told that he cannot sin, then when he does, he redefines sin to his own spiritual detriment."[17]

Elder Claren Williams, a black Old Regular Baptist pastor of a remarkable integrated church in Red Fox, Kentucky, used the inner and outer man belief to touch on perfection:

> You know in the Scriptures, God created man from the dust of the earth, but he wasn't living until He breathed the breath of life. Now the breath of life was the soul of man. The outward man dies someday, but the soul never dies. . . . It goes somewhere, goes to Paradise with God until the Resurrection. People think that there is just one part to man. . . .
>
> The inward person—when you get that new birth in Christ—it is perfect. It will sin no more. But this outward man, it sins daily. There's enough sin in this outward man that it's got to die. Sin kills this outward man. Then when this outward man is resurrected on the Resurrection Day, God makes it perfect, just like he does the soul. They unite and become one at Judgment. The inward part is the soul man, and the outward man, that's another man. He's corrupted. That's what causes it to die. If it was perfect, it would never die. You have perfection only in the soul.[18]

The Latter Days

In talking with people about the human condition, I often heard the belief that we are approaching the Latter Days, that human nature and the world are growing worse and worse and that Jesus will soon come again to gather the faithful. Some talked of drugs, divorce, violence at home, terrorism, and wars abroad as evidence that the world and the human condition are growing steadily worse (contrary to the common hope that religion, education, and human relations will bring steady improvement), fulfilling biblical prophecy. When asked whether he thought people are getting better through education and other modern advances, Garfield Sloan, a retired miner and carpenter, replied: "No, they can't get any better. Paul told what people will do in their latter days, and he said it would be soon. He said the time would come when they'll kill you and believe that they are doing their Father's will. And he said that there will be many deceived by the great signs and wonders. All kinds of people have been deceived."[19]

Pansy McCay, the Pentecostal evangelist from Mt. Vernon, Kentucky, worried about the sinfulness of the world and the unconcern for spiritual things and saw these as signs that the end of time is coming soon:

> My main concern is that people are forgetting God. In the revivals now very few people are touched. Not many people any more have a burden for sinners. They have their minds on other things. They are too worldly minded. They are not thinking about the coming of the Lord like they ought to, to make preparation to meet Him, and try to help others. People are not concerned about their souls. Twenty years ago people were eager to hear the Gospel. They would accept it, and it would change their lives. The families were closer. The children respected their parents more than they do now. And the parents don't seem to worry now about what their children are doing. I think it is just ridiculous what they are teaching our children in school now [sex education]. I think it is just egging them on. It [sexual permissiveness] is just getting worse all the time, and it is going against the Word of God, and I know God is not pleased with the way our young people are living. I think the way people are doing is going to bring on the coming of the Lord.[20]

Elder Claren Williams also talked about how modern ways and material gains have changed people in terms of religious zeal:

> Used to be there were sisters who sang and shouted and praised the Lord and some of the preachers would preach until they would about fall dead. They couldn't thank the Lord enough, because they were so mean, and just think how good God was to come along and save them. Now I see people who won't hardly sing, won't hardly shed a tear, never see them shout, while others may be all over the house rejoicing. We don't have shouting like we used to. A lot of the old sisters are dead and gone. The women today don't shout like the old ones did. A little pride has moved in among the children of God. When I was a boy, there might be four or five preachers preaching at the same time and maybe eight or ten women shouting and rejoicing, but you don't see that like you used to.

Money's come in, fine clothes, fine homes, cars, all that sort of thing, and that chokes down your mind a-thinking of the Lord I don't rejoice like I used to. There are a lot of things on my mind. The more business you've got, it'll deprive you from serving the Lord. See, when people didn't have but little, they'd thank the Lord.[21]

Rev. Phillip Banks, a Freewill Baptist, also preached that the end of the world is soon coming. He talked of what the Christian's purpose is in such a world and about the remnant of true believers who will be spared. Although he was coming from a different theological point of view, this belief in the salvation of only a small remnant is similar to the Calvinist view that only a few were predestined to be saved. He believed, too, that sin prevents the improvement of the world and that the Christian's purpose is concerned with the hereafter:

I think we are shaking up the last days. Things are in chaos and confusion, and they don't know where to turn or what to do. Our purpose [as Christians] in the world is to give witness to Him until He comes again. When He comes He's taking His people out of this world.

He promised us a Messiah in Genesis, promised a savior. He promised a seed, a remnant to be spared, and regardless of sin, of Satan and everything else, there is going to be a remnant people that is going to be saved for the glory of God. I think the ultimate purpose of God's people here is to witness to the glory of God until Jesus comes and then wait for the Rapture to be with Him.

I don't think we are here to get the world better and better. I think that is a lost mission. I don't find anywhere in the Bible where we are told to do that. We are told to witness, to bring people to the Lord that they might be saved, that they might escape eternal damnation.[22]

Rev. Fred Lunsford also questioned human progress in the world and mourned the loss of community ties and commitment to one another:

One of my main concerns is the apathy on the part of the people, the loss of genuine concern for their neighbors. We had closer community ties in the old days than we do now. We are more dispersed now. In some areas we are making technical progress. Morally, I think we are slipping backwards, generally speaking. This is a big concern of mine. Every week, I have had from one to a dozen young people come to me for counseling who are involved in drugs. I think they are seeking fulfillment of life. There is an emptiness, a void in their lives. I believe that this can be filled with a proper relationship with Jesus Christ. I've seen it happen.[23]

Elder Lovell Williams, brother to Claren Williams, also espoused the belief that we are in the Latter Days because of all the evil in the world—family breakups, wars, and other signs:

You can read the signs that it [the Second Coming] is getting close. The New Testament speaks of wars and rumors of war in diverse places—famine, children's disobedience to their parents, nations against nations, kingdom against kingdom, men's feet swift to shed innocent blood. Now we see those signs, and people are not taking any heed. It's getting closer.

According to the Scriptures, the world will wax worse and worse until the end. That's the way they done in the days of Noah. Noah preached about a hundred and twenty years to them, telling them about the flood that was coming—built an ark. They just made fun of him, didn't believe him. When the rains started coming, it was too late. We have to live in the world, but still yet, Christ said, "I'll choose you out of the world. Therefore, you are no more in the world."[24]

Rev. Jeffrey Simpson, pastor of the Parkway Church of God in Clay City, Kentucky, preached a sermon on Latter Day disobedience to God and our failure to see the warning signs, using as a text Jeremiah 6:10, "To whom shall I speak, and give warning, that they might hear? Behold, their ear is uncircumcised, and they cannot hearken: behold, the word of the Lord is unto them a reproach; they have no delight in it."

We are living in a day when people are not too careful to sit up and listen . . . to abide by the warning signs. . . . Now, God's got some warning signs, people . . . , and you know that these warnings are ignored consistently by the majority of people. They're not deaf, but they don't want to hear. We are living in a day when people are determined to do their own thing and do it their own way [more] than ever before. There has never been a time when the people are more determined to be independent and self-willed than they are right now. That's why so many people are lost. . . . Have you ever seen a time when people were more bold in their sinfulness? There's never been a time when our nation is more perverse that it is right now. We're almost in the days of Sodom and Gomorrah. Our young people have—if I may use a mountain expression picked up from my mother—gone hog-wild and pig-crazy. Dope, sex. It's the spirit of the devil that has caused this. . . . They're going deeper and deeper into sin. They have forsaken God, backslidden, gone in the opposite direction. They are just like an old stubborn heifer. If you've ever tried to lead a heifer that's not been trained, Brother, she'll set her toes and pull you. She'll give you a hard old time. God's people are like that.[25]

Josephine Martin, from Floyd County, Kentucky, shared the belief that although some things are better socially, we are getting worse in the moral sense. She saw the devil winning:

In one sense I think people are living better now, and there is more money in circulation, better homes, more programs. Morally . . . we're very low. I hate to say it about a good old honeycomb nation like we've got, but we've got just about as low a moral standards now as we've ever had. . . . I hate to say a thing like that about our nation, but I really feel it, that we have degraded ourselves, degraded one another. For one thing, I think that people's tongues have become so vile and possessed with the devil that they don't care what kind of words they use in front of a child. . . . I think we've got one of the most sex-crazed times that we've ever had. There is no self-respect, no modesty. They'd just as soon go nude or with next-to-nothing on the body. I think it is a heathen generation.[26]

The late Herbert Barker emphasized a belief that the world is already a lost cause, that God is trying to save not the world but only lost people:

I don't think the world will get better—a utopian condition that some people preach. I think it is going to get worse. In automation and progress, in the field of science, know-how, technique, and all the rest, yes, it is progressing, but I don't think it is becoming more God-conscious, more spiritual. . . .

Jesus said, "Save yourselves *from* this wicked generation." It seems to me that in some of the preaching you hear today, they are preaching to save the *generation*. Jesus was saying that the generation is already under the wrath of God and that we should save ourselves *from* it. You save yourself from this generation by turning to God.[27]

Finally, Elder Frank Fugate had concerns for the modern world and lamented that people have forsaken God: "God first said that the time of distrust, the time of discontent, the time of fear that we are living under today would come by God's people departing from the faith. . . . Instead of seeking God to guide them, they have departed from divine guidance. . . . Human nature is one of the most corrupt things there is, and that is why we need God to overcome this nature of ours."[28]

Although many Upland Christians think we are in the Latter Days and that there is no hope for the world and those whose hearts are hardened, others believe that if people would turn to the Lord, the world and human nature would get better. Many believe that the world, being part of nature, is beyond help, but others feel that repentance and salvation make us new persons and that we can then have an influence on others and on the world. Several Christians talked to me of their hope for improvement in the world and spoke of what they expected of Christians. Rev. Fred Lunsford, a North Carolina Baptist, said his main purpose in life is to help others to "rise to a higher level of life and to have a proper relationship with God and man." He commented that Baptists "have been very strong on the past and on the future, and we forget that we are living in the *now.*" His point is that we have responsibilities to others in addition to our quest for personal salvation.[29] My brother, Garnett Jones, a Baptist deacon, raised the question of what manner of person we should be as "trustees of the Gospel": "We ought to be the kind of person who will tackle problems of not believing deeply enough, and trying long enough, and loudly enough, to de-hypnotize himself from his own impossible thinking, and who will let God be God, and let him be God's man in God's place and time, to do God's work at God's direction, and who will search for the ultimate but be content to accept what he has."[30]

I heard a woman in a Baptist church in the Arkansas Ozarks testify: "I just want the Lord to get after me and say, 'Irene, you get up from there and do what's right.'" The preacher in the same church, Wallace McConnell, quoted from 2 Timothy 1:6 ("stir up the gift of God, which is in thee,") and then said: "How do you stir up that gift? You stir it up by getting on your knees and crying out to God . . . , and whenever God tells you to do something, do it! Don't wait till something else comes along and says, 'Don't do it.' The second voice *will* come along. I've told people that if God ever laid something on me to do, I'd go do it."[31]

Family Relations and the Roles of Men and Women

The late Elder W. J. Berry, a Primitive Baptist, in an editorial in his magazine, *The Old Faith Contender,* dealt with a more sensitive issue for this age, that of the modern world's influence on the breakdown of what he thought to be the proper order and authority of the family:

> With every PROGRESS in culture, science, commerce, manufacture, education, entertainment, and government, etc., each resulted in another subtle but sure means of undermining and weakening the foundations and bulwarks of marriage, family, and local community; the one vital, God-ordained foundation for human society. With the breakdown of the foundational order in the family or home life, came the consequent moral deterioration of its members. . . .
>
> Husbands and wives, fathers and mothers, began to sink to the lowest depths of unfaithfulness, children thus neglected, forsook their parents and became "heady, high-minded," and disobedient to parents. 2 Tim. 3:4. The lives and examples set by fathers and mothers lowered their God-ordained high position, until the words of father and mother lost their original authority and influence. This, and much more has taken place, until now we have a society weakened, confused and demoralized to the lowest and most critical point in human history. Why?—All because of man's sin, depravity and departure from God's order for man and woman, husband and wife, father and mother.[32]

This raises questions about the role of men and women in the family and the church. The Primitive Baptists are perhaps the most strict in their views, relying mostly on the Apostle Paul's words, as in this excerpt from a Primitive Baptist publication:

> Let your women keep silence in the church; for it is not permitted unto them to speak; but they are commanded to be under obedience, as also saith the law, And if any will learn let them ask their husbands at home, for it is a shame for women to speak in the church. 1 Cor. xiv: 34–35
>
> Let the women learn in silence with all subjection; but I suffer not a woman to teach, nor to usurp authority over a man, but to be in silence. 1 Tim. 2:11–12.

The Primitive or Old School Baptist believing the above Scripture, are not advocates of the modern practice of women preaching. This practice originated, not with Christ and his Apostles, but with George Fox, the founder of the Quakers . . . , who lived in the seventeenth century.

But while women are not, by God's word, permitted to teach publicly in the church, yet all speaking is not prohibited; they may speak their experiences to the church; give an account of the work of God on their souls, speak to one another in Psalms, hymns, and spiritual songs, and speak as evidence in the church case. They may also teach privately their children . . . , teach other women . . . , and teach men also. . . . But to exceed the limits of God's Word and to assume the position of preachers or public teachers is contrary to natural modesty, and bashfulness of the sex, is a shame to themselves, a disgrace to the church, and betrays uncommon pride and vanity, and unnatural boldness and confidence.[33]

Even in more modern churches I heard reservations about women taking the lead in services. Lillian Olinger, a black member of the Town Mountain Baptist Church near Hazard, Kentucky, had this to say:

We don't have women deacons. I like to see men step out in front. We women have plenty to do. We don't have to get into some things we get in. Over in Titus, Paul told us what to do—teach the young ones. That's an everyday job. Support and love our husbands, treat our husbands nice, like that woman over in Proverbs 31.

But I think men have laid down on the job. If men get on the ball, and get on their job, things can look up in America. 'Cause us women, we love men, and they can lead a long way. They can lead us way down the road in sin, and they can pick us up again. They need a helpmeet. Women can be behind their husbands, pushing them, encouraging them. . . . When he walks out on the street, they know he's got a good wife at home. The Scriptures say it. That's what it is, a husband and a wife, and that man going out front, standing tall, and her right by his side—then things can be different. I believe that. About four or five years ago, God laid it on my heart to pray for men.[34]

Mrs. Olinger's sister, Mable Jones, a retired schoolteacher, added the following: "If we women would do like Paul said, I believe there'd be less divorce. I have saved three marriages through counseling. That's what it took—just the Lord's words. . . . That's why I know the Lord doesn't want me in the pulpit, preaching. I'm going to preach on the couch, or in a chair. I can deliver the Word. I can witness."[35]

These black Christians from Hazard spoke admirably of the Promise Keepers movement and thought it was a good thing. But others have reservations about the Pauline order of things. Ruby Dotson, a Freewill Baptist from Dickenson County, Virginia, had different ideas about the role of women in church:

> There's a lot of people who don't believe in ladies speaking in church. They always say that if they want to know anything, they should ask their husbands at home. Well, if he isn't a Christian, he couldn't tell them. I think when the Lord tells you to speak, to speak. If the Lord calls on her to testify and she doesn't, she's quenching the Spirit. If we feel led to pray and we fail to do that, we're quenching the Spirit. If it isn't right to testify or to pray [aloud] in church, I don't think it would be right to shout, if we felt like shouting or singing. I think we should be led by the Spirit.
>
> Christ's first message after the resurrection was by Mary [Magdalene], and if he hadn't aimed to use women in His work, He wouldn't have sent the message by Mary when there were other apostles close by.[36]

Sister Anna Mae Cook, a longtime black preacher and member of the Church of God Militant Pillar and Ground of Truth in McRoberts, Kentucky, also went back to Mary Magdalene as evidence that God intended women to carry the Word. When I asked her why some Christians object to women preachers, she said:

> Well, that's because they don't read—they read but they don't understand what they read. It's in the Book. It has to go back to Mary when Jesus rose [from the tomb]. Mary was the one that brought the first message when Jesus rose. He give the first message to Mary. He said, "You go tell my disciples."
>
> Yeah, we've run into problems. Lots of people don't believe in women preachers, but you see, that don't change it. It's just like telling about hell—it's hot—but if you don't believe it, that's your business.[37]

Bishop Willie Lamb, a World War II veteran and former miner and union leader who is now the pastor of the McRoberts Church of God Militant Pillar and Ground of Truth, having been the bishop of related churches in Kentucky, added: "I don't have any problem with women preachers. Most Pentecostal churches I've been in have women preachers. The Bible says that 'there is neither Jew nor Greek, there is neither bond nor free, there is neither male nor female: for ye are all one in Christ Jesus'" (Gal. 3:28).[38]

Sister Lois Thompson, also a member of the McRoberts church, said this on the subject:

> You was wondering if we have a problem with women ministers. We don't, because we've always had women ministers, and we believe that God speaks to whom He please. He said, "There's neither male nor female." So, if there's not male nor female in God's sight, there is no difference. If He call a man, and a man don't do it, He's going to call a woman. And He'll call a woman anyway. If God wants you, He wants you. A woman preacher—I'd just as soon hear them as a man. . . . If God can speak through a jackass, why not a woman? See Numbers 22 [referring to Balaam's ass, which the Lord caused to speak to its master].[39]

Several people saw changes in gender roles and a decline in church attendance as a cause of family problems and troubled children. Mable Jones commented: "That's why parents are losing their children. The parents leave God out, and they're so wrapped up in their jobs . . . , they're not really dealing with their children. When it comes to the real thing [parenting], they're not doing it. They [the children] don't give honor to the parents, and they don't give it to the children. I'm going to deny myself for my children's sake" Lillian Olinger commented similarly, "My generation, we were used to staying at home and taking care of the home. The husband worked and took care of them [financially]. When the woman left that home, that brought on a lot of divorces, I believe. I knew one woman who went off and left five children with her husband. Five children!" Pansy McCay said: "The divorce rate is too high, and that is not pleasing to the Lord. Right now the family hardly eats together. I just don't like the way families live now. I think families ought to have some time together." Rev. Phillip Banks echoed the same theme: "Family and church go hand in hand. As the family has deteriorated, so has the church. How can there be a home life when the man works one shift and his wife another? There is no home life."[40]

Most church people blame the world with its opportunities and enticements, and sometimes the devil, for people's leaving the church and not paying close enough attention to the family. Some, however, feel that people have become more self-centered rather than family and church centered. The Town Mountain Baptists, in Hazard, Kentucky, talked a good deal about maintaining modesty and not being lifted up in pride.

The Value of Humility

I have long been interested in the high value that Upland Christians put on humility. It is an important idea in the Bible, which has some seventy occurrences of some form of the word, and thirty-one instances of *meek* or *meekness*. I have heard numerous sermons that preached the necessity for humbling ourselves before God, in comparison to whom we have much to be humble about. Most mountain people believe that humility is the only proper stance to take with one another, as well as toward God. Upland Christians have been profoundly influenced by biblical quotations such as the following:

> Whosoever therefore shall humble himself as this little child, the same is greatest in the kingdom of heaven. (Matthew 18:4)

> And whosoever shall exalt himself shall be abased; and he that shall humble himself shall be exalted. (Matthew 23:12)

> God resisteth the proud, but giveth grace unto the humble. . . . Humble yourself in the sight of the Lord, and he shall lift you up. (James 4:6,10)

> Likewise, ye younger, submit yourselves unto the elder. Yea, all of you be subject one to another, and be clothed in humility: for God resisteth the proud, and giveth grace to the humble.
> Humble yourselves, therefore, under the mighty hand of God, that he may exalt you in due time. (I Peter 5:5–6)

Howard Dorgan, a professor of communication arts at Appalachian State University and the author of several books on mountain religion, is also the author of an interesting paper, "The Art of Deference and the Science of Humility," about elections of church leaders within one Old Regular Baptist association. He describes this art, or conviction, in this way: "Strongly controlled by one value that permeates much of the faith's thought and conduct—meekness, modesty, and self-depreciation ('giving God the glory')—Old Regulars seek position and power only by seeming to run from these honors, constantly deferring to the goodness and wisdom of others, while claiming little or no virtue or insight for themselves. Only by humbling one's self can one possibly be lifted to eminence."[41]

This humble stance is a Southern tradition that is intensified in mountain churches, where some may appear to try to "out-humble" one another. One story is that a Baptist deacon was given an award for his humility, but it was taken away when someone heard him bragging about it. One old woman, when asked whether she had seen Halley's comet when it passed by in 1910, replied, "Well, only from a distance." People have difficulty accepting a compliment and may try to explain it away or to deny it outright, saying something like, "Well, I really didn't play well at all. Maybe if I'd had time to practice I might have done better." I've even heard people pass off a compliment directed at one of their children, saying, "Well, I guess he does pretty well with what he's got to work with." They will say self-deprecating things such as, "I was hiding behind the door when the looks [or brains] were passed out." It is also common to resist a call to serve in the church or elsewhere by deferring to others, as Dorgan points out, suggesting always that others will do a better job. Although humility is a religious conviction, I have long noted that it is part of the manners system of the Uplands. It is part of a negotiation process of determining whether one is truly wanted for the job at hand.

So humility and deference are common both within the church and without. We are quick to notice that some people elsewhere take themselves very seriously and are quite willing to extol their own qualities. Uplanders want to make sure that they are not accused of acting as if they are better than they actually are. This strong belief in humility and leveling flows out of our view of the human condition based on religious beliefs. I have heard people say to their children, "You are as good as anybody else, but no better."

Arthel "Doc" Watson is quoted on humility and his relationship with God by Jock Lauterer in his *Runnin' on Rims: Appalachian Profiles*. Watson, born in the Blue Ridge Mountains and blind since birth, knew much of poverty and hard times, but he is now recognized as one of the best folk guitarists and traditional singers in the country. He is much admired by fellow musicians, including some country "superstars." His comments on stardom, modesty, and faith are a fitting summation of Upland views on humility:

> I don't care about being a big star. I don't want people to worship me. I just appreciate people enjoying it if I do a good job—just like you'd compliment a carpenter or a plumber if he did a good job. I don't want any stardom. The good Lord didn't intend people to live like that. These young men who get to be stars get up so high on it that when it all comes down they have to use liquor or drugs to keep them up. . . .

Some of these young stars become arrogant toward the world. What have I got to be arrogant about? Ask Rosalee [his wife]. Sometimes I'm as ornery and no-count as can be.

You've got to put God in his place and stardom in its place. Nobody is better than anyone else son. And I'll tell you what's the truth—that's what it's all about. One man might do something better than another man, but that's no reason for him getting all puffy or self-righteous about himself. . . .

And I'll tell you what's the truth buddy—the good Lord was with me every step of the way.[42]

Human Nature and Race Relations

Many Christians have done what they thought the Lord expects of them and what the Bible teaches. Others have been unable to overcome temptations of the world, such as the pull of culture and the mind-warping power of prejudice. Too many church members throughout the country have not lived as if they believed that "God hath made of one blood all nations." Yet I have been fortunate in meeting Christians, black and white, in the Uplands—a part of the South—who have been cordial in their relationships with one another. I want to use race relations, then, as an example of how some Upland Christians have tried to follow Christ's teaching rather than act out human nature or give in to cultural pressures, as many of us do.

I discovered three churches in the eastern Kentucky coalfields that have always been racially integrated: the Little Home Old Regular Baptist Church at Red Fox, part of the Old Indian Bottom Association; the First Baptist Church of Town Mountain, near Hazard, a member of the black National Baptist Association; and the Church of God Militant Pillar and Ground of Truth, a member of a Pentecostal association of the same name, in McRoberts.

The Little Home Church is in a Knott County mining community of blacks and whites scattered along the road and creeks in an integrated fashion. In 1911 several black members of the Old Carr Regular Baptist Church of the Indian Bottom Association (organized in 1876, although the original Indian Bottom Church dates to 1810) asked to organize a new church that would be set up especially for the black members of the association. This request was granted, and the Little Home Church was organized with the oversight of Old Carr officers. However, many of the white members of Old Carr and other churches in the association began to attend services at Little Home, since Old Regular Baptists meet in their home church only once a month, allowing members to visit other churches when their own church is not meeting.[43]

Presently more white people than black attend the Little Home Church. Even in the membership whites predominate, although the moderator and other officers have always been black.

In the following comments, black and white members, as well as others who attend the church, talk about this interracial body and their life together. Elder Claren Williams, the stately black moderator of the Little Home Church, who quit mining to become a building contractor, talked of the community of Red Fox: "As far as this neighborhood, the white and colored growed up together. We understood one another. We never had any problems. I have never known in all my life a white person killing a colored person, or a colored person killing a white person. Everybody knows one another—growed up together, worked together, always did."[44]

Elder Lovell Williams, Claren's brother, commented on the church, the Red Fox community, and the benefits that integration has brought to both races:

> Well, to me it makes you feel closer. You've got a white brother or sister having the same mind you've got. You can walk along together, you can preach together, sing together, rejoice together. You've got the same thing. You eat at the same table. That draws you close together. . . . Black and white have all lived together, were all raised up together. If we hear of somebody in need—that's one of our basic beliefs, helping people in need, regardless of whether they're in the church or out of the church—we give a helping hand. . . . It's [the Little Home Church] been integrated since it started. No problems between blacks and whites. Everybody got along good.[45]

Elizabeth Ashley was a spirited ninety-year-old white member of Little Home when I asked why her attitude toward blacks was different from those of many white Americans and why she was a member of this church: "I just walked the Lord's way. We're all God's people. It must have been the Good Lord's work that we got along so well. I never heard of any trouble between the races in Little Home Church. People have never said anything about me going to Little Home. It wouldn't have mattered. They don't put bits in my mouth and lead me around. I said, 'I'm in Little Home Church, and I'm at home. I'm not a Rambling Sam, going from one church to another.'"[46]

Elder Jesse Hagans, a descendent of respected black preachers, said this: "As far as members, we make no difference in persons. We go on the old-time way, the way the Bible teaches us, and just our inward feelings. That's the way we are—love one another the way God has told us to do. We have no prejudiced feelings against anybody, black, white, yellow, or whatever. . . . It's always had white members as far back as I can remember."[47]

Vance Blair, a disabled white former miner who drove a school bus for a living, spoke fondly of the Little Home Church, referring to it, as did Mrs. Ashley, as his home:

> We've had a lot of people come to see about us. They can't understand how whites and blacks can get along so good. Like I've said, our hearts have been made over with power from above. We're easy to get along with. We've always got along good—white members and black members. I joined that church in 1955, and my wife joined Little Home in 1983. I just felt that the Lord led me home to the house of my Master and brothers and sisters. We are all created, and I had nothing to do with my body being white, and the black man had nothing to do with his body being black. We've got good in the black and bad, and good in the white and bad in the white. . . . I think God's people can't be prejudiced if they've really been forgiven from above. I grew up with the black people.
>
> I was sick most of my life [as a result of rheumatic fever], and I said to the Lord, if You'll let me live, I'll do your will. . . . It's nothing great I've done. It is His mercy.[48]

The late Elder Alonzo Watts, a white member of Old Carr Church, regularly attended the Little Home Church. He had strong feelings about the relationship between black and white members of the association:

> I joined Old Carr Church, [but] we have fellowship together. . . . Little Home is the only colored church. We fellowship together because we love one another. Me and you, everybody that's been born again, we can't hate nobody. We must love everybody's soul. We can't hate each other. We just can't do it. . . . When people are born again, they love one another, and color doesn't have anything to do with that love. That's why we are Old Regular Baptists, and we mix and mingle with one another because of that love. If we let Satan interfere with that love, some confusion would come. We don't let Satan enter our hearts enough to lose that love. . . . I love to go to every meeting. I love to go![49]

Howard Dorgan became interested in the Little Home Church after reading an article by Ron Short, an actor and writer whose people are Old Regular Baptists and who stated, among other things: "As long as I can remember, there have been black preachers and members in the Old Regulars. I think that it is important to point out that while this country has labored under the burden of continued racial strife, this Church has maintained the equality of people as a natural part of the Christian ethic, not as defined by the legal limits of a person's civil rights."[50]

After studying Old Regulars and the Little Home Church, Dorgan agreed that Short's assessment was accurate. He concluded in a paper: "Surely no cluster of mankind can be so idyllic in social virtue that it avoids every element of racism. Man is far from perfect, and his institutions mirror his imperfections. Nevertheless, Old Regulars appear to have fared better than most Southern or border-state religious factions in establishing fellowships in which a high degree of black/white racial harmony exists."[51]

Despite the warm testimony of the good relationships in Red Fox and in the Little Home Church, some blacks speak with more humor and irony than bitterness about racism in the community in the past and hints of it in the church. One remembered when school-bus drivers would pick up all of the white students first so that the black students had no seats and later put a curtain in the back, making the black students sit behind it. Another talked, when asked, about white attitudes toward blacks within the church. "Well, you know, God judges the heart, and we look on the outward appearances. . . . I feel there are some people who feel that way [that they are better]. I'll be honest with you, but they have to come down off that before they can get to heaven. They're Christian people, but they have to come down from that."

Even though there are lapses from ideal attitudes, I found the Little Home Church and Red Fox to be a remarkable church and community. We see evidence that a good number of mainline churches have had a change of heart after the civil rights movement and now welcome black members, but I believe the kind of relationships at the Little Home Church, with its working-class people, is still a rarity in the Uplands and in most places in the country.

The Town Mountain Baptist Church was organized in 1882, and a building was later placed on ground donated by two former slaves, Jack and Bill Combs. The Combses, who were brought from Virginia, were soon joined by the Olingers, also from Virginia. The Combses were frugal and hard working, and they eventually owned more than a thousand acres on Town Mountain. They sold parcels to others who wished to build houses there. Several white people, described as poor, were among those who built there.

Some of them attended the Town Mountain Church, and there was some intermarriage between blacks and whites.

Through the years more blacks came from Virginia and the Deep South to work in the mines and for the railroad, and they built houses on Town Mountain. Eventually nearly all the people on Town Mountain became related to each other through marriage. Blacks and whites acknowledge common ancestors. Residents claim a high level of respect and trust between the white and black people of Hazard, although there was trouble in the past brought on by the alleged rape of a white woman by a black man and the lynching of a black man following the death of a white man in a fight.[52]

When asked why there are good relations in Hazard and why there have always been white members in the church, three members of the Town Mountain Church responded in this way:

D. Y. Olinger: I'd say that when we were kids, we didn't have that much race problems. We played together every day. The whites lived on one side of the mountain, and we lived on the other side, and we'd go across the mountain every Sunday and play base-ball—black team play the white team. We never had any problems. Now this was back in the thirties.

Our foreparents told us that we had always had white members in our church. I'm sixty-nine, and I remember we always had white members when I was a boy. They lived in the community. Town Mountain was an integrated community.

Lillian Olinger: We were mostly black. A lot of the white people that we had [in church] were poor. Our grandfathers [the Combses and Olingers] had land, and they would let them build them a house and live on it free of charge. I guess we showed them love, and that will win people, you know. They lived in the neighbor-hood, and they joined the church. Others came and visited who maybe didn't join. The people of that area were always well thought of. They were respected and honest. It's a family church. Those who are not kin are related some sort of way by marriage. We've had a great church in terms of people being just who they are, honest, hard-workers, believe in their families, educate their children. It's unusual for a little church like that.

Mable Jones: They [the original settlers] were not lifted up in pride. They were humble people. I believe that's a lot of hindrance now to the church. . . .

We lived with our grandfather—us three girls—and we'd take in anybody at night [black or white]. We felt that wasn't the right thing to do, but he said it was, said, "You might need the same help."

D. Y. Olinger: When we lived out on the farm, people walked through, black and white. I remember my mother getting up at midnight, fixing a meal for somebody who was walking through, said they wanted to spend the night. She would feed them and give them a place to stay.

Lillian Olinger: You might look and see anybody coming towards your house. They'd be looking for a place to stay all night, looking for a place to eat. You didn't turn down nobody. I don't care who they were.

My grandfather had to go to different places to get saws, bring stuff in here that we didn't have here, for his lumber business. He said white people who kept them were good to them, and they could teach us to love people.

D. Y. Olinger: They'd ride rafts of logs down the [Kentucky] river to Beattyville and coming back up the river, the people they spent the night with would be white.[53]

Bill Morton, a former mayor of Hazard, Presbyterian layman, and an owner of a lumber company that employs blacks, also spoke highly of black citizens and race relations. "We had very little trouble with school integration, which came shortly after the *Brown* decision," he said, adding, "They [the blacks] were honest people who always paid their bills, and that was important to people." He remembered as a boy seeing black and white miners going by his house to the mines. "I think working together probably made for good relations. They held substantial jobs in the community."[54]

David Olinger, now a Justice Department attorney, grew up in the Town Mountain Church and remembered that there was discrimination before the *Brown* decision and civil rights laws, but he also described black people who were strong and able and who held important jobs or owned businesses in the community:

The United Mine Workers had a lot of influence on race relations. That's why I am so pro-union as an adult. You were able to work and make a good living, which allows a lot of other things to work themselves out. My understanding is that the union didn't tolerate overt racism, but during the years of separate-but-equal, you did have mostly black mines with very few whites working there. But so far as the medical benefits and all that, you were not denied those.

I wouldn't say everything was perfect. . . . We used to go play with our white friends in the Little League. Some people would frown a little bit, but they wouldn't say anything. I remember one time a lady asked me to go out of a little restaurant—she said she'd rather we sit on the steps. As I got older, I realized what she was talking about. We had access to theaters; we just had to sit upstairs. I played basketball in high school. During the time I went there, the team was predominantly black. . . .

There was some intermarriage, [but] there wasn't that much as I remember growing up. As you look at my skin color, it's hard to tell anyway. They wouldn't say anything to you, because they weren't sure at times.[55]

Roy Moore, white friend and high-school and Berea College classmate of David Olinger and now a professor of journalism at the University of Kentucky, remembered cordial relationships between whites and blacks in the Hazard area:

There wasn't a "we versus them" syndrome, "We're black, they're white; therefore we are different." I never sensed that at all. . . . I just never thought of it in that way. I think a lot of it had to do with the fact that we were interacting on a daily basis. Some of the brightest students when I was in high school were black students.

David and I used to go have lunch down at Fouts Drug Store and some other places downtown. There was never anybody to say, "He's black and, therefore, we're not going to wait on him."

There were several interracial marriages. . . . We'd see the families when they came to school events and so on. Of course, I may have grown up in a different [kind of] family, but there was never any discussion about it—certainly not negative comments. . . .

If anybody had made prejudicial comments in a classroom—teacher or student—it would have been immediately challenged. That was not considered to be the appropriate or ethical thing to do."[56]

The Reverend John Pray, the seminary-trained pastor of the Town Mountain Church reared in Washington and Philadelphia, offered several thoughts on race relations in Hazard and eastern Kentucky:

> I have been impressed on the relations between the races here, and I've often wondered just why it was. . . . They've been very close-knit here, worked together all these years. They all had the same difficulties—the people here—had their trials as families, and they kind of looked to each other for support, regardless of their color. And I also discovered that many of these people are blood related. . . . They worked together, they commingled, they married, they raised families together.
>
> The founding of the church was by black and white people who were related. It was a family thing, starting out, even then. . . . Two sisters [now] in the church, their great-grandfather was brought over by the [white] Combses who first settled here. This [white] Combs, who came from Virginia, brought two slaves [Jack and Bill], and my understanding is that [one of the slaves] was [actually] Combs's son.
>
> It's interesting, when you attend funerals now, especially of the older people, you'd be amazed at what you see. Whites come in for the funerals of black relatives. I had some white people to tell me, when they found out I was Jim Lunce's son-in-law, they said to me, "Well, Jim is my kin."
>
> One thing about people in the mountains, they don't treat people with disrespect. When I first came here, I worked for UPS [United Parcel Service]. A man came from Chicago to interview [me]. He kind of gave me a little rundown on what I might encounter in the mountains, as if it were very primitive, that I might be doing it at my own risk. . . . And I was amazed that wherever I went . . . they were so friendly, helpful. I'd deliver a package, and people would want to know if I'd come in and sit down and eat—that sort of thing. Coming from Philadelphia, that was strange to me. In all my lifetime, I'd never seen anything like that. In short, I saw a different white man in Kentucky. . . .
>
> I wish the whole world would come and see what has happened here. . . . They've done something that we've been struggling with for decades—trying to mold some kind of Christian band. . . . In spite of obstacles, they've come to something very decent.[57]

The Church of God Militant Pillar and Ground of Truth was founded in McRoberts, in Kentucky's Letcher County, in 1919 by Bishop G. W.

Keith and Mother Alma R. Walker. There are now several churches of the M.P.G. of T., whose headquarters are in Columbus, Ohio. The present pastor of the McRoberts church is Bishop Willie Lamb, a former coal miner who grew up in the coal town of McRoberts, which sprawls up and down several hollows, although many houses now stand empty since the decline of mining has led people to look for work elsewhere. In the past some of the hollows were mostly either black or white, although some were integrated. Presently several of the communities are integrated. Lamb's church is in Tom Biggs Hollow, which has both black and white people, and his church, although mostly black, has some white members. It is a Pentecostal church, and it differs from the Little Home and Town Mountain Baptist Churches in that it encourages women to take a strong lead in church work. Regionally and nationally the Church of God M.P.G. of T. has a number of women pastors, and there are three women who preach in the McRoberts church.

I spent a morning riding with Bishop Lamb up and down the hollows of McRoberts and to the nearby towns of Neon and Fleming, all once prospering coal towns, and then went to his church to hear a concert of religious music by the Golden Voices of Bluefield, West Virginia. The audience was integrated. Brother Lamb, a veteran of World War II's European theater, is one of the most appealing church leaders that I have met. He was greeted with enthusiasm and affection by both black and white residents in the three towns. Reuben Watts, former judge executive (a county administrator) and former sheriff of the county, commented, "Willie sees no enemies and no strangers" and went on to say that Lamb had won his family's eternal gratitude for visiting Watts's dying mother when she was in the hospital. Following are Bishop Lamb's comments on various topics relating to hard times and interracial life in the hollows:

> I started preaching in 1967 when I was still in the mines, and I then started pastoring in 1969. I preach more white funerals [here] than anybody. I know the people to the fourth and fifth generations. . . . If any of the old settlers die, the young preachers don't know as much about them as I do. . . .
>
> Our church here was founded in 1919 and was always integrated. We have a white assistant pastor. We have three white members right now . . . but we had as high as fifteen or sixteen, but they died out. The membership is down to twenty-seven. The older ones have died out and the younger ones have had to go get jobs. . . .
>
> I went into the mines in 1941, and I retired in 1977, with the three

years and two months in World War II. I am a union [United Mine Workers of America] miner, and I served on the pit crew for twenty-some years. Their [Consolidation Coal and later Bethlehem Steel] policy was that every man would be treated right, and the union was the same way. When a man went into the union, he took an oath that he wouldn't betray a brother, regardless of degree, color, national origin, whatever. He was a union brother. And whether he wanted to or not, he had to live up to the obligation. If he didn't, the union would run him away.

We got along fine here. I played with these white boys here. We fought, we played ball, we went swimming together, and we worked together. . . .

My father-in-law was white, and his wife was colored. They lived in Virginia . . . had these children, and like I tell people, if I got a problem with race, I got a problem with my family. I didn't have it before I married my wife, and it's certainly not going to be there now.

You talk about race relations here. I was raised here, and my mother had fifteen children here in the coal fields, and if it hadn't been for the white people helping my mother during the depression in the thirties when times was hard—Hoover Days—we'd starved to death. My father was a coal miner. . . . My mother'd send down to one of our neighbors, send a dime down to get buttermilk in a gallon bucket. The woman would fill that bucket up and give her a pound of butter. People helped each other.

I'm going to tell you something, if people have a problem with [integrated] services down here, they'll never go to heaven. There's no way in the world for you to go to heaven, if you can't serve with one another. . . .

If people respond to the truth—them that's trying to go to heaven—if a preacher is out here preaching the Word, and the Word of God hits a person, you're not going to look up there and say it's coming from an Indian, or from an African-American, or coming from a white man, or whatever. You're listening to the Word. The Bible says that with God there is no respect of persons. There's neither Jew nor Greek, barbarian, Assyrian, neither male nor female.[58]

I asked Anna Mae Cook, a black preacher and member of Bishop Lamb's church, whether it was unusual that black and white were worshiping together at the McRoberts Church of God:

Well, it may be, but that's just "isms" of men, for God made all of us. He made every man and every woman—Adam and Eve, the mother of us all.

A lot of churches have got mixed race around through here. Down in Pikeville, it's white and colored in one of our churches. There are even colored and white marriages. We just believe what the Lord say. We have colored and white here in our church. We just lost our assistant pastor. He was white.[59]

I have presented these three churches as examples of black and white people—mostly working-class people in the coalfields of Kentucky—living in harmony. I tried to find out why this area is different from elsewhere. The Red Fox people talked of their Christian love for one another. Bill Morton spoke of the people working in the mines together. The Town Mountain Baptists and their pastor, Rev. John Pray, suggested other reasons: living closely together, a sense of hospitality, and personal relations. Willie Lamb talked of everyone's knowing and helping one another and of the influence of the United Mine Workers union and coal-company policy.

William Turner is a coauthor, with Edward Cabbell, of *Blacks in Appalachia*. He was born in a coal-mining family in Lynch, Kentucky. In a telephone interview he spoke to me about racial harmony in the coalfields:

I believe in those places the fact that you didn't have these major class cleavages created conditions where black folk and white folk saw each other for what they were, and that is that we're all about the same, except for that which we get imposed upon us by society. One finds that particularly when there are such a small number of blacks, the white people get to know them very well, and they tend to accept people for who they are, even if inside one family one has done something heinous. They don't let that become the mark of the whole clan, but that one can be a good person inside an otherwise bad situation. So group identity doesn't become so important as does individual identity.

Going all the way back to the union effort with John L. Lewis, especially, there was always in many districts—I remember in my home district, Daddy's UMWA District 19—there was the idea that you'd alternate between a black and a white head and vice president of the union. I believe that the common toil and labor and that special camaraderie that gets generated when people are in a situation where they depend on each other to live for nine or ten hours a day tends to develop strong bonds down there in the belly of the earth. I think that carries over into their activities when they come outside the mine to a greater extent than it does with industrial workers in a factory in Chicago. In addition, the geophysical space is so restricted in a coal camp that you don't have a place to go hide from each other. There's just one road going up and down the hollow, so everybody sees everybody all the time. People came to form what the sociologist Durkheim called organic solidarity, as opposed to that mechanical solidarity that some people have because they're on the same bus. When you're on the same mantrip [the vehicle that carries miners into the mines], it's a whole different look. My father used to talk about so-and-so being a good old boy. He had whites that he flat-out didn't like, but there were others that he did like, and he made a distinction based on their individual characteristics. He'd say, "Now that's a mean SOB there." He didn't mean it as though he was a mean *white* SOB. They would never be the type to say, "Some of my best friends are . . ." They'd be the type to say, "I'm not saying this because he is black, but I just don't like him." I've heard that a thousand times.

But there's an indisputable fact that when mechanization came in the early fifties, blacks got laid off at much higher rates than whites did, and one cannot dispute that whites did have exclusive rights to certain positions, such as mechanics, the people who maintained the trains and the motors, the welders, the highly skilled jobs.[60]

Turner ends on a negative note, and certainly Upland people have not always been exemplary in race relations. Evelyn Williams, the subject of an Appalachian Film Workshop documentary video in its "Headwaters" series, spoke of problems in the coalfields:

I saw the Klan march when I was a child in 'twenty-five. . . . The Klan would march through the black camp, and I remember one night they'd set that cross afire. It came one of these pouring rains, and it drenched the cross. And they left the cross up there. We lived on the other side of the mountain, and when you came out you'd see that cross up there. I never thought too much of about that cross until my son was killed in Vietnam. We went out to the cemetery, and they'd put these little crosses with flags, and I looked at those flags . . . and it had such an effect on me, because all I could see was that cross burning on the hill over there, and the way that he had died. . . . I had to be sedated. And I said, "You never know the impact that these things have on youngsters." . . .

It was April 10, 1934, and we were in Vicco at a ball game, and someone came in and said they had lynched Rex. We heard the noise. I'll never forget that Rebel cry, that squealing, the jubilee, of that time.

The [black] men went back and they worked with them. It was just one of those things. They talked about it, but they were powerless. . . . I guess at that time it dawned on me what powerlessness meant, and injustice. . . .

When I left here, nothing had been done, and when I came back here in the seventies, there were several who pointed out different ones that had been involved in that lynching, and nothing was done. . . .

Up at the company store they had a canteen—whites sit over here and blacks over here. . . . They would put a speck of black paint on the bottom of a glass [for blacks] so they wouldn't mix them. And some of the blacks protested, and they wanted to know why we didn't have the same service that they did. "Oh, there's nothing about it—nothing about it," they would say. Then they stopped the black paint on the glass.

But there was always something there to let you know that you were separate and unequal.[61]

Even though there has been overt racism in the Uplands, the ordinary people in these three churches and communities have done better than have people in most American communities. There have been other examples where Upland Christians have fought the negatives of human nature and have shown Christian charity in many ways.

Death

The concern that overarches the lives of common people is the final experience: death. In interviews I found a preoccupation with death. We all fear not being. Religion and human imagination deal with this basic dread. Common people try to understand death and the mystery of life through religion but also through folklore, superstitions, myths, and legends. Numerous stories abound of ghosts and other spirits that appear from the Great Beyond. Religion, however, is the main source of information and speculation about life and death and what may lie beyond. *Strong's Exhaustive Concordance of the Bible* has more than a page—three columns—of references to death. Perhaps the one verse that encompasses the Christian Gospel best is John 5:24, "Verily, verily, I say unto you, He that heareth my word, and believeth on him that sent me, hath everlasting life, and shall not come into condemnation; but is passed from death unto life." The most-quoted passages at funerals is from 1 Corinthians 15:54–55: "Death is swallowed up in victory. O death, where is thy sting? O grave, where is thy victory?"

I believe that rural Uplanders have an organic and natural relationship with the cycle of life and death, seeing it always around them. Ordinary folk talk more frankly of death than do those who may feel that dwelling on death and tragedy is somehow unsophisticated. James K. Crissman, in his book *Death and Dying in Central Appalachia,* asserts that most contemporary Americans are reluctant to talk about death and dying, and they employ substitute terms such as "passed away," "expired," or any of sixty-seven other euphemisms that have been identified. He suggests that Appalachians, because of their relative isolation, have retained an older attitude toward death: "Death was commonplace, but that didn't make the death of a loved one easy. The peculiarities of this culture and especially family closeness gave rise to a distinctive relationship with death that allowed for honor and dignity for the deceased and grieving and comfort for the survivors."[62]

John Ferry Moore, a North Georgia Baptist minister, told of his growing up in a Christian home and being taught early about death:

I can remember Mommy believed and taught us that one had to die. She was not afraid to talk about death. Neither was she afraid for her children to hear, "That it is appointed unto men to die." She also believed that one should live. Must live here, and must live now, until the hour of death. And that both the living and the dying experience needed to be considered with common sense. And that this common sense consideration would produce a desire, and the will to work and prepare for living, today, tomorrow, and next year, and also to face death squarely when it appears. I recall one day, when I was a small boy, Mommy told us that a baby was dead in the community. . . . Mommy said, "I am going to the funeral at two o'clock." After we had eaten dinner, Mommy got ready to go. Then she got me ready. She held my hand as we walked down the winding road a mile and a half to the church. . . .

The mother, a tall, strong woman, was beside herself, torn with grief, such as I had not known at that time. Mommy quietly wept with her. As the people passed the coffin, Mommy took my hand

and we looked at the child for a moment. . . . The men nailed the lid back on the coffin. One man lifted it gently and carried it to the little grave in the churchyard. . . .

As we walked home I asked Mommy . . . what I really wanted to know. I had not cried, and I was not upset, but I was somewhat troubled about the hole in the graveyard with the ugly red dirt piled up beside it, and the little coffin going down into that cold, red, hard ground. So I asked Mommy about it. She told me very simply how that when people die, they must be placed in the ground and be covered with earth until the Goodman, the Lord, should come. Then the graves would be opened and the baby, with others, would be alive again. I knew the certainty in Mommy's voice. I knew that she was telling the truth, and I liked what she said, and I believe it now.

The things that Mommy settled in my mind, however little I understood then, have stood me in good stead many times as it has been my responsibility as a Christian and as a preacher to sing a song or say a word of comfort while standing at the casket of one who has faced this thing of death, of the loved ones and friends who seek for some understanding of, and a glimpse into the day of the dead living again.[63]

No matter what the belief is in terms of the end of time, the Second Coming, or the Resurrection, Upland Christians connect death with the hereafter, with heaven as their promised place where there will be no more earthly cares. Charlie Cole, a Southern Baptist deacon from Carter County, Tennessee, put it this way: "I think every child of God is really looking out yonder to heaven. We've got hope in that direction. We think of heaven as being a place of happiness, freedom from sorrow, no disappointments, or chaos. . . . We appreciate the fact that we have a final place of happiness for us."[64]

The human condition is seen as a precarious one in the Uplands. The economic underpinning for many people is shaky. Social position and thus self-respect may be low, poor health is likely, and death is inevitable. From the religious point of view, we are always in danger of being led astray or failing to live up even to our own expectations because of our inherent weakness and fallibility. Many believe that we are depraved from the time of Adam's fall, that we will never be able to withstand temptation and trouble by our own strength, and thus that we can achieve goodness and eventually salvation only by the grace of God. Others, of course, believe more in the efficacy of people to look to their own salvation and to prepare themselves by studying the Scriptures, by attending Sunday Schools, church meetings, revivals, and the like, by actively seeking the Lord and salvation, and by resisting temptation and striving mightily to be Christlike. Whatever our theological orientation, for most of us, meaning in life and understanding of the human condition are largely religious matters.

2 *God*

O Lord, thou art my God; I will exalt thee, I will
praise thy name; for thou hast done wonderful
things. . . . For thou hast been a strength to the
poor, a strength to the needy in his distress, a refuge
from the storm, a shadow from the heat, when the
blast of the terrible ones is as a storm against the
wall. . . . He will swallow up death in victory; and
the Lord God will wipe away tears from off all faces:
and the rebuke of his people shall he take away from
off all the earth: for the Lord hath spoken it.

And it shall be said in that day, Lo, this is our
God; we have waited for him, and he will save us:
this is the Lord; we have waited for him, we will be
glad and rejoice in his salvation.

—Isaiah 25:1–9

We Upland people also ask the big questions: How did we and all around us come to be? Is there a God who created us and everything? If so, what is His nature? Why did He make us as we are, and what is His purpose for our lives? Is there something beyond this life, and if so, what is it like? How is God related to us and all around us in this day and time? What answers we have come mostly from the Bible and what we have been taught in other ways. Meaning for us starts with Genesis, where God the Creator emerges, as does His nemesis, Satan, and humankind. Thus we share a system of meaning directly with the Judaeo-Christian world. Through myth and other spiritual systems, however, we share meaning with a much larger portion of the world's people.

No doubt we have nuances of meaning here that differ from understandings found elsewhere, but mostly we are like people everywhere. Our questions arise through mystery, layer on layer. We, the world in which we live, and the unknown beings and things beyond knowing are too marvelous, too intricate and complicated, for us to believe they just happened without a grand creator, but we know we will understand only partially, even though we spend our days somewhere in the back of our minds pondering these imponderables. We come to conclusions sometimes aside from the Bible, but mostly we rely on its teaching, accepting the answers it gives and chewing endlessly on the questions it raises.

The words I have gathered in this chapter are mostly oral testimony, musings, or strongly held convictions given voice by people of the Uplands in talking about God and their experience in seeking Him. Some speak directly, whereas others tell stories that illustrate something important to them about the nature of God and our need for Him. Some have had an encounter with God, whereas others have not. Yet most have firm beliefs about Him. Some of these statements will not be different from what you might hear from Christians anywhere, and this illuminates the fact that there are more similarities between Upland people and others than there are differences. This is not to say, however, that the differences are not sometimes distinctive and profound.

The Need for God

Rev. John Ferry Moore, a North Georgia Baptist pastor, told about becoming lost with friends on a nighttime coonhunt and walking many miles only to find that they had circled back on their own trail. He compared this to life's journey and our need for a guide:

> I found out later what an old man had meant when he told me, "If you get lost in the woods, don't just keep going. Set down agin a tree, put yore face in yore hands, between yore knees, and just set there, and think slow. Don't keep on walkin' if you don't know where you're going. But it'll come to you atter while and you can find yore way."
>
> In unfamiliar territory there must be some object, the sun, a mountain peak, a tree, that can be seen, now and again to guide you straight.
>
> Life itself is like that. It is all unfamiliar territory. Every day is twenty-four hours to walk through. Never before has there been one like it. Never will there be another one like it. Yet there is One who

has walked every step of it before us. He knows the end from the beginning of every day. If He is the object by which our steps are to be guided, we can walk, even "through the valley of the shadows of death," we can "come through the wilderness."

However if I refuse to turn my steps toward the One who stands at the center of the universe. . . . This one who calls, every hour from the heart of life itself, and who Himself is the Fountain of Life, . . . if I refuse His light and His call, my steps soon circle back to my own selfishness. To my own littleness, and my own pride. Hopelessly floundering in my own self-righteousness. With no peace and no happiness.

If anyone would take my old friend's advice. Just let him stop walking, and scrambling, and falling, and circling back to stumble over the same trails again. . . .

There is One who has broken the trail through the dismal swamp. He made a way through every thicket of thorns, even wearing some on his brow. He climbed the last mountain. There He opened the gate to life and happiness, for this world and the world to come.[1]

We all have our doubts at times about God and what we have been taught. Elder Frank Fugate, an Old Regular Baptist, said, "You may doubt—is there a God? Look all around you. You can see God's presence everywhere. It would take a crazy person to doubt that there is a God, whenever they can see His life all around them and experience His life in our existence."[2] Elder T. G. Bates, another Old Regular Baptist from Hazard, Kentucky, believed, "The greatest thing for all of us is to fear God," and added: "What does it mean to fear God? It is the beginning of wisdom."[3] For these Christians, God is ever-present around them. They do not doubt His existence, although they may debate His nature.

The Nature of God

Pastor Henry T. Mahan, of the Thirteenth Street Baptist Church of Ashland, Kentucky, spoke of God from what we think of as a Calvinist orientation, in terms of His throne—of glory and majesty; of holiness, justice, and righteousness; and of grace—contrasting these characteristics to those of the human condition:

His throne is a throne of sovereignty. . . . Is anything too hard for God? The Scriptures say that the Lord rules over all. God is God! He declares the end from the beginning. . . . God's rule is an everlasting dominion, and . . . He doeth His will in the armies of Heaven among the inhabitants of the earth. . . . God is sovereign. He worketh all things after the counsel of His own will, and that's in creation, and that's in providence, and that's in salvation. That's the God of the Bible. He said to Moses, "I'll have mercy on whom I'll have mercy. I'll be gracious unto whom I'll be gracious to."

None can stay God's hand. If He sets out to save, He'll save. If He sets out to damn, He'll damn. He has the key to Hell and death, and the One who carries the keys is the one in charge.

And then, His throne is the throne of wisdom (Psalm 104:24 and 136:5). That's the God of the Bible, the God of creation. That's the living God. That's the God of the universe. That's my God.

They said to David, "Where's your God?" All the heathens and pagans talked about their little peanut gods, the gods they'd whittled out of their own imaginations, these little idols, etc. He said, "My God's in the heavens." "What's He like, David?" "Whatever my God pleases, He does, in heaven, earth, and the seas, and all deep places. . . ."

Our God is God, glorious, magnificent, majestic, eternal, sovereign, just, holy, righteous, wise! Great God, how infinite are Thou! What worthless worms are we. Let the whole race of creatures bow and worship only Thee.[4]

Elder Steve Casteel, a Primitive Baptist who lived in Berea, Kentucky, when it was my fortune to meet and interview him in 1981, added to this image of an all-powerful God: "We're talking about a merciful God, an all-wise God and an all-purpose God. He is so sovereign that He can do whatever pleases Him, and we dare not question it. That's what the Scriptures teach me, and I think that is the general teaching of His church, whether it bears the name of Primitive Baptists or Church of Christ. God is all-wise, almighty, everlasting. He knows the end from the beginning, and nothing surprises Him. He surprises us, but nothing surprises God."[5]

Debbie Isaacs, a Pentecostal believer from Rockcastle County, Kentucky, also saw God as almighty, all powerful: "Yessir, see, God said there was all power given unto Him, and if He made heaven and earth, He can do anything. If He could make you and me out of clay, He could do anything. . . . Yessir, if He could make a living being, a human being, and could breathe in his nostrils and make a living soul, He could do anything."[6]

Elder Virgil Combs, of the Indian Bottom Association of Old Regular Baptists, spoke of God's all-knowing nature in a sermon:

God knows all about me. He knows all about you. He knows where each and every one of us is at today. He also knows what we stand in need of. God knows the very intents of our minds and hearts. When I ask someone to pray for me, God knows whether you pray or not. He knows what you've got in your mind, and He knows what you need in your heart. He knows that you need Him if you don't have Him. God knows so much about us. Many years ago if He knew where a mule was at, surely He knows where we are at. . . . What I'm trying to get across to you is what a powerful God we've got. I believe He knows every ant that crawls in the woods and every bird that flies in the air. Everything there is in creation, He knows all about. . . .

God knows you today. He knows you by name. He's not going to get you mixed up with somebody else. If He did, you wouldn't know who He was talking to. This God knows every individual here on this earth, this great big wide world, not just in this country, nor just here in the state of Kentucky, not just in the United States, but all over the world. God knows every man and every woman. This day is set aside for Christian people to worship God, and in many places all over the world they're worshiping God this day, and many prayers have gone up, but He's able to hear them every one. We wouldn't be able to do that because our puny minds just wouldn't handle it. . . .

God knows whether you are a sinner or saint today. He knows those who are not His. When I got in trouble over my sins, God knowed what I had done, and God's got a record of your life, but twenty-two years ago God forgave me of those sins. They will never be remembered against me no more.[7]

The late Elder Frank Fugate, one of the great spirits in Upland Christianity, talked eloquently and fervently about God, stressing our earthly inability to see and understand Him:

If only all people could understand this God who is everywhere out there around us. God is light, a God that we can't see with these eyes. We feel him. He has promised in His Scriptures that He would teach all men, that He would write His laws in our hearts and print them in our minds. That is written in the minds of all adult people, whether they can recognize it or not, because God speaks to us in feelings, in knowledge. We never go to commit a wrong but what we feel in our minds, understand, that it is wrong. Well, that is the law of God written in our hearts and minds. He works in the minds of people. We'll never see God with these eyes. We are going to have to die and be resurrected, and the fullness of us is going to have to be achieved in the Lord, and then we are going to have eyes that can see the beauty of God, the God that is in you and over you and under you, the God that these eyes can't see.[8]

Elder John Sparks, from Offutt, Kentucky, is a young college-educated United Baptist preacher who is as articulate and knowledgeable as any person with whom I talked. He is humbled, and thus hesitant, in trying to describe God: "God is a spirit, the creator of the universe, heaven and earth, everything therein contained. I would like to be able to find the words to adequately describe God, but they fail me. Even to call God the creator of all things in capital letters, it seems to me, is to do a disservice."[9]

God's Power and Human Response

Elder Johnny Blackburn, a Primitive Baptist from Pike County, Kentucky, believed that God knows His purpose and will exert His will whether or not we have prepared ourselves and invited His help: "People will get up and tell you that the Lord will do so and so if you'll let Him. You know, I'd hate to believe in a God like that—that has to wait and see what you and me's going to do. I'll tell you what, that's not Israel's God. That's not the God of Abraham, and that's not the God of Isaac. The God of Abraham, Isaac, and Jacob is a God that does His will in the armies of heaven and earth, and none can stay His hand."[10]

An unidentified Pentecostal minister had the opposite belief, that is, that God will not enter our lives until we ask Him to. "God will be where we let Him be." He went on to say that because the congregation wanted God to be with them in their service, "I have no doubt that God is here tonight. I feel His presence here. I have no doubt that God is real. He is able tonight. God's willing tonight. God is concerned tonight, hallelujah! He can help us tonight. He can save you tonight, Glory to God!"[11] Elder Squire Watts, an Old Regular Baptist, also felt that God speaks to us only if we open ourselves to Him. He believed also that you have to be willing for God to save you:

Do you hear God's voice today? If you ain't listening, you'll never hear it. If you don't want God to speak to you, He sure won't. If you don't want to do His will, you never will. . . . This voice can speak to your heart today. If you do what that still small voice bids you to do, you'll wind up in heaven. My friends, there ain't enough devils in the world . . . can get you when you get inside that fold. You can't keep yourself. You'll be kept by the power of God, through faith in His Son. . . . If you do what God wants you to do, what God bids you to do, you'll be all right. . . . The hardest thing I ever done in my life was to get willing to do God's will—to lay my pride down, be humble to follow that low still voice, do what He wants me to do.[12]

Coy Miser, a Kentucky Pentecostal quoted by Deborah V. McCauley in her book *Appalachian Religion: A History,* thought that God can live only in our hearts, but we have to be willing to let Him in. Mr. Miser's emphasis on the heart as the seat of religion is common in the Uplands:

In order to have religion, we've got to have him in our heart and that's the only place he's got to live. Of all, as big as the world is . . . , as many people as there are, that's the only place that God has got to live in this world is in the hearts of people, men and women. He's big enough to fill the universe, but yet he is small enough to live in our hearts. . . . that's the only place that he has to live in this world because he can't set foot in this world until it's purified. . . . But the only place right now he's got to live is in the hearts of people, and that's just the ones that let him come in.[13]

The Reverend Douglas Jessee, pastor of the First United Methodist Church of Cary, North Carolina, spoke in a way that would be approved by many of the Old-Time Baptists, in terms of God taking the initiative in our lives: "You and I are unlikely choices. But God can work through us, sometimes in spite of ourselves. . . . Our baptism, however it occurred, is an objective fact. In our baptism God moved toward us. We didn't find Him; He found us. We didn't choose Him. He chose us."[14]

All those people quoted believe fervently in God and what the Bible says about Him. To them, He is all-sufficient, and they believe that to recognize this makes us wiser. Lizzie Combs, an Old Regular Baptist from eastern Kentucky, added to this certainty: "People change, but God is the same forever and ever."[15]

God and Human Equality

When Edgar Miller, a Southern Baptist, spoke of God being no respecter of persons, he meant that God does not think more highly of one person than another because of status or accomplishments. I have frequently heard this egalitarian belief throughout the Uplands, the idea that one person is no better than another, temporally or spiritually: "God is love. He is holy, and He has no respect of persons, that is the greatest part of all. As He looks down on us, you know we can't buy our salvation. You know that one person can't buy and be a little better than the other one. When God looks on us, we're all equal. We're just alike, and that's the way He has no respect of persons, see, and you know if He had respect of persons, a guy like me could be left completely out. Somebody would get ahead of me and push me back."[16]

Millard Scott, pastor of the Free Pentecostal Church in Laurel County, Kentucky, also spoke of God's not being a respecter of persons: "You get saved by faith. Anything you get from God you get by faith. He is the rewarder of them that diligently seek Him. You won't get by just because of who you are. God is no respecter of persons. . . . Thank God, He loved the black man just as He loves us."[17]

God and the Word: Calling His People

Elder Frank Fugate spoke on the effect of God in the lives of people and the consequences of their turning away from God. Reflecting a non-Calvinistic belief bordering on perfectibility, he claimed that we will be better people if we seek salvation and that this will make the world a better place:

> If we had God in our lives, it would make better fathers and mothers. God in the lives of people makes better judges, better sheriffs. If all people had God in their lives, we wouldn't need sheriffs and officials and jailhouses, as we have today. . . . God's people has forsaken Him. They have growed cold. They have been caught in the swift current of nature, which is hate, which is prejudice, which is partiality. Our minds have got to be renewed and made alive.
>
> If only our religious world hadn't of lost and turned its back on God, our world wouldn't be in the condition it is today. The millions of dollars that are being appropriated are not going to solve this. We might think we have the answer, but we do not. Money won't achieve these things.[18]

In some Old Baptist associations there is a tradition of assigning someone to write a "circular letter" for the printed minutes of the annual association meetings. The writer usually picks a subject that he thinks is important for the health of the association and its individual churches. He may also use the occasion to proclaim his own faith in and understanding of God. Elder Claren Williams, moderator of the Little Home Old Regular Baptist Church at Red Fox, Kentucky, gave his view of God and His work with His people:

> The thing that bears upon my mind is Love. God tells his people to love one another, and he that is born of God is born of love. Brothers, I believe that sometime in our lives God will visit every man and woman upon this earth, and will let them understand that they are sinners and a savior is needed. . . . I believe every nation shall be taught of God. . . . I believe in the general resurrection of the just and unjust, and I believe that all will stand before God in judgment and give an account of their behavior here upon this earth, whether it be good or bad. I believe God is merciful unto all, and will give every man and woman a chance to be saved, if they want to bad enough, they will have to lay down their sinful life. . . .
>
> Brothers, I hope we will continue in the good old way, neither turning to the right or left, but hold just to which is right and trust in God. I feel sometimes that I have had my share of heartaches and trouble, but then I think of the promise that God said, that he would not suffer his people no more than they are able to bear. . . . I hope that as we travel through this narrow land of life, that we could pray a little more, so that God could strengthen us and give us a little more understanding that we might be a little stronger, and our lights be a little brighter.[19]

Elder Teddy Ball, of the Coon Creek Primitive Baptist Church in Pike County, Kentucky, spoke of God's putting a godly sorrow in our hearts so that we will repent and turn to Him. His belief in predestination is evident throughout his statement:

> He has mercy on whom He will have mercy. He has compassion on whom He will have compassion. God does His will; we must be still and know that He is God. I believe that if you will read the Book God will bless you to understand it. . . . We believe that God has to work a godly sorrow in your heart before you will want to repent. We believe that godly sorrow is set up in men and women's hearts and induces them to humble repentance.
>
> Certainly I never thought that my preaching ever saved anybody, but that it is through Christ. If I could save you, I wouldn't have any-

where to put you after I saved you. I'm glad that the one who does the saving has prepared a place for us before He did the saving.[20]

The late Elder Banner Manns, from Hueysville, Kentucky, one-time moderator of the New Salem Association of Old Regular Baptists, limited the idea of predestination to the act of God in enlightening "every intelligent adult person on earth, through His reproving spirit, which teaches us that we are out of the ark of safety and living in a state of condemnation before God." He went on to discuss the seven spirits of God mentioned in Revelation:

God is a spirit, and he has many spirits. We read in the Bible where he had seven spirits [Rev. 1:4, 3:1, 4:5, 5:6], and those spirits visit people, living people here on earth, to teach them and to show them that the wages of sin is death; but the gift of God is eternal life through Jesus Christ, our Lord. . . . He has the spirit of wisdom, spirit of knowledge, the spirit of love, and the spirit of love and compassion. He has a spirit that loves all of His creation, because the Bible says, "For God so loved the world, that he gave his only begotten Son, that whosoever believeth on him should not perish, but have everlasting life" [John 3:16].

God's Call to Preach

Elder Manns continued eloquently on the subject of his being convicted by God's Spirit and then saved, and he explained his belief about what that entailed. Then he talked of his call to preach, his resistance to the call, and his explanation of the way God reveals religious truths and His purposes to those whom He has called, even those who have little formal education:

When this Spirit of God came to me, even early in life, I at that time loved sin. I enjoyed sin; but after I came to the point where I believed, then it moved me to seek the Lord. . . . And at the time, at the end of my suffering and travail, which means trouble, I offered God everything I had. I don't mean by that to say that I offered God money or land. I offered Him my life, my very life, if He would save me from sin. At this time I was on my knees in public for the first time, praying to God for forgiveness. God's Spirit had come in such a way that It moved upon me, that I felt the Spirit of God in my face and all over my body. When prayer was completed, I rose from the earth [and] for the first time used this phrase and said, "Blessed be the name of the Lord. . . ." God's promise to me was if I was to come to Him through faith, that He would save me from sin, that I would become dead to sin, which means no longer in love therewith. . . .

What inspired me [to preach] was the visitation of the Holy Spirit of God that taught me that He had chosen me as a vessel or minister of the Gospel. I argued with God. . . . The Spirit made contact with me, with my mind and with my spirit, just like you would set around and study a book and this would open to you. The Spirit talked to me, and of course, I told God that I just couldn't. I told Him that in my mind, probably with my tongue . . . , that I was not qualified. I told God that I was uneducated. I told God that He should call somebody with more education and better prepared . . . to serve Him and deliver the message of the Gospel to men on this earth. . . . I was telling God . . . that it was so serious to preach, that I feared I might sow the wrong kind of seed in the lives of men and women, that I might cause them to believe the wrong thing. Because I hadn't considered that God's Spirit would come in due time and at God's own time and transform my mind from the natural things on earth into the spiritual things of God and the realities of God.

We speak—we don't speak, but the Bible speaks—of a revelation. Now revelation means to me that God's Spirit opens our understanding, that God's Spirit interprets for us the great mysteries of God, a portion of it. It [revelation] makes me different even from the lay members . . . of the church that God hasn't chosen to preach the Gospel. It makes me able to understand portions of the Scriptures, especially the necessary things that God wants the congregation to hear, to believe and obey.[21]

An unidentified Pentecostal preacher spoke also of his call to return home and preach. I have heard many such testimonies from preachers about God's call to preach, their efforts to avoid the call, and God's persistence: "I was working up in Indianapolis, making good money. I'm from Kentucky . . . , but I couldn't wait to get away from here, I was so tired of the place. But, my friend, God dealt with my heart. He said, 'I want you to go [back to Kentucky],' and He put something inside of me that made me content. Hallelujah! God is real! Like Jonah, I tried to run from God. He needs to shake our lives at times. Sometimes the Spirit of God has to come down and get ahold of you and shake you, Glory to God, He brought me home to preach!"[22]

The Trinity

For most Christians, God is in three persons—Father, Son, and Holy Spirit. Yet we are ambiguous when we speak of the Trinity, using names interchangeably at times and using several names for each element: we call God either Lord, Father, Creator, or Almighty; His Son we call Lord, Jesus, Christ, Redeemer, Savior, and Son of Man; and the Holy Spirit is also known as the Holy Ghost or simply the Spirit. Perhaps the Trinity is more a mystery to all of us than we care to discuss. The constitution of the Burning Springs Association of Regular Primitive Baptists in eastern Kentucky deals with the subject in this way: "We believe in only one true and living God, Father, Son and Holy Ghost, equal in essence, power and glory. Yet there are not three Gods, but one." Perhaps this article of faith partially explains why the many titles of the Trinity are interchanged.

Some Upland Christians, however, resemble Unitarian Universalists in rejecting the Trinity; these groups include the Pentecostal Apostolic churches and other small Appalachian groups such as the Church of God in Jesus' Name Only.

It seems to me that we also see another threesome in the equation that most concerns us—God, the devil (often tied to things of "the world"), and humankind. In this chapter and others we hear Upland voices discussing God in three persons, but always in a context that includes the devil (and the world) and people. An unidentified North Carolina Methodist states the issue this way:

> Yes, the devil has his side and God His, the devil on the left side of mankind and God on the right side. The devil brings up the things of the flesh and tries to draw man away from God. Sometimes he makes it. Sometimes he makes a good strike after it. Sometimes he draws us away from God, and we find ourselves in the path of disobedience to God, and God has to call us back. And because He calls us, we hear that voice that says, "Overcome evil with good." That's what makes us come to church; that's what makes us bow our heads at the door and ask God to move all evil things out of the way, that we might worship God in spirit and truth.[23]

I have heard the Trinity described in several ways by different Christians. Although many use names of the three facets of the deity interchangeably, some find scriptural bases for definite ideas about the discreet purpose of each. Rev. L. O. Johnson, pastor of the Evangel Church of God of Prophecy, Cumberland County, Tennessee, said: "We believe in the Trinity. We believe in God the Father, and His Son, and the Holy Ghost. . . . Each represents the other, and they are inseparable, and yet they are three distinct divine beings."[24] G. A. Perry, of the Riverview Baptist Church in Knoxville, said this:

> God the Father, God the Son, the Holy Ghost—they are the Godhead, the three. Each has a separate office, doing particular work, and they are counted as one. And God was the Father, the Jesus the Son, and the Holy Spirit or Holy Ghost is the Comforter who came in Jesus. After He departed this world, why then He sent the Comforter or Holy Spirit to minister in His place. We know that Christ is the only one that has been perfect. He was even victorious over death in the grave, and He lives today in the hearts of those that know Him and are believers.[25]

Bishop (his given name, not a title) Pentz, a Presbyterian from Allegheny County, Virginia, added:

> I think it is a little difficult for the layman to really understand . . . three persons in one and be able to have a mental picture of God in three persons. I have never been able to do that. I can't say that God looks like this or that or something else. It's something you have to think of and feel in your mind, as a spirit, as a mental activity without any particular form, and from that viewpoint, you can see God as the Father and that Christ came on this earth and lived as a man. We have all sorts of mental pictures of Christ, but when you get to the Holy Ghost, you run into a difficult problem that has to be seen as a mental or spiritual activity, rather than something with form. If you see all three as a mental or spiritual activity, then you can see them as three in one.[26]

Upland Christians express gratitude that God sent his Son into the world to save us, and most of their emphasis is on Jesus. Sister Diane Harrison, a Pentecostal, said in a radio testimony: "I thank God today—I praise and honor Him—that Jesus is real, and I don't have to profess [Him]; I can possess [Him], and that means a lot. He is just a prayer away."[27] Elder Elwood Cornett, an Old Regular Baptist, said: "Jesus is a special Savior to the believer. It's not that He is a special Savior to the rich, well-off, highly intelligent. He is a special Savior to the believer, whoever he is. I thank God that is the way."[28] Elder John Sparks, United Baptist, said: "That is the purpose that Jesus was sent to earth, because what we lost in Adam, we gain in Jesus Christ. We have eternal life through Him. We have fellowship with God which is what He wants for His creation."[29]

In its 1979 minutes, the New Salem Association of Old Regular Baptists reprinted a circular letter by Elder N. T. Hopkins from the 1922 minutes. He emphasized the human state of Jesus, comparing Jesus' role in the church to Moses' role in ancient Israel. Here are excerpts:

> For Moses truly said unto the fathers: A prophet shall the Lord your God raise up unto you of your brethren like unto me; him shall ye hear in all things, whatsoever he shall say unto you. So Christ was to be raised up of his brethren in the church, just the same as Moses was of the tribe of Israel, and was their leader; for Moses says, he is to be like unto me, and the children of Israel were to hear Moses and to observe all things that he spake unto them; so we are to observe all things that Christ said unto his brethren in the church. . . . He [was] just as much a member of the church as Moses was a member of Israel. He could not have been like unto Moses if he hadn't taken up fellowship with his brethren; so we see him coming to John the Baptist and demanding baptism of him and John baptized him in the river Jordan and thus laid the corner stone in Zion as was prophesied by Isaiah 18th chapter 16th verse, Therefore saith the Lord God, Behold, I lay in Zion for a foundation, a stone, a sure foundation, a tried stone, a precious corner stone. . . . I will also cite you to Deut. 18th chapter 15th verse: The Lord thy God will raise up unto thee a Prophet from the midst of thee, of thy brethren, like unto me, unto him shall ye hearken; verse 18th, I will raise them up a prophet from among their brethren, like unto thee, and will put my words in his mouth; and he shall speak unto them all that I shall command him . . . All the foregoing scriptures show that he was wanting and was willing to be equal to his brethren, for as much as the children are partakers of flesh and blood he himself likewise took part of the same for verily he took not on him the nature of angels; but took on him the seed of Abraham, and so being found in fashion as man he humbled himself down with his brethren and took up fellowship with them in the church. . . .
>
> "The servant is not greater than the master, neither [is] he that is sent greater than him who sent him. . . ." So precious brethren and sisters, cheer up and do all your Christian duties and keep yourselves unspotted from the world; keep your lamps trimmed and burning,

ready to meet the bridegroom, the husband of the church, our elder brother.[30]

Grace Jimson, a Southern Baptist from Transylvania County, North Carolina, also spoke of the importance of Jesus' being on earth in the flesh. Jesus is frequently mentioned as a "personal Savior," emphasizing one of the deep values in the region, that of personalism:

> Well, I think it is a wonderful thing to know that Jesus came to live on earth, and came in the flesh. By Him coming in the flesh, He could sympathize more with the people that are living in the flesh now. By Him living in the flesh, why He could have more sympathy for us. . . .
>
> If it hadn't been for the love of God in sending His Son to us, we wouldn't have any hope, so it's through His love that we have the hope of eternal life.
>
> I think that though He was here without sin that He had compassion for us because the flesh is so weak we are easy to fall into temptation, and I think that's why God is so ready to forgive us these things, because of course Jesus is our intercessor to God.[31]

Brother Turner, pastor of a Kentucky Pentecostal church, stressed the personal nature of Jesus and His being right here with us: "Jesus is still the same as He was, and I know He's right here. I've already felt Him. I don't have to call up to heaven to get Him down because He's already here. I don't have to shout at the top of my voice because He's already here. He's right here!"[32]

Calvin C. Wyatt, a member of the Church of God of Prophecy in Cumberland County, Tennessee, also talked of a personal Christ:

> It's a great consolation to me to know that when I go out to work or play, whatever it might be, even though I am not in service, I can still have Christ with me. I have the assurance that Christ said that He would be with us always. I don't have to go out there alone, but I have the Lord with me always. I can always feel Christ with me, in working or in playing or in church or wherever I might be, because you can always call on Christ, and if we have Him with us, we don't have to go somewhere else to find Him. We can feel Him, and He is our very present help in time of need.[33]

Old Regular Baptist elder T. G. Bates, then eighty-seven years old, with sixty-three years in the ministry, said these interesting words at a memorial service for a departed fellow minister, also emphasizing the personal nature of Jesus' gift to us:

> The strangest thing about the Bible came over me last night. I never had that thought before. Three things the Son of God must accomplish. The Bible tells us that Jesus has conquered death, hell, and the grave. What came over me is that He did that for Himself. . . . [but] He [also] conquered death, hell, and the grave for me. . . . I've got to go through death—and the plan of God will bring that to pass—for me. . . . The victory is in the Lord Jesus Christ, who brought it to pass and gave personally to me and to you that believe in the Lord Jesus Christ a victory from death and from hell and from the grave.[34]

Edward Hicks, a coal miner and member of the Church of the Brethren in Dickenson County, Virginia, succinctly summed up Christ's primary purpose:

> I believe that when Jesus Christ was born here on this earth, He came for one purpose. That was the saving of the souls of men. He led the life that was given to Him through the spiritual consolation of His Father, and He came to earth to be thirty-three years old, completed that course, and give His blood that we might live, and He laid the plan of salvation. I believe today that if every man, every woman, would take up and follow where Christ laid down, gave his life, that they are preparing for them a home in glory. And I find in the many commands He gave that He left no way for to turn back, or to go back and commence over, but to press forward onward to reach a mark.[35]

It is important to many people that Jesus was sent to live an earthly life so that he could intervene and save a lost people. Jesus is thus seen in a personal way, as approachable, understanding, empathetic, and desiring to save us, whereas God is almighty, remote, and less approachable. Jesus, because he had an earthly experience, is closer to us, knows our earthly troubles, and can intervene with the Father to plead our case. Some, like Brother C. A. Williams, a Free Pentecostal from eastern Kentucky, believe that we cannot speak directly to God but should pray to Jesus, who will interpret us to God:

> We don't believe that a man can speak directly to God. In fact, Jesus, has to relay what we say to God, because we believe that God is so

much above us, and Jesus died and is sitting at the right hand of the Father. That's His position, and He is pleading our case in this world here tonight. I believe that the Bible says He was made a high priest forever after the order of Melchizadek. And there always had been a high priest between God and man, because no man could ever look on God. And so that's why Jesus took our place. He knew our infirmities, our weaknesses, and so we don't go to a priest or somewhere to confess our sins, but we go directly to Jesus, and Jesus goes to God Himself.[36]

The Holy Spirit is the third person in the Trinity. The word *spirit* comes from the Latin *spiritus,* "breath," that is, something that has a presence and yet cannot be seen. It is also something that animates or brings life. Some connect it with the soul of a person. The New Testament presents the Spirit as connected to God, however, as in Matthew 3:16, which says that after Christ was baptized, "he saw the Spirit of God descending like a dove, and lighting upon him." The Spirit is seen also as a gift from Jesus to His disciples, as in John 20:22: "he breathed on them, and saith unto them, Receive the Holy Ghost." In addition, it is seen as a presence within each believer. Some stress the nature of the Holy Spirit as the Comforter that Jesus mentioned in John 14:16, 26: "And I will pray the Father, and he shall give you another Comforter, that he may abide with you forever. . . . But the Comforter, which is the Holy Ghost, whom the Father will send in my name, he shall teach you all things, and bring all things to your remembrance, whatsoever I have said unto you."

Among Holiness-Pentecostals I have heard much emphasis on the baptism of the Holy Spirit, as in the Day of Pentecost described in Acts 2:2–4, 4:31–32: "there came a sound from heaven as of a rushing mighty wind . . . and they were all filled with the Holy Ghost, and began to speak with other tongues, as the Spirit gave them utterance. . . . And when they had prayed, the place was shaken where they were assembled together; and they were all filled with the Holy Ghost, and they spake the word of God with boldness. And the multitude of them that believed were of one heart and one soul."

United Baptist elder John Sparks said, "We believe that Jesus works right now through the Holy Ghost exactly the way He did in the body when He was on earth."[37] Bonnie Garrett, a Pentecostal believer, said: "The Holy Ghost is a comforter that Jesus said He would send back when He went away. You know you have it [the Holy Ghost] by the evidence of speaking in other tongues. That is the evidence of the Comforter."[38] Victor Williams, of the Free Pentecostal Church in Laurel County, Kentucky, also spoke of the

Holy Ghost as the Comforter: "The Bible says He seeks us to worship Him in Spirit and in truth. So many times it speaks of the Spirit in the Bible. It says without the Spirit of Christ you are none of His. In fact, He is our example, and we need His Spirit. He said, 'It is expedient that I go away. If I go not away, the Comforter will not come, but if I go, I will pray the Father and He will send you another Comforter,' which means to all of us the Holy Ghost."[39]

Rev. Charles W. Davis, a Southern Baptist from Chattanooga, emphasized the Spirit as that which leads us to truth and gives us security: "The Holy Spirit also was sent for an express purpose of God, to guide us into truth. Jesus said that the Holy Comforter would come to guide us all into all truth. In Ephesians the Holy Spirit promised that which is our inheritance, the down payment, you might say, on our salvation. The Holy Spirit is given us as a seal, as our security, a seal to the promise."[40]

Will Igon, a Pentecostal from DeKalb County, Alabama, felt that being a Christian requires an experience of the Holy Ghost: "We cannot be a real Christian without the Holy Ghost with us. I will say . . . that when we are converted and love comes in, why that's the Holy Ghost, and it makes us have a feeling that nothing else has. There's nothing can cause the feeling to come in your body, your soul . . . like that of the Holy Ghost. That's the thing that comes from God."[41]

Mrs. Charles Davis, a Baptist from Chattanooga, talked of the Holy Spirit bringing a conviction about sin to the souls of the lost: "We believe that when we pray for lost friends, we pray that the Holy Spirit might convict their souls, and that is one of the reasons we pray to the Holy Spirit, because we realize that we cannot save lost people, but the Holy Spirit can convict them of their sins and through this conviction they come to Jesus."[42]

Rev. Bailey Sadler, pastor of the Fairview Baptist Church in Boyd County, Kentucky, had a different view about having the Holy Spirit:

> A man asked me, he said, "Do you have the Holy Ghost?" and I said, "Sir, that's the least of my concern. I am not worried one bit about whether or not I have the Holy Ghost. The only thing I'm concerned with is, 'Does He have me?'" I don't know what I would do with Him if I had Him. He'd be so great! That reminds me of the dog that chases the car or the truck. He barks and barks, and he carries on, but what would he do if he caught it? He couldn't operate it could he? But if we give ourselves to the Holy Spirit, to God the Father, God the Son, and to God the Holy Spirit, either or all of them are able to take us and use us for His glory.[43]

The Holy Ghost is central to Pentecostal Christians; they see it as an indwelling spirit that brings a feeling of joy and enables them to do extraordinary things, such as speaking in tongues. An eastern Kentucky student at Berea College commented:

> We believe in speaking in tongues, so we believe in appealing to the Holy Ghost. It is hard to explain what it is like, but if you ever experience it, it is one of the most pleasurable things you've experienced in your life. It is something that makes you feel that God abides in you. . . . It's something that guides your life, and even if you are not thinking about it, it is there telling you whether you are doing right or wrong. It just plays a major role in your life, but you have to be willing to let it, you know, rule your life, for if you don't you would just be wasting your time.
>
> Sometimes—I hate to say it—but sometimes people put on a show [by dancing and shouting], and it's the thing to do. Sometimes the biggest devils are the ones up shouting. You don't necessarily have to shout to feel the Holy Ghost down inside. Some people aren't shouters. Different people have to be led in different ways. It depends on the individuals and their way of expressing what they feel.

Here are further comments on the Holy Ghost made by three more Berea College students from 1974:

> It is an inner peace that God has given you. It's God's presence always being your guide. It's something that you want to understand and experience for yourself when you know that God is always there. He's always there to listen. He's always there to give you divine direction in everything that you need to do. No matter what you need Him for, He's always there.

> Attaining the Holy Ghost is something more than emotional. If you have the Holy Ghost you can sing and shout, but you don't need anybody to hold you down. He's an all-right God. He's not going to let you get hurt. When people get hurt, it's just emotionalism. It's not the Holy Ghost.

> The Holy Spirit is there to remind you not to go in the wrong direction. I've seen people shout and get up and dance. It doesn't hit me that way. It begins in my stomach, like a tightening; it grips my side or girds it. It's a feeling that comes over you. I don't consider myself that

emotional, but I often catch myself crying. It is a different experience, an exciting experience and a wonderful feast that you will never experience in any other way. It is kind of like a conscience. It kind of guides me in what I should and shouldn't do. It was gradual with me. That doesn't mean it can't come all of a sudden with others.[44]

Some people relate the conscience to the Holy Spirit. Members of an American Baptist church in Preston County, West Virginia, discussed this question.

Harold Trickett: I think God speaks to one. That would be your conscience.

Doris Davis: Well, that is what I was thinking of, but . . . it looks as if conscience and the Holy Spirit are something different.

Lloyd Wiles: If you do some act that you know is wrong, I think God will condemn you through your conscience, and He will keep driving at you until the next time you want to do it, you won't do it.

Harry Yeager: I think conscience can be defined as those things which you are conscious of. Many sins you may not be conscious of. We may have a subconscious act through our daily living that we know nothing of. In no way could God speak to us if He had to speak through only what we had knowledge of. . . . Our conscience, then, is not, in my opinion, the Holy Spirit. . . . I think your conscience is not a safe guide. We can sear our conscience. We can do the same thing over and over again, and after a while the Holy Spirit doesn't speak to us any longer. We become so hardened we don't hear the Holy Spirit.

Opal Elliott: I think people who don't believe in God has a conscience. They don't recognize God, but still they won't steal. They won't lie. What is that but their conscience? Isn't that what guides them? Your conscience wouldn't be the Holy Spirit. You don't have the Holy Spirit until you have accepted Christ.[45]

These people speak in an intimate way about the Holy Spirit and how It comes to them and communicates in thought and feeling. They also believe in communicating to one or more persons of the Trinity through prayer. Prayer will be dealt with in chapter 6.

I end this chapter on God with a portion of a sermon, "The Throne of Grace," by Pastor Henry T. Mahan, of the Thirteenth Street Baptist Church in Ashland, Kentucky, who speaks of God, of Jesus, and of the most important gift of God, grace, in terms I have heard preached in other pulpits in the Uplands:

> The throne of God is the throne of majesty, a throne of glory, holiness, and justice, righteousness, sovereignty, everlasting throne of wisdom. Is that all? If that's all, if that's the only character revealed of our God, then we'll bow down and die and perish today. That's right. If that's all you've got, if that's all the character that's revealed in this Bible about God, then there's no hope for sinners like you and me. We'll remain, as Paul said, aliens, strangers, foreigners, without help, without God in this world.
>
> But wait a minute, here's good news! That's what *gospel* means, good news. Paul, in our text, Hebrews 16, calls the throne of God a throne of grace. I love these other attributes, because if He's not almighty, He can't be gracious. If He's not sovereign and glorious, then He can't be gracious. If He's not holy, He cannot make us holy.
>
> What is grace? Grace is not justice. Grace is free, unmerited, unearned, undeserved mercy. Grace is God giving us what we don't deserve, and mercy is not giving us what we do deserve. In Christ, mercy and truth are met together. God is going to deal truthfully with us, and mercifully with us. How can He? If He deals truthfully with me, He'll damn me. If He deals mercifully with me, He'll save me. How can He deal both ways? In Christ. . . . In Christ, mercy and truth are met together. Righteousness and peace kiss each other. God set forth His son to be a propitiation, a covering, a sacrifice, and atonement that He might be just and justifier of all who believe. If you only perceive God on His throne of glory, His throne of holiness, His throne of justice, of righteousness, you can entertain no hope at all, but if you see God on the throne of grace—free, unmerited, unearned, undeserved grace—then you can entertain some hope.
>
> The throne of grace started with God. He loved us first. He chose us, in Christ, before the foundation of the world. Christ is the surety of God's covenant. Christ's blood is the blood of the everlasting covenant. Christ's death and resurrection is the assurance of God's covenant. God said, "I'm going to save them. I'm going to show mercy to them." This all originated before the foundation of the world. Christ

was a lamb slain before the foundation of the world. . . . He is the great shepherd of the sheep through the everlasting covenant. It originated with God. His throne of grace is old, old, old. . . . It is from the beginning. God has chosen you from the beginning for salvation. . . . God was in Christ reconciling the world to himself. When our Redeemer died on the cross, under the weight of our sins, He died for the just and the unjust that He might bring us to God. . . . So God was glorified in it all. I can come to the throne of God. . . . I'm coming as one against whom justice has no charge. The Scripture says, "Who can lay charge against God's elect?" It is God who justifies. Who can condemn me? Christ has died so I can come boldly to the throne of grace. I don't owe justice anything. Christ paid it all. God is reconciled. God doesn't have anything to be angry about. There is no sin. There's no guilt. There's no charge. There's no judgment to them that are in Christ Jesus. . . . He's reconciled. The debt is paid. Christ paid it all.

The throne of grace is God receiving sinners, like you, like me. . . . There's no sin we haven't committed in word, thought, or deed or in potential. The throne of grace is God receiving sinners in Christ. That's the only way He can receive them, the only way He will receive them. Jesus said, "I am the way, I am the truth, I am the life. No man cometh to the Father but by me." These are the three things Adam lost in the garden. He lost the way to God. He lost the truth of God. He believed a lie, and he lost his spiritual life. And in Christ all three are restored, the way, the truth, and the life. The message of the Gospel is twofold. It is substantiation and satisfaction. Christ bore our sins and paid our debts.

So then, Hebrews 4, verse 16, "So then let us"—people like you and me, folks up the hollow, on the mountain, by the river, folks like you and me—"come boldly," confidently, come with liberty, sincerity, come in faith, come at all times, come. Where? "To the throne." Come to the throne of grace, not to the altar, not to the hand of the preacher, "come to the throne of grace, that we may obtain mercy." Mercy, like the thief on the cross, like blind Bartimeus. God's plenteous on mercy. Come to find mercy, and find grace to help, sufficient grace, saving grace, sovereign grace, free grace, redeeming grace, grace in time of need.

When is your time of need? All the time. I need grace to worship. I need grace to preach. I need grace to pray. I need grace to forgive and grace to give and grace to live and grace to die. I need grace in prosperity and grace in poverty and grace in sickness and grace in health. I need grace in old age and grace in death. And I know where it's found—at the throne of grace, before God of all grace.[46]

People of the Uplands have a concept of God that is as valid as any held elsewhere. I have found them to be fervent though awed believers in an almighty God. I believe that most see themselves as unworthy in God's sight, and thus they are grateful for Christ's sacrifice for them and for the grace that gives them "sweet hope in their breast" for heaven.

3 *The World and the Devil*

> Put on the whole armour of God, that ye may be able to stand against the wiles of the devil. For we wrestle not against flesh and blood, but against principalities, against powers, against the rulers of the darkness of the world, against spiritual wickedness in high places. Wherefore take unto you the whole armour of God, that ye may be able to withstand in the evil day, and having done all, to stand.
>
> —Ephesians 6:11–13

In the several mainline churches I have visited in recent years, I have rarely heard the devil mentioned in a sermon. A few times, however, he has been used as a metaphor for evil in the world. I examined a dozen recent books on religion and found that only two listed the devil or Satan in the index. I realize that this absence may say more about the orientation of the authors than about the religion of the people about whom they have written, but given the prominence of the devil in the Scriptures, it is nevertheless cause for reflection.

In contrast, in the Upland nonmainline churches I have visited, Satan (the devil, the Evil One, Lucifer, Beelzebub, or Old Scratch) is a powerful presence to be reckoned with and is a frequent subject of sermons and conversation. In my study I found that the name *Satan,* most often used in the Old Testament, means an adversary, the opposer of good, of those who would follow the Lord, and that the devil, as he is usually called in the New Testament, is the accuser or traducer; that is, he seeks to expose and vilify and embarrass the faithful.

The Nature of Satan

In searching the Scriptures, I found that the devil is first referred to in 1 Kings 11–14, "And the Lord stirred up an adversary unto Solomon." In 1 Chronicles 21:1 we are told that "Satan stood up against Israel." Upland Christians know how Satan came before the Lord to suggest testing Job's faith by taking away his prosperity. The Lord asked "From whence comest thou?" and Satan answered,"From going to and fro in the earth, and from walking up and down in it."

This answer indicates that Satan is always up to something. The Lord said to Satan in regard to Job, "All that he has is in thy power" but "upon himself put not forth thy hand." Satan then had the Sabeans take Job's oxen and asses and kill his servants, after which Satan brought fire from heaven to kill his sheep and more servants and had the Chaldeans steal his camels and kill additional servants. When Job persisted in his faith, Satan said, "But put forth thine hand now, and touch his bone and his flesh, and he will curse thee to thy face." And the Lord replied, ""Behold, he is in thine hand; but save his life." Satan then afflicted Job with boils and so forth. Job kept his faith in God, but this story demonstrates the wiles of Satan in enticing even God into a scheme to test Job.

In the New Testament, with the coming of Christ to establish a plan of salvation for lost people, the devil becomes more active in his opposer role. In Matthew 4 he tempts Jesus in the wilderness, but Jesus, after the forty-day fast and the temptations, says, "Get thee hence, Satan: for it is written, Thou shalt worship the Lord thy God, and him only shalt thou serve." In Mark 4:15 Satan steals even the word of God out of the hearts of those who might believe. In Luke 22:3 the devil enters Judas so as to lead him into betraying Jesus, and in verse 31 he influences Peter to deny Him.

Jesus chose Paul and caused him to be converted and sent to the Gentiles "to open their eyes and to turn them from darkness to light and from the power of Satan to God, that they may receive forgiveness of sins" (Acts 26:18). Paul warned the Corinthians of "false apostles, deceitful workers, transforming themselves into the apostles of Christ," and went on to say that this shouldn't surprise them because "Satan himself is transformed into an angel of light" (2 Corinthians 11:13–14). Revelation 12:7–9 tells the story of the war in heaven between Satan and his angels and archangel Michael and his angels, "And the great dragon was cast out, that old serpent, called the devil, and Satan, which deceiveth the whole world: he was cast out into the earth, and his angels were cast out with him."

So the religious reality in the Uplands is that Satan is down here among us, working his wiles. Elder Squire Watts, an Old Regular Baptist, emphasized this point: "The sons of God were called together one time. . . . and God looked, and lo and behold, there sat Old Satan right in the middle of the congregation. The Bible tells me that God said, 'Satan, what are you doing here among my people, and where have you been?' [Satan said], 'I'll tell you where I've been. I've been down on the earth that you created. I've been down there just as plain as day. I've been down there among your young men and women, seeking whom I may desire. That's where I've been.'"[1]

Satan's domain may be hell, but the main concern is that he has permeated all that is worldly. Upland Christians constantly worry about what is of the world and what is of God. Their struggle is between the worldly and the spiritual—the natural and the supernatural, the "inner" and the "outer" person. The natural person is attracted by the things of the world that may lead us away from the spiritual, from the love of God.

Since they believe the Scriptures, Upland Christians accept the reality of Satan, the source of evil, among us. One prevailing notion about him is that he is capable of appearing as "an angel of light" to beguile and deceive us. Therefore, we must always be on guard against him, and the best way to prevail is to ask God to save us and to strengthen us against him.

Dealing with Satan

I recorded the following unidentified radio preacher speaking of the need to be prepared when fighting the devil given that modern ways weaken our resolve. He is familiar with both worldly and scriptural weapons:

> If you want to have an effective warfare against Satan, then you must have the right equipment, my friend. You don't go against your enemy who has a .50 caliber machine gun with a derringer. . . . You must have the whole armor of God, and you don't get that from a rock concert, nor do you get it from listening to rock music on a radio or record player, nor do you get it from the world's amusement parks. You get it from the Word of God. Consider, my friend, Ephesians 6, verses 12 through 17, "For we wrestle not against flesh and blood but against principalities, against powers, against rulers of the darkness of this world, against spiritual wickedness in high places. Wherefore, take on the whole armor of God that ye may be able to withstand in the evil day, and having done all, to stand. Stand, therefore, having your loins girt about with truth, and having on the

breastplate of righteousness. And your feet shod with the preparation of the gospel of peace. Above all, taking the shield of faith, wherewith ye shall be able to quench all the fiery darts of the wicked. And take the helmet of salvation, and the sword of the Spirit, which is the word of God."

People's problems today is that they have not put on the whole armor of God. How many of the Sunday School teachers do you know who are real Bible teachers? The majority of them are quarterly [periodical Sunday School study materials] readers. They know absolutely nothing about the word of God. As Jesus said, "If the blind lead the blind, they both will fall."[2]

I also recorded a radio broadcast by Brother Ozell Bunch, a Pentecostal preacher from Lafollette, Tennessee, expressing confidence in his fights with Satan; his confidence was not in cunning, however, but in the power of God:

Brother, I'm not afraid of the devil. He'll trip you, he'll lie to you, and he'll do anything in the book to you, but I'm not afraid of him because the Man that lives in me is greater than he is. I know in whom I believe. I know God. I am here to do a job for God, to fill the church, and to preach a great God to a great people, and I believe that when people get their minds on God, and God gets His mind on that people, there are not enough devils in hell to keep them from growing, to keep them from building, to keep them from shouting, to keep them from going forward in the name of Almighty God![3]

Two unidentified testifiers in the Green River Pentecostal Church in Lincoln County, Kentucky, also offered their thoughts on the devil; each spoke also of God, the only shield from the Evil One:

I thank God for the Full-Gospel Pentecostal movement, where we hear the full word of God preached. I just love God for this good way, and I know that I'm saved and have got the good joy and peace in my soul, and I just want to keep it there to endure to the end. I don't want the devil to steal my victory. I know that's his job. He's going to do everything to steal my victory, but if I hold on to God, I believe I can make it to the end. I don't believe the devil will defeat us.

The devil will do all he can, but he cannot take you away if you hold on to God and do the very best that you can. I heard of a church—I ain't a going to say what church—where they said that the devil didn't work in that church. If they've got a place like that, the devil's got it the way he wants it. That's what I'd say.[4]

Brother Wayne Gillespie, whom I recorded from an unidentified West Virginia, radio station, preached that Satan can work on our emotions to foil our good intentions, but he also asserted that God gives us the kind of strength to persevere: "The devil will get under your skin, get your goat, keep you from staying the course, but the Spirit of God will give you the courage and patience to stay that course."[5]

Most Christians see that the armor spoken of in the Scriptures is the biblical Word of God. Our access to God is through the Word and the Holy Spirit. With this help we can withstand the wiles of the devil. A Pentecostal testifier had this to say:

> I thank God I'm still saved, filled with the Spirit. I love the Lord to-night, and I want to step out by faith, do more for God, let my light shine, and endure to the end. I believe it's going to take some enduring. There's the old devil out there fighting. He's going to attack us in our bodies, any way he possibly can to try to get us down. I believe that if we are children of God, we can be more than conquerors through Jesus Christ. I thank God for the Word. We may not feel good, but we can go to God's Word and tell the devil that what we have we have because of the Word of God. The Word says that I'm saved. I've got the Holy Ghost, can speak in tongues, because the Word of God says I am. I believe God's Word. I thank God for the Pentecostal movement so that we can hear the full Word. I just want to keep it. I don't want the devil to steal my victory. With God's grace I can hold on till the end.[6]

I remember the late Daisy Myers, a fine Baptist woman who was my neighbor at Brasstown, North Carolina, testifying in a revival meeting about the work of the devil. She said that on her way to the meeting, she passed by a store and saw some cloth in the window that she thought would make a nice dress. Through most of the service, all she could think about was the cloth. She attributed this distraction to the devil and testified that she would deny herself the cloth because she thought that she would be succumbing to the devil if she bought it.

Sister Sue Cox Cole, a Pentecostal minister from eastern Kentucky, also gave the devil credit—or blame—for people's failures to lead Christian lives:

The devil has blinded people until they don't have their values straight. People used to would not work on Sunday. . . . We used to have a store that closed on Sunday, and they advertised "The Day is Worth More than the Dollar." Evidently [now], the dollar is worth more than the day. . . .

There was a Frenchman [Alexis de Toqueville], years ago, came to America, and as he looked over America trying to decide why this country was so much greater than other countries, he would go to different places, and he felt that he had just not found the key, but when Sunday rolled around, and he saw all of those people going to church, he said, "This is what makes America great. America is great because she is good." If she ever ceases to be good, she'll cease to be great, because the devil is working hard.[7]

One of the great Christians I have known was Buell Kazee, a Southern Baptist from Magoffin County, Kentucky. Heavily influenced in his youth by the Calvinism of the United Baptists around him, he felt that the customary evil and threatening image of the devil, with hoofs and horns and pitchfork, is misleading to a lot of Christians. He was more worried about the subtle ways of the devil in getting people to do "good works" that would lead them away from the worship of God:

Religion is popular now; it's good business and good entertainment, but it's shallow, nothing rugged about the old cross now. Well, it's got a lot of good things in it . . . but there's a lot of difference between "good" and that which is from God. Keep in mind, a Christian must never ask, "Is it good?" He must ask, "Is it from God?" That's where the Christian's life is centered, and he must not become absorbed with the goodness of the world as if it were the godliness of the Lord.

But you understand, the devil's not mean; he's not got a tail and horns; he's a god, but he's a counterfeit god. He's going to be as much like God as he can without being God, and he wants you to have religion. He wants everybody to have religion. He wants to divide and have all kinds of religion for everybody. The devil's got more religion going on than the Lord has, and it's *good* religion. It has humanitarianism in it; it's got morality in it; it's got all the marks that we are looking for as *good* in it. But godliness . . . , that's something else. . . . It's not the fellow who's not honest. He's working on good, honest people, the most consecrated religious people. That's where he's working. But the deception lies in the devil getting them to believe something other than the Word of God. You have to be guided by *that Word!* But when you begin saying, "I feel this," and "I hear this voice," and "The Lord told me this. . . ." Well, that's where you can get deceived. That's where Satan works, in your feelings and directions.

Why, the Lord wouldn't have all of these denominations. The devil fixed that up, you know. "Doctrine" lies at the base of all of that. We were divided on doctrine, but now we don't know enough doctrine to keep us divided, so we are melting together. That's what's happening. Satan is in the saddle. He's coming to the apex of his reign. And he's going to have all religions melt into one, and it'll look good, because man's looking for "good." He can't see *God,* but he's looking for *good.* And he's just being deceived. And religious people, saved people, preachers that are saved, God's preachers, are being deceived by a lot of this. They think they're headed in the right direction. Success now is numbers . . . quantity. How many people? How much money? How will this stand in the judgment?[8]

Listening to Kazee's assertion that denominations are the work of the devil and conversely his suspicion of ecumenical movements that attempt to meld people into one denomination that has some sort of common-denominator set of beliefs, I was reminded that I have heard others in the Uplands debate these same conflicting ideas.

Three black Baptists whom I interviewed in Hazard, Kentucky, had similar ideas about the beguiling nature of the devil. They also spoke of an ill-defined figure mentioned only in Paul's epistles to John, as in 2 John 7: "For many deceivers are entered into the world, who confess not that Jesus Christ is come in the flesh. This is a deceiver and an antichrist." Such a person or persons were predicted to come in the last days to lead people away from Christ. Mable Jones, D. Y. Olinger, and Lillian Olinger spoke of the Antichrist, linking him with the devil, and questioning whether we will have enough faith to withstand him:

Lillian Olinger: I got to wondering about that yesterday, of just how sure we're going to be that we're in the Lord, 'cause you aren't going to be able to stand, according to the Scriptures. I don't believe we'll go right after him [the Antichrist], but he's got everything everybody's looking for. He's going to have peace, he's going to have prosperity, and he's going to have love to throw around—act like it's love—just bring everybody together. He's even going to set up in the synagogue. The devil and the Antichrist go together, just like the Father, Son, and Holy Ghost—the Antichrist, the devil, the false prophets.

It's real important to be satisfied in Christ. There is no way for the world to satisfy me. I have to be satisfied in Christ. But when the Antichrist comes you're not going to be concerned with all of that. He's going to come, you know, full-blown, and we're just going to have to be able to stand firm in the Lord Jesus Christ, not be carried away with that.

D. Y. Olinger: That's where he is fooling people today. He's showing all of the pleasures of life. As long as they don't question these pleasures of life, he's not going to tell them another way. He's not going to question anything. He's just going to let them go as they are going—like [using] drugs, alcohol, and all those other things. That's all the people who don't know Christ, or who are doing evil. A lot of people are really enjoying life. He is not going to discourage them. He's just going to let them go, because they're his children.

Mable Jones: Don't be tossed by every wind or doctrine, so says Paul. There are plenty of things that are the work of the devil, and we think they are the work of the Lord. He's the Antichrist, and he's going to give us all those good things.[9]

Satan's Worldly versus God's Spiritual Values

It seems to me that Upland Christians have a clear sense of spiritual matters in conflict with temporal ones. The devil is lurking, whether or not he is specifically mentioned, in the obvious sins of sex and drugs and prurient entertainment, but to many he is also in those things that we love, such as sports, the movies, secular music, and the like. Elder Squire Watts, an Old Regular Baptist, commented on movies, dancing, and bluegrass music as examples of the problems such things raise to those who try to be faithful in in his particular association of churches:

Movies are probably very well accepted, [but] if one kept going to movies that weren't too good, that'd create a problem. Partying and dancing, that would create a problem. A large percentage of the people in the Old Regular Baptist Church were brought up with bluegrass music. At the old-time box suppers, pie suppers, and things, they always had a square dance. That was in a community. Going to a bluegrass festival would probably be frowned on. I like bluegrass music. I sure do. I'd say if a member occasionally wanted to go to a bluegrass festival to enjoy it, it probably wouldn't be a problem, but if they really got into it, it probably would be a problem.[10]

Even though the devil is a real person to many Christians, he is nevertheless also a symbol or metaphor of evil in the world and within us all, and we know that each of us has to confront this evil and deal with it. Rev. Phillip Banks, a Kentucky Freewill Baptist, spoke of the need for proper teaching and regeneration: "There is no way you can change evil and injustice unless you change the hearts of men. Therefore, you come back to the need for family life and the church. Our hearts have to be changed and regenerated. Without that, evil is going to stay with us."[11]

The late Rev. John Ferry Moore, a North Georgia Southern Baptist, believed that when we are at our worst, we become like the devil. He discussed the problem of anger building up within us as an example:

Modern philosophy seems to be that you must let yourself go and let off steam ever so often, otherwise it will build up inside and you will explode. Seems to me to say, if you feel like it, just cut a wide swath. If anybody is in the way, cut them down. If a heart is wounded, let it bleed. Speak your mind. Do your thing. You have your rights.

In my own experience I find that things do build up inside. Little things. Always the little things. The bigger things must be faced and are faced. The little things eat like a canker. Then the steam letting. The scalding. The hurt. Then the aftermath. The payoff. The remorse. . . .

The thing that has built up inside is nothing more or less than anger. Yes, call it justification, and my rights, and other good-sounding words. But it is still just anger. . . . So when I speak in anger, I talk like the devil. And when the payoff comes, it without fail is in the coin of the realm of the devil. Every time I have been the loser.[12]

John Ferry Moore believed that all good things, such as food and even labor-saving inventions, come from God and that Satan works to destroy or discredit such creations or their equitable distribution:

My firm belief is that every good thing comes from the intelligence, and grace, and mercy of the God who created man. I believe the purpose of Satan is to tear down and hinder and destroy the creation of God. Even mankind. Since his only work is to wreck and devour, I am sure Satan does not rejoice when our bodies are relieved from backbreaking toil. I believe that Satan would never inspire a mind or give skill to one's hands or provide patience for one's heart to invent a lightbulb. Satan would rather have men live in darkness. He neither provides the materials nor the knowledge for a man to construct a comfortable house for his family.

However, I am sure that Satan does rejoice when we forget that "Every good gift and every perfect gift is from above, and comes down from the Father of lights, with whom is no variableness, neither shadow of turning." When our good automobiles and our good roads, our automatic devices and instant services, our comfortable homes and circumstance, provide us with so much more time to indulge our own selfish desires, I am sure that Satan gets a certain twisted pleasure from that. While we beg and bribe our children to eat rich foods on their plates. While other millions of children beg and cry for a bit of food in their hands. While the greatest minds among us have never found (or perhaps have never tried to find. I do not know which) a way to distribute the bountiful food supply of our world. Satan must derive some satisfaction from these things.[13]

Elaine J. Lawless reported similar beliefs from Beula Estes, a Pentecostal woman in southern Indiana, where many people from the Uplands have settled in this century:

During the years of friendship with Beula, I learned of the cultural world to which she belonged. I recognized a traditional, even Puritan view, which syncretized notions of witches and devils with a Holy Ghost and a personalized Christ figure. Everything that happened in Beula's world had something to do with God's will or with Satan's wily intervention in her life, and for me, at least, it was largely indistinguishable which force was at work. If she lost something, it was the work of Satan; when she found it, it was because God showed her where it was. If difficulties became more than she thought she could bear, it was Satan tempting her and God testing her faith at the same time.[14]

John Ferry Moore applied Satan's work to our daily lives in the world and how we make choices every day, and he was concerned with how we view our choices. The meaning he derived from life allowed new techno-logical developments in our worldly state. He, like other Christians, was concerned about our being led away from our spiritual commitments and concerns by new fads and inventions rather than keeping things in perspec-tive. Sue Cox Cole, one of the few women preachers I met, also warned against embracing the successful things in life: "Some people think that if something's going big, God is in it. Well, if it went that way, the Superbowl, the Cincinnati Reds, the Kentucky Wildcats, and all that kind of stuff is big. I don't care how many people go out to the Superbowl, I doubt that God cares who wins. I figure that it is a bunch of foolishness to Him—that a nation could get with something like that, so frivolous. People care more about pleasure than they do God."[15]

Those interested in how sports, as one pleasure, have taken over our lives and corrupted or distorted everything from higher education to the church (not to mention the family on such days as Superbowl Sundays) should read my friend Robert J. Higgs's *God in the Stadium.* I've noticed a couple of other items that suggest that sports have become the main priority for many peo-ple. On January 6, 1996, a great snow and ice storm, with constant travel-ers' warnings, failed to stop 25,000 people from throughout the state and beyond from attending the University of Kentucky–Old Miss basketball game at Lexington's Rupp Arena (Kentucky won, 90 to 60). The next morn-ing news sources reported that most church services had been canceled in Lexington and elsewhere in the state because of the bad weather. Herald-ing the Olympics in Atlanta in the summer of 1996, the head of the Inter-national Olympics Committee was reported to have said that "the Olym-pics are now more important than the Catholic religion."[16] This left me wondering how the chairman believes the Olympics stand in relation to Protestantism and other world religions.

Buell Kazee spoke to me of his concerns about "successful" religion. He accused television evangelists of taking money away from the local church-es so as to build big programs and to attract attention to their crusades, inviting people who were successful in worldly endeavors, such as sports heroes, to appear with them. He explained:

> There isn't a man or woman who can appear on Billy Graham's pro-gram who hasn't been a "success" *in the world.* That is to say, his suc-cess in the world qualifies him to appear on the crusade program. He has to be a headliner in the world.
>
> I'll give you an[other] example. In Lexington [Kentucky], they had a crusade, the Bill Glass Crusade. Well, everybody on that cru-

sade was a star athlete or a star of something else. I don't mean that this was "sinful," in the sense of immoral or anything like that, but that sort of thing is just not of the Lord. . . . The whole worldly thing is going to pass away. . . . Now, one's an athlete. Another's a beauty queen or something else, maybe the Roy Rogers and Dale Evans type. They have to be something pretty spectacular *in the world* before they're qualified to appear in a crusade.

They had a fellow who was the world's champion yo-yo artist on this program in Lexington. Now, he came not because of his great Christian life—he was a Christian, maybe—the point is, he was there *because he was a champion yo-yo artist!* Now, I've preached fifty-seven years, and my witness beside his wouldn't be worth two cents, because I can't yo-yo. . . . You see what I'm driving at? You've got to be a "world figure" and be prominent in the world before you can be used in one of these great crusades as a witness for Christ. And this, as you can see, is pure sham, because most of the people who are dedicated to Christ in the real sense wouldn't have any time for any of that other stuff.

Kazee thought also that worldliness has pervaded the local churches as well as the crusades. When I asked him what the function of the community church is in society, he replied:

Mainly preaching God's Word and seeking the lost. This, of course, presumes separation from the world. What has happened to church life is that it has *blended with the world.* The idea now is to make a man "feel at home" when he comes to church. Well, socially he should be made to feel that way, but spiritually, if he is not a saved man, he should feel like a sinner. . . . I don't mean that they should not be friendly or have a "holier than thou" attitude, but there ought to be something that would convict a man that he is wrong. . . . I mean Christianity ought to be far superior to anything that this world has to offer, so that man who is clinging to the world would be inclined to let loose.[17]

Sue Cox Cole was as concerned as Buell Kazee was that the world has pervaded the churches and that people have lost their sensitivity to worldliness:

The church world in general is not as spiritual as it was. A lot of the church is worldly. I'm not saying everybody, for I see churches and families that are a lot more dedicated to God than they've ever been, but in general I'm appalled at the lack of conviction people have. Nothing, nothing bothers them. It's as if they have no conscience any more. They can do almost anything and say, "Why, I don't feel bad about it." So sad.

We are living in a society where it seems almost anything goes. The divorce rate is so bad that it is almost unbelievable. So many homes are broken. I see the hurt. I see the children that are broken. I see the dreams that have been destroyed. I see the crushed lives because of divorce. I don't like the careless, haphazard way of this generation. We ought to teach our children that when we get married, it is for life. I'm afraid that we are taking things too lightly. We have an eight-year-old son, and I ask myself, "What in the world is it going to be like for him?" I want some preachers still around preaching the old-time holiness. I want some preachers still around preaching separation from sin.[18]

Elder Elwood Cornett, moderator of the Indian Bottom Association of Old Regular Baptists, is a person I admire greatly in both his profesional life (before retiring he was a Distinguished Educator under the Kentucky Educational Reform Act) and his religious leadership role. In his former position as director of the Kentucky River Educational Cooperative, he associated with a variety of people, some of whom are worldly by his standards:

My job is to direct an organization that is governed by a board made up of superintendents of the area, and theirs is a political position under the laws of Kentucky. I maneuver within that course. One of our positions [in the Old Regular Baptist Church] is no alcohol, and I'm as strong as I can be on that. I don't drink—period. But the people I run with—the conferences I go to—they have their happy hours, receptions, and that sort of things. That's very worldly. I stay out of that. I don't have any problems staying away. I know before I go I'm not going to fool with it. I know that nobody is going to entice me. Nobody's going to push me into it. It's been interesting, but I've never really had any problems with people trying. There have just been one or two instances when somebody has tried to push me a little bit. It didn't take long to get that straightened out.[19]

Elder Frank Fugate, Old Regular Baptist, spoke of a worldly vice he had with no worldly cure and in doing so introduced another aspect of the separation between the world and the realm of the spirit and the need for divine intervention to overcome pleasures and problems of the world:

> I was one time overcome with alcohol, and I tried every means that this world had to deliver me from the thirst of that and from the joy of that. I tried every remedy. There was no remedy. This world had no remedy to break me of the thirst and from the lust and from the effects of that alcohol. The time came when God verified His promises. He intervened in my heart and my mind and made me see. My mind was poisoned with it. I was diseased with that alcohol, just as the minds of youngsters are diseased with this dope. We've got to be delivered by the goodness of God, and made to hate that—love the things we once hated and hate the things we once loved. Then you will know that you have been born again.[20]

I want to point out here just how important Upland religion and the church are in redeeming people like Elder Fugate, who had a terrible problem that he overcame with the help of his beliefs. The point is that his faith community and friends in the larger community accepted him as a new person, and in fact he became one of the most admired elders in his church. Sometimes the really big sinner, once forgiven, is lifted to heights of respect because he or she has overcome so much.

Satan as the Great Adversary

Many Christians see the devil not as just corrupting us and our best intentions but as a mighty antagonist who has to be fought tooth and nail. The late Brother Herman B. Yates, pastor of the Grace Baptist Church in Dingess, West Virginia, spoke eloquently and graphically of Satan in a sermon entitled "The Elect of God." He saw a titanic battle being waged by God, or Christ, against Satan for the souls of those who are rightfully God's.

> Christ has never tolerated any truce with the Evil One, and He never will. There is a deadly, implacable, infinite, eternal enmity between Christ and the sin of which Satan is the representative. In this battle no compromise can ever be thought of, and no quarter can ever be given. The Lord never will turn from His purpose of casting Satan into the Lake of Fire. . . .
>
> Although man's heart was intended to be the throne of God, it's now become the palace of Satan. Adam was the most obedient ser-

vant of the Most High and his body a temple for God's love, but even he who was the sire of the whole human race was overthrown by this awful enemy in the early days of his innocence.

Through the Fall, we have become the servants of sin and our bodies have become the workshops of Satan. . . . Sampson was known as the avenger of Israel, and he slaughtered many Philistines, yet even that strong man fell victim to this stronger fiend of Hell. That mighty hero, who could literally tear a lion apart, was no match for that Lion of the Pit. . . . Solomon, the wisest of men, was outwitted by Satan, for his heart was led astray by his tempter.

Ah, Beloved, this awful spirit is so strong that if all of us could combine against him, he'd still laugh at us, just like Leviathan laughed at the spear. He is strong, strong in strength, and also in cunning he is strong. He knows just how to tempt us, and when. . . . He is strong with a vengeance. It is a great blessing for us to know that there is a stronger than he. The might of Satan could crush you to powder, if it were not for the almightiness of Christ coming to our rescue. He's not only strong, but it says here he is armed. He's never without weapons. His principal weapon is the lie. The sword of God's Spirit is the truth, but the sword of the evil spirit is the lie. It was by a lie that he overcame our race in the beginning, robbed us of purity and perfection, and he continues to forge and to use lies to destroy the souls of men. . . . He has a way of making the worst appear to be the best. He can make people believe that it is to their own advantage to do the things that are literally destroying them. He can make them dance upon the brink of Hell as though they were on the verge of heaven. Fools that we are, how readily do we receive these lies and let them prevail against us.

Then, there is the weapon of pleasure—the lust of the flesh. He doesn't offer the same to everyone. To some he offers only a dainty dalliance, maybe, and the overflowing cup of sin that looks so good to the eye, he offers to others. To the greedy, he offers great wealth. Fame and the applause of men he offers to another. . . .

The evil spirit is well-supplied in that which protects him against all earthy weapons. Prejudice, ignorance, evil education, all of these are chain armor with which Satan girds himself. . . .

It is also said that he is watchful. Satan does not put this armor on in order to sleep in it. You may find sleeping saints, but you'll never, ever find a sleeping devil. No, no. The restless activity of fallen angels is awful to contemplate. The Scripture says they rest not, neither day or night, but like ravenous birds they go about seeking their prey. . . . When Satan enters a man's heart, he takes care to watch if there is the smallest danger that the truth will come in and drive him from his throne. He puts a double guard on the person who is under the sound of the Gospel. . . . So be aware that when the Spirit of God is working, our great enemy is sure to be active. . . . While men sleep, he sows tares, but he never sleeps himself. He is always about the business of watching over his black sheep.

Is there a reason given here as to why Satan is so watchful over the heart in which he dwells? Why, yes, there is a reason given. It's because he considers man to be *his* property. They are not his by right. Whatever goods that are in the house of mankind must belong to God who built the house, and who intended to dwell there, but Satan sets up a claim and calls everything in the man his goods.

What are some of these goods? Well, man's memory, for one. Satan stores evil things there. His judgment is another. Satan perverts judgment so that the scales never give a true weight, never tell you the truth of the matter. And love, he perverts, so that man loves what he ought to hate and hates what he ought to love. His imagination he twists with foul delusions so that he doesn't get a right picture. All the powers of man Satan claims. . . . He claims the whole man is his. What a sad thing it is, that we accept his claim so readily. For mankind thinks that he hears music in the clanking of the chains that Satan uses to bind them with. Men cheerfully obey the Prince of Darkness. . . .

Satan does with men the same as the fabled sirens were said to have done with the ancient mariners. They sat upon the rocks, and they chanted such beautiful songs that no mariner having heard that sound could resist steering the ship towards them. So each ship that went that way was soon dashed to bits upon the rocks. It's not in poor mortal flesh and blood, unaided by the Spirit of God, to stand against this thrilling witchcraft. . . .

Oh, that God's servants would serve him as joyfully as those do who serve Satan. I've seen his servants. I've seen them in a lot of places, in many different countries, and in more cities in this country than I care to remember. You can see them in every hospital. . . . They'll offer their body and soul to be consumed as a whole burnt offering that they may serve Satan with all of their hearts.

O Beloved, that we were as faithful to God as Satan's servants are to him. O, pray, that the eternal God will drive them out. If not, there is no hope. No hope apart from that.[21]

Brother Yates was typical of a good many men of God with whom I became acquainted during this study in that he had limited formal education but used his impressive native intelligence, devout faith, and prodigious reading and study to become an eloquent and powerful preacher. He was a butcher by trade but always a student of the Bible. He died in 1995 while waiting for a heart transplant.

Sin

I sometimes jest that I grew up when preachers spoke bluntly of sin rather than social problems, psychoses, family dysfunction, or economic and political conspiracies that lead us astray. Upland people still believe that sin is central to the problem of evil. Sin is often mentioned throughout the entire Bible, starting with Genesis's account of Cain's sin against his brother, Abel. God's judgment and wrath are quick in the Old Testament. Many passages in the New Testament suggest that we all are sinners but that Christ has paid the price for our sins. Paul said, "where sin abounded, grace did much more abound" (Romans 5:20) but asked, "Shall we continue in sin that grace may abound? God forbid. How shall we who are dead to sin live any longer therein?" (6:1–2)

I am used to people speaking forthrightly about sin. Harry Yeager, a West Virginia Baptist, said, "To me, sin is sin, whether it is large or small." Fellow Baptist Lloyd Wiles commented, "It is just the opposite of God."[22] Mrs. John Thomas, a West Virginia Methodist, said: "Sin is as old as the human race. Sin entered the world in the Garden of Eden. . . . It brought murder into the first household. . . . The devil is the author of all sin, and all that is wicked and sinful is the workings of the evil spirit of the devil."[23]

Calvinists and Arminians are divided over the question of sin and salvation, some seeing the human condition as an inescapably sinful one, with any perfection coming only in heaven. Some perfectionists believe that the true Christian is one who lives a sinless life. Others array themselves somewhere between these poles. Some feel that we cannot escape sin, but that if we are saved, it is forever. Some believe that we ought to avoid sin, but if we fail, we must ask forgiveness and be saved all over again. Most see a struggle always to do the will of God in the midst of the devil's temptations.

Elder Mike Smith, a Kentucky Primitive Baptist, stated boldly that sin ceases only when we are dead. "We are sinful creatures. That's what I've got to pray to the Lord about, what he'll save me from."[24] Yet Mrs. J. A. Ledbetter, a member of the Evangelical United Brethren Church in Charleston, West Virginia, believed that the Christian should be able to live without sin: "I think that when we talk about going along with the crowd that there are a lot of Christians who might as well go along with the crowd, because you're a Christian or you're not. There is no such thing as a half-Christian. If they want a good time they might as well go along . . . because they are not a Christian. They stand in sin. For me, a little white lie is as bad as the biggest black one that has ever been told. Sin is sin, and that is all you can say about it."[25]

Earl Tanner, another West Virginian, a Methodist, held similar views: "A little fib is sin as much as murder. Murder is sin, but a small sin is just as bad as any great big sin, any little thing that we do wrong. I believe that the use of alcohol to get drunk, that is a sin, or if we break the law of man, that's sin."[26]

But Mrs. Bill Hamlin, an Alabama Pentecostal, tried to separate serious sin from the many mistakes we inevitably make. She said, "Well, I think that sin . . . is something that you actually do that you know is sin because inside, your conscience is telling you, but a mistake is something that you don't have to ask forgiveness for."[27] Mary O'Dell, a West Virginia Methodist, brought up the sins of omission: "Sometimes it isn't what we do, it's what we don't do that's a sin. The Bible says that if we know to do good and doeth it not, it's counted as a sin against us."[28]

The following Old Regular Baptists held other views of sin. They believe in the "inner" and "outer man" and in this way try to explain the basic problem of the worldly and the spiritual in each of us. Elder Fon Bowling spoke of this inner and outer man:

> Now my dear brethren, I am not trying to tell you that this natural man, in this flesh, is perfect in this life. But there is a part of this man made perfect through the new birth in Christ. The inner man or soul, by being born again of the spiritual birth, can't sin or die. Heaven bought, heaven bound. . . . He can't do the things he once did, such as lying, getting drunk, adultery and fornication. Because He that is in you is greater than he that is in the world. Then you are not your own keeper, but kept by the power of God, ready to be revealed in the last times. Although through the weakness of the flesh, we do our trespasses, errors and our mistakes for which we have to suffer. But brethren I don't believe we will go beyond that and commit vile crimes.[29]

As a Baptist I grew up hearing about the age of accountability. It is no certain age but rather a time when the question of sin and the need to be saved from it begin to weigh on you. For me the age was thirteen, when I repented, was baptised in Little Brasstown Creek, and joined the Little Brasstown Baptist Church. Old Regular Baptist elder Clifton Hampton spoke of the age of accountability but also of Satan's efforts to thwart our hope of salvation: "Poor weak creatures that we are. When we reach the age of accountability, God puts His law in our hearts and teaches us that it is good to do good and wrong to do wrong. Then the old Tempter comes along and we override the low, still voice in our hearts and do the things that are not right. Therefore we become sinners. He who knows to do good and does it not, to him it is sin. And when sin is finished, it brings forth death. Then we are dead in trespass and in sin."[30]

Brother Paul Jacobs, another Old Regular Baptist, summed up the sin question and its solution with a Calvinistic interpretation:

> So Brethren, if . . . we believe the Bible is true—we must conclude that man in his sinful condition is only the recipient of God's grace. If it wasn't for God's grace we would all be doomed. We have all sinned and come short of the glory of God.
>
> The old timers used to preach, "Man sold himself for naught and had nothing to redeem himself." God has provided us with a way to escape from this sin-cursed world. It is a strait and narrow way. It is freedom from the damnation of hell and [brings] peace in troubled times. The way is a lamp unto our feet, and a ransom for the debt that we couldn't pay.
>
> God's son, Jesus Christ, stood as a lamb slain from the foundation of the world to release his people from the stronghold of the adversary.[31]

Rev. Darrell Mullins, an eastern Kentucky Holiness radio preacher, spoke of the pleasures of sin that once enticed him away from God, as they continue to do for other young people:

> Before Saturday morning I was most of the time broke because of sin and its pleasures. Now, let me tell you something, my friends, a lot of people think that they are having a good time, and the world will tell the young people that they are having a good time when they drink and use drugs and all those things, but let me tell you something, the pleasures of this world are only for a season, but the gifts of God are eternal, and God's love will feed you and take care of you. He takes care of the sparrows of the air. He takes care of the wild animals of the woods, and he'll take care of you.[32]

Rev. Darrell Elam, another Kentucky Pentecostal radio preacher whom I recorded, stressed the wages of sin and the futility of trying to hide it from God but also noted the saving power of the blood of Jesus:

> Listen to me, my friend, sin will take you further than you want to go. It'll cost you far more than you'll want to pay. Where sin is, the Spirit of God won't be there. . . . There's people today that's tried to hide things from God, and He said there's nothing that won't be revealed. . . . Remember today that the wages of sin is death, but the gift of God is eternal life. If there's sin in the camp, God knows all about it. You may try to hide it in your tents, but God knows. But all you've got to do is lay it aside and look on Jesus, the author and finisher of faith. . . . It's up to you what you do with that sin you got hid in your camp. You can take it to the Lord, and He'll cover it with His precious blood. . . . Today is the day of salvation. Get rid of sin, and let's go home together.[33]

Pearl Spence, a West Virginia Baptist, also stressed the joy of being saved from sin: "Whenever we sin, disobey, and sin in the sight of God, we have condemnation upon us. Then we feel a guilty conscience, and then we ask God to forgive us, and He forgives. Our joy is restored, and this condemnation is removed from us, and we feel all right in the sight of the Lord, before God and before man."[34]

Brother Vernon Harrison, an eastern Kentucky Pentecostal preacher, preached that sin brings death and hell but that God's gift through Jesus can bring eternal life, no matter how venal your sins:

> The Bible says that when sin has brought forth its complete works, it brings forth death, but the gift of God is eternal life. . . . One of these days you're going to die, and you're going to open your eyes, and you're going to be in torment, and you're going to ask somebody to take one drop of water to wet your tongue, but there hain't a-going to be any water down in the pits of hell. There hain't a-going to be any help for anyone that is cast into the lake of fire. Why would that be a-happening? Why? Because sin has taken over in your life. Your members have been members of unrighteousness.
>
> They's people listening today that thinks God could not save their poor soul because of some of the wicked things they've done. You're thinking, "God, there's no hope for me. I've been cast out of the sight of the great I Am." But you need to know that, praise God, hal-

lelulah, that there's only one unforgivable sin. That's blasphemy against the Holy Ghost. Everything else is repentable, and the blood of the Lamb will cleanse you of all unrighteousness, whether a little sin or a big sin. Everyone listening today needs to know that sin will take you to hell. Sin is nothing but works of the devil. If you don't know Jesus, you need to be falling down upon your knees and repenting of your unrighteousness.[35]

And finally, Brother Harold Kelly, another eastern Kentucky Pentecostal preacher, warned against the devil's deceptions in leading us into the things of the world that may appear grand to us but that lead us away from God and into sin:

Sin and the devil are deceptive in every age. Just as sure as a compromise in attitude pulled Lot astray in his day, that same spirit will entice us today if we allow it. . . . People are fooled by the promises that sin makes unto them. . . . Sin today has been renamed, kindly whitewashed, been put in a place of prominence until people are fooled today into thinking that because a lot of others are doing wrong, they'll be able to get by also. Satan is deceptive in every age, and we're not wise enough not to follow the multitude, if the multitude is not following the hand of God. They have erred from the faith and pierced themselves with many sorrows.

This business of going after financial gain that this world has to offer at the expense of our soul is a temptation; it is a snare. It is a deceptive move that Satan has worked on mankind for thousands and thousands of years. We're living in a time when materialism is elevated so that it seems people can never be satisfied. . . . I say we need to wake up and wise up and get things in the right priority.

There are people today who have pushed God aside for a little bit of social prominence for them and their families. There are people who are denying the truth of God's words so that they may be accepted and looked upon as being socially prominent in the world. . . . There are people who'd rather have their name in *Who's Who* than in the Lamb's Book of Life.

Today it seems like the church has begun to mix and mingle so much in the world that the world doesn't pay much attention to us. We've watered down the Word of God. The preachers are trying to make the message socially acceptable to people who want to live in sin and pattern after the world—go the way of the devil—transgressing the law of God. We dishonor God by bestowing so much honor upon the wrong things of this day and hour in which we live. . . . I pray today that if you've drifted, if you've strayed, that you'll humble yourself and turn back to God.[36]

Satan, Witches, and Ghosts in Folklore

Satan is also frequently found as a character in ballads and folktales, showing that earlier Christians viewed him as a constant threat. The fact that these ballads and tales are still sung and related in the Uplands indicates that he is still a concern. One of the oldest ballads collected in the Appalachians is "The False Knight in the Road," in which Satan appears in the guise of a knight to lead a small boy astray. The boy is too brave and smart for Satan, and thus the ballad teaches a strong religious lesson:

> "Where are you going?" said the knight in the road.
> "I'm going to my school," said the child as he stood.
>
> *Refrain*
> He stood and he stood, and he well thought as he stood,
> "I'm going to my school," said the child as he stood.
>
> "What do you study there?" said the knight in the road.
> "We learn the word of God," said the child as he stood.
>
> *Refrain* (ending with the last line of previous verse)
>
> "What're you eating there?" said the knight in the road.
> "I'm eating bread and cheese," said the child as he stood.
>
> *Refrain*
>
> "Oh, won't you give me some?" said the knight in the road.
> "No, not a bite or crumb," said the child as he stood.
>
> *Refrain*
>
> "I wish you were in the sea," said the knight in the road.
> "A good boat under me," said the child as he stood.
>
> *Refrain*
>
> "I wish you were in the sand," said the knight in the road.
> "A good staff in my hand," said the child as he stood.
>
> *Refrain*

"I wish you were in a well," said the knight in the road.
"And you as deep in Hell," said the child as he stood.

Refrain[37]

I know several folktales in which a hero named Jack has contests with the devil and wins. In one they have a hammer-throwing contest. The devil heaves his hammer skyward, and it takes three days for it to come down. Jack takes the devil's hammer, asks everybody to stand back, and then cups his hands to his mouth and yells: "St. Peter, open the gates! Clear the angels away and have them stay way back from those golden streets up there, for I'm going to throw this hammer right through the Pearly Gates!" At this point the devil says, "Wait a minute, I don't want to lose that hammer." So he takes it and goes back to hell. Satan is thus depicted as the greatest of all antagonists, and when the boy Jack outwits Satan, just as the lad in the ballad does, the tale takes on religious significance and suggests to ordinary Christians that they too can prevail against Satan.

People are not too pious to make jokes about Satan. I have collected many devil jokes. One is about a fellow who dressed up as the devil for a Halloween party. On his way home he went by a country church having a revival meeting. He thought it might be fun to walk in. When he did, the preacher and his flock jumped out windows or bolted for the door. One fellow was trapped in the corner, unable to get around the masquerader. He said, "I've been a member of this church for twenty years, but I've always been on your side!"

Some Upland people also believe in other evil supernatural beings, such as witches and ghosts. The word *witch* goes back to the old Anglo-Saxon word *wicca,* or "wizard." There are warnings against witchcraft in Deuteronomy 18:10 and in Exodus 22:18, in the admonition "Thou shalt not suffer a witch to live." In the New Testament, only Paul mentions witchcraft and sorcery (Acts 8:9 and Galatians 3:1). Thus it appears that notions of witches have come down the generations more through folklore than through the Bible.

The late Wilse Reynolds, a fiddler and former miner in Whitley County, Kentucky, talked to me freely in 1972 about witches and their ability to cast spells on human beings. His beliefs were influenced almost as much by current news stories about witchcraft and Satan worship as by traditional belief. He associated witches with Satan:

Some people don't believe in witches, but it's a fact—witchery is a fact—there's no question about that. It's really getting a start in

America now. Out here in San Francisco, California, there's a church of Satan. Well, England's infested with witches. We've been bothered with them here, but a lot of people don't believe in them.

There was one told me one time—I was just about seventeen years old—said, "I'll tell you something. If you tell it I'll draw you in a knot." Well, I went just as straight to where I was staying there and told it, said, "That old lady out there said she'd draw me in a knot if I tell this. I'm going to tell it and see if she can do it." And I'm a son-of-a-gun if she didn't. I couldn't walk all winter, couldn't walk from the bed to the fireplace without holding to chairs, and my legs would draw, and I'd might' nigh draw double, and the insteps of my feet was like a sore tooth. Well, I was thataway about six or eight months.

One day I was talking with this woman's grandchild, and she said, "Wilse, didn't you know that you can be witched?" I said "I don't know, but she said she was gonna do it. I know one thing, I couldn't hardly walk all winter." She said, "I'll tell you what—you can judge—if you've been witched you won't dream a dream for two years." And I never dreamed a dream for two years. Now that's a fact.

This same one told me this, said "Do you know Aunt E——— M———?" I said yes. She said "She's a witch. You know that hump on her back?" She had a hump on her back, this lady did. She one time asked my brother for a chew of tobacco, and he cussed her, and she said, "You'll pay for that!" And he got so sick and like to have died, and they went to Tellico [Plains], Tennessee, and got these two to help them. They drawed that knot on her back and like to have killed her, and she had to let my brother alone.

These fellows that's got this [strip mining] job right here—everybody that fools with that coal stripping gets in trouble, gets broke up. There's been two companies owned it now, and everything they had broke down. There was [another] company come in here, and everything they had broke down. They bought a new loader, and it broke down every day—a brand-spanking new one. I'm not saying this [witches] is what caused it. I'm just telling you what happened. There's a fellow buried right out there. There's a big cedar tree, and he's buried right next to the cedar tree, and his people is the ones I'm telling you about. His ancestors were all witches. I told them fellows, said, "Somebody's got a jinx put on you fellows." This fellow up there at the mine has never run more than three weeks in three years—stays broke down all the time. It's because that fellow's buried up there, and they didn't want them to go around and bother his grave. That's what I thought could happen. I'm just a-telling you now what people tell me, and what looks like it might be.[38]

Reynolds, who in retirement from coal mining was a watchman for the strip-mine site that he talks about in the preceding quotation, was a complex man who continued to surprise me during our friendship. I once met him at Renfro Valley, Kentucky. "What have you been doing, Wilse?" I asked.

"Well," he said, "I've been reading Gibbon."

"Gibbon?" I asked, with a rising inflection.

"Yeah, you know, *The History of the Decline and Fall of the Roman Empire.* I'm interested in the period between Constantine and Luther. You know, the Catholic Church had old Satan under control in that period, but with the rise of the Protestants, Satan has been on the rampage all over the world. Why, I read about a church of Satan out yonder in California just the other day."

Wilse Reynolds was taken away by a combination of black lung disease from his mining days and cancer, but he confidently treated himself to the end with a potent mixture of holly berries and various tree barks marinated in moonshine whiskey. He was an independent man in both physical and spiritual realms.

Some Uplanders believe in demon possession. David Kimbrough, in his book about serpent-handling Pentecostals, *Taking up Serpents: Snake Handlers of Eastern Kentucky,* reports that "The Devil surfaced frequently among Holiness congregations [and]. . . demons permeated everyday life and were likely to be given credit for a bucket of spoiled milk, a strange dream, and an untimely death." He went on to say:

> With the problems that had emerged with industrial capitalism, demons and spirits played a larger part in explaining everyday problems. Community anxiety and social interrelationships fed belief and fear, and accusations of demon possession grew more common. . . .
> Each community explained demons and witchcraft by the local standards, and belief in demons took distinct forms. For example, some saw witchcraft and the Devil as being one. . . . The Holiness people saw society as a war between agents of the Devil and the servants of God. . . .
> Many reports of demon possession exist in the Appalachian highlands. . . . It is commonly believed that a person with a weak spirit, or one who does not believe in God or demons, is a particular-

ly good candidate for demon possession. Mrs. Doyal Marsee of Bean Station, Tennessee, claims that she saw her father cast out demons throughout rural Appalachia. She believes that demons are floating about looking for a "weak soul" to enter and that they cannot enter the soul of a strong Christian.[39]

Beula Estes talked familiarly about the presence and work of witches:

I want to show you a piece out of Sunday's paper. This is about a witch named Aileen Davis. Now I knew her and she *was* a witch. She lived just down the road from me and we all knowed that she was a witch. Oh, yes, and we believed in them, too. Well, you know, they are Scripture. The Bible talks about witchery. They've got a contract with the devil, you know. My daddy used to tell us about witches. Back then, though, you knew who was witches and you knowed what they did. I remember once during thrashing, the thrashers would help each other, twenty or thirty of them at one farm, and the women would gather and cook a big meal, spread big tables. When the men came in that day they said, "Well, the horse has been be- witched." They knew who it was, too. A woman had been there to borrow something. "Don't let her have anything," the men said. She had a teacup, wanted to borrow some sugar. But the women turned her down. She came three times, see. "Don't let her have it," they said, "and it will break the spell." Well, that made her mad. She'd made that horse sick, see, but then the horse got well.[40]

I have heard many people in the mountains and elsewhere talk matter- of-factly about witches. Some are skeptical but nevertheless love to hear and tell witch stories. Folklorists have collected stories all over the region and have tried to systematize the beliefs in witches by listing characteristics of witches, methods for becoming a witch, and what they do. Ethel Owens wrote of witch beliefs in Kentucky:

Having believed that witchcraft perished in Salem in Colonial times, I was rather surprised to find in my adopted county of Breathitt some people who professed belief in witches. Upon inquiry I learned that becoming a witch is not impossible, even though rather difficult and dangerous.

There appear to be several methods of attaining this goal. One is to take a gun at sunrise, fire the gun and curse the Lord. After the gun has been fired, tie a silk handkerchief over the end of the gun barrel, turn the gun down toward the ground and the blood will run out. This must be done for nine straight days. If this method is too tedious, take a black cat and boil him alive at midnight. While the cat is in the kettle boiling you must curse the Lord three times and say you love the devil.

Another way is to dress up in black from head to toe, leave only the eyes and mouth to be seen. At midnight sneak up on a black cat and kill it with a broom. Taking the same broom, go to the dark part of the forest and get on the broom as if you are riding it. If you have passed the test, you will start flying; if not, you will fall off and die. No wonder witches aren't exactly numerous.[41]

Donald Wallace reported more information on witches from the eighty-year-old widow of a McCreary County, Kentucky, coal miner:

1. If a witch dislikes a person, she will borrow some object from the person, work her magic through the object, and the person will get sick and die. . . .
2. If a witch says the word *God* while she has a spell on a person, the spell will be broken. . . .
3. If a person looks a witch in the eye, the witch can cast a spell on him. . . .
4. If a witch is injured in another form, the injury remains on her body after she resumes human form. . . .
5. If a person refuses a witch's request for something, whatever the witch requested will suffer harm. [Elsewhere it is reported that witches can be foiled by refusing to give or lend them anything they request, even a drink of water.]
6. A silver bullet can kill a witch or destroy her power. . . .
7. A witch can make a cow go dry.[42]

There is belief in other supernatural beings in the Uplands. Ghostlore is plentiful. Even though the alleged activities of ghosts are sometimes much like those of witches, they are not usually linked to Satan or to witches. Witches are thought of as being living persons with extraordinary and usually evil powers, whereas ghosts are the supernatural form of a deceased person. W. K. McNeil does not discuss Satan in his *Ghost Stories from the American South,* although he does deal with witches. William Lynwood Montell, in his *Ghosts along the Cumberland: Deathlore in the Kentucky Foothills,* makes no mention of Satan and has only two references to witches and witchcraft.

Ghosts are frequently mentioned in the Uplands, although not all people believe in them. Like witches, ghosts are mostly part of the folklore of the region and usually are not connected to religion. However, I believe they help to explain events that appear to be supernatural, and thus are part of the belief system. Montell, introducing ghostlore in his *Ghosts along the Cumberland,* gives the following information about the element of belief in ghosts among those from whom he and his students collected:

One reason certain hillcountry people believe in ghosts is that for the most part such persons are products of their cultural matrix; that is, the milieu in which they were reared was one in which ghost stories were part of the culture trait. If parents or grandparents told ghost stories to frighten children into submission, or if ghost stories were a part of the folk process of entertainment and were told often, the active participants in these traditions would believe in ghosts more than those persons who were brought up in an environment to which ghost narratives were alien. One informant stated emphatically, "I'm afraid of ghosts and refuse to have anything to do with them." Another commented, "I didn't like to hear them [ghost stories]. That's the reason I don't know any. . . ."

Some stories give a definite reason for the return of a spirit. Specifically, in the order of appearance in this book, the explicit reasons for the return of ghosts are as follows: tombstone for a dead man not yet erected over his grave; person had died of starvation and his ghost had returned to eat food; fireplace hearth had been built over the grave; body was restless in the grave; a workbench had been erected over the family burial plot; ghost returned to finish playing a tune on the piano; and mother returned to inquire about baby's whereabouts. Other reasons for the return of ghosts were: to retaliate because a woman's husband had re-married at her death; to seek vengeance; to determine who had picked pins from the dead person's shroud; to look at former students; to re-enact death; to haunt husband; to identify murderer; to punish for theft of part of corpse; to haunt man who pocketed money; to punish man for drinking; to search for money; to torment the killer into admitting guilt; to reveal hidden money; to haunt spot where murder occurred; to get occupants to give up their claim to house; and to play a prank.[43]

I have heard stories of numerous other supernatural phenomena that help to explain mysteries of life and death and otherworldly matters. Some are in the category of superstitions, such as the following: if you step over a grave, it will lead to bad luck, perhaps death; if someone walks in the tracks of another, he will die; if someone dies on Monday, someone else will die before the week is over; if you see lights where no light is present, someone will die; if a bird flies through the house, someone will die; and if there is one death, there will be two others before long. I know people who believe that dreams have special significance in warning people of the impending death of a loved one, such as stories of persons dreaming about loved ones, often away at war, and knowing by the dream that they have been killed or that they are safe. Also lights, loud noises (usually waking one from sleep), shadows, or strange animals in the night are believed to foretell an impending death or other tragedy. In some stories the strange creature encountered is believed to be the devil himself, or sometimes an angel.[44]

It is difficult to separate theology from folklore in regard to Satan, witches, ghosts, and other supernatural beliefs. The Bible deals with all such phenomena, but strong beliefs have also come through the oral tradition, influenced greatly by Germanic, Anglo-Celtic, and African American folklore. As mentioned earlier, the ancient ballads, folktales, and fairy stories are laced with supernatural motifs. All people are superstitious, meaning that we believe all sorts of things that aren't necessarily true or provable. We laugh at other people's *superstitions* while defending our own *beliefs*. Superstitions, myths, and belief in supernatural phenomena are means of making sense out of a puzzling world. Some things cannot be explained in a rational way, so through time, people invent a rationale that attempts to explain the inexplicable. The devil of the Scriptures explains evil in the world. Belief in witches also explains our experiences of bad things that we don't feel we deserve. Ghosts and other unexplained happenings bring meaning to some about things they don't understand. Stories about all these matters intrigue something in us and even bring a special delight. We all fear death, and we are fascinated by superstitions and folktales about death. We seek any clue about what may follow it.

Upland people, like people everywhere, have to deal with evil in the world and in ourselves. What we see people doing to one another and to themselves is not understandable in purely human terms. The Bible teaches that Satan is the root of evil, and thus he remains a constant presence in the Uplands. Other supernatural beliefs also help people to understand and deal with evil, tragedy, and death. For many Christians in the Uplands, however, Satan is more than folklore or a symbol for evil. He is a strong presence in our religious belief system.

Primitive Baptist elders and officers at a meeting of the Tates Creek Association held at the Rock Springs Primitive Baptist Church on the Owsley-Jackson County line, ca. 1920. *Front row, left to right:* Elder John Gilbert, Elder James J. Gilbert, Elder Nathan Culton, Elder James Anderson, Elder George Seale, and Eli Taylor. *Second row:* Merida Gabbard, Riley Shepard, David Deaton, unidentified, unidentified, William B. "Buck" Metcalf, James Metcalf, Allen Rutherford (or Rupard), and Elder John Hinkle (1851–1941), a preacher for fifty-six years who is quoted in this book. (Photo and identifications courtesy of Jess D. Wilson.)

Plains United Methodist Church and Cemetery, Haywood County, North Carolina.

United Baptist Church, Knott County, Kentucky.

Church of God Militant Pillar and Ground of Truth, McRoberts, Kentucky.

Presbyterian Church, Monroe County, Tennessee.

Faith Assembly of God Church, London, Kentucky.

Moore's Chapel Freewill Baptist Church, Letcher County, Kentucky.

Island Home Missionary Baptist Church in morning mist, Anderson County, Tennessee.

Cemetery with open meeting house, Leslie County, Kentucky.

Crosses in southern West Virginia.

On the Daniel Boone Parkway, Clay County, Kentucky.

Fields of the Woods, Church of God of Prophecy, Cherokee County,
North Carolina.

The Narrow Way Church of God in Jesus Name, Madison County,
Kentucky.

Seventh Day Baptist Church, Harrison County, West Virginia.

Church of Christ, Monroe County, Tennessee.

First Baptist Church of Town Mountain, Perry County, Kentucky.

Quiet Dell United
Methodist Church,
Harrison County,
West Virginia.

Mt. Joy Church of the Brethren, Rockbridge County, Virginia.

Grace Baptist Church,
Buchanan County,
Virginia.

Red Lick Holiness Church, Madison County, Kentucky.

Hallsburg Missionary Baptist Church, Harrison County, West Virginia.

4 *The Word*

The word is nigh thee, even in thy mouth, and
in thy heart: that is, the word of faith, which we
preach; That if thou shalt confess with thy mouth
the Lord Jesus, and shalt believe in thine heart that
God hath raised him from the dead, thou shalt be
saved. For with the heart man believeth unto
righteousness, and with the mouth confession is
made unto salvation. . . . For whosoever shall call
upon the name of the Lord shall be saved. How then
shall they call upon him in whom they have not believed? and how shall they believe in him of whom
they have not heard? and how shall they hear without a preacher? And how shall they preach, except
they be sent? as it is written, How beautiful are the
feet of them that preach the gospel of peace, and
bring glad tidings of good things. . . . So then faith
cometh by hearing, and hearing by the word of God.

—Romans 10:8–10, 13–15, 17

It has been made clear to me that the center of belief and the source
of meaning in the Uplands is the Word—Scripture—which is studied and reflected on by each believer or preached by those who are called to
that work and who have the insight and the divine revelation to interpret
it. Faith is based on the meaning in that Word.

Importance of the Word

Sylvester Hassell, an early Primitive Baptist scholar, wrote about the centrality of the Word:

The Highest Critics—Jesus Christ and the Holy Spirit—put the stamp of their Divine authority on the Scriptures of eternal truth. The Old Testament was "Our Savior's Bible," and was always referred to by Him, with the greatest reverence, as the infallible, the literally and the perfectly true testimony of God; and more than two thousand times did the Holy Spirit move the writers to say that not only their thoughts, but their words, were God-breathed or inspired of God. . . . No other book or document of human literature bears these marks of divine authority; and, therefore . . . the Old and New Testaments [are] the only infallible rule of faith and practice. "All flesh is grass and all the goodliness thereof is as the flower of the field: the grass withereth, the flower fadeth, but the Word of the Lord shall stand forever," I-Peter 1:24, 25.[1]

Elder Hassell speaks for the Old School Baptists in this excerpt, but I believe his statement is relevant for most Upland Christians, because the Word in the Old and New Testaments is all important to discerning meaning in life. Most groups emphasize the Bible as the sole authority for faith and practice, not priests, seminary-trained preachers, or other earthly ecclesiastical authorities installed by human beings. Brother Harold Mullins, a Holiness preacher on the other side of the continuum from the Old School Baptists, stated well the centrality of the Word in Upland Christianity:

We must live by the Word of God. The Word of God will deliver us. He's got words for everything. When there's a death in the family, He's got words that will console us. The 23rd Psalm is some of the best consoling reading that you can ever read. In the moments of need, He said He'd never have His people begging alms. . . . God is able to deliver if you'll just stay true to His Word. In the Word of God there is food, and there is hope for our souls. This is more important than anything our body could ever need. Our soul must have God, or it will die to be lost for eternity.[2]

Rev. Henkle Little, a North Carolina Southern Baptist pastor, stated: "I take the Bible every day. I apply it to my life. I make it practical to my day, and it's always worked for me. The Lord's blessed me in so many ways."[3] Brother Harold Kelly, pastor of the Church of God, West Bend, Kentucky, stressed the Word over human endeavor as the way to salvation:

Where is the glory among people? Where is the power to deliver from sin? Where is the power that men and women can lay hold on for real salvation? . . . God help us, we need to get back to the Word of God. We need to get to the place where we can preach enough Gospel that if anybody wants the Lord, they know how to get loose from sin. There are people today who have lost all the glory. I've been in some churches and they're dead. They're cold. They're so formal. The Holy Ghost is gone. There's no glory, there's no shouting, there's no conviction! God's just gone away! You want to know why? It might be the people in the pews. It might be in the pulpit. They've backed up on the Word of God, compromised on what God has revealed to them![4]

Herbert Barker, whom I visited with in Point Pleasant, West Virginia, before his death, said: "I believe in the Bible. I believe it is the infallible, inspired Word of God."[5] James Tanner, a Methodist layman in Nicholas County, West Virginia, extended this basic belief in the fundamental integrity of the Bible:

I believe every word in the Bible. There's nothing in there that I've ever found anything wrong with. It's all good and I get lots of good from reading the Bible. It helps me, and it teaches me. . . . The New Testament part is a picture for me. It teaches me many things. It teaches me how to live, and it teaches me how to treat my brothers and sisters in Christ, and it teaches me everything that I know is good. I didn't know much about the Lord Jesus and no one else in the Bible until I was converted and went to reading and studying it. . . . I learned a lot from the Bible, and I think everything in it is good.[6]

Hassel Mullins, a Church of the Brethren layman and farmer from Dickenson County, Virginia, spoke strongly about the Scriptures being the infallible Word of God:

I believe a man should first read the Word so that he understands and knows the will of God. . . . He must realize that God inspired the prophets and the writers to write the Word, and I believe it so strong that God was holding the pen Himself. If He'd wanted one more letter added, He'd a added it. If He'd wanted one left out, He'd a left it out. I believe that if men today, preachers, church leaders, Sunday School leaders, if they begin to read the word of God and understand, and preach what the Word says—the divine Word of God—what it says, and not what they think, we'd be getting somewheres.[7]

Brother Ozell Bunch, a Holiness minister from LaFollette, Tennessee, also emphasized the infallible nature of the Bible: "I believe that all of the Bible is real. If this book isn't the book of God, you'd better throw in the towel, for there is nothing else that will stand the test like this book. I'll tell you frankly that I have been talking with Jesus, and His word lives in my heart. . . . There are not enough devils under the sun to make me doubt that this is the infallible Word of God, because I have read it, and what I needed jumped right out of the pages into my heart."[8]

An unidentified Dickenson county, Virginia, Church of the Brethren member emphasized the basic belief of the Upland faithful that Christian truth lies in the Word of God and not necessarily in the words of those who try to interpret it in our times:

Belief in the Bible is something we have to say is our top word. Without the Bible, we're lost. We have no guidance. We have nothing to stand on. We have nothing to lean on. The Bible is the full salvation of man. The Bible is the way built for us to go. Looking into the Bible is as though we might be in a classroom listening to Jesus give His lectures. When we read the Word of God, it is the same as if we are taking lessons. . . . We must be willing to obey, to follow, to live the things that are laid down in God's Word.[9]

Rev. Dennis M. Moore, pastor of the Isoline Baptist Church, Cumberland County, Tennessee, added to the basic belief that the Word is sufficient to our day and that all is embodied in Christ: "I believe with all my heart that the Bible is the holy Word of God, that He inspired men through the Holy Spirit to write the Word in order that they, not only in that bad time, but in the day in which we live, in this instant of time, might be able to receive the Word of God. Now, the Word of God is Jesus. Jesus was the Word. He was the light, and He brought light unto all men that we would believe upon Him."[10]

I believe the Word is perhaps more important to those church members who do not have published creeds or confessions than to those who do. To them the Bible is the sole foundation and the guiding principle for their churches and for their lives. An unidentified preacher in a Kentucky Pentecostal church commented: "Obedience to the Word of God will get us to heaven. . . . The Word is one of the most powerful forces in the universe. . . . It surmounts all things. . . . It is through it that I can have the meat and drink for the soul."[11] Rev. Marvin Kincheloe, a Tennessee Methodist, said: "To me, it's a mirror; it lays bare the heart. . . . God speaks to me through that written revelation."[12] One of my favorite preachers, Elder Danny Dixon, in a sermon at Cedar Grove Old Regular Baptist Church, Letcher County, Kentucky, said: "The Word of God is quick. It's powerful, the most powerful thing that has ever been. It's sharp, sharper than a two-edged sword, piercing even to the soul and to the spirit, to the bone and marrow. . . . It's a discerner of the intent of the heart, and when you have heard the Word, the truth, the Gospel . . . you can be filled with the Holy Spirit and the promise."[13]

Mary O'Dell, a Nicholas County, West Virginia, Methodist, talked of the practicality of the Word in everyday life: "I think we should read it all. It does us good. Many times we can be cold and blue and troubled, and we can pick up the Bible and read it and it lifts us up and cheers us along the way."[14] Dianne Harrison, wife of Vernon Harrison, pastor of the Church on the Rock, Clay City, Kentucky, also saw the Word as being helpful to those in great need, but she went beyond this to talk of her wish to live by the Word and thus to be an example to others:

> He says if we can come to Him with a broken heart and a contrite spirit that He will in no wise cast us away. That's the Word of God, and I know it's true. When everything else is a lie and wrong, I know I can count on the Word. I've been a-learning lately that I need to do more of the Word. The Bible says not to be a hearer only but a doer of the Word. That's talking about the Word coming through you and living like it says to be, and that's what I want in my life. I want to be a walking testimony for Jesus. I want the Word to be in me and let it live and shine through me.[15]

Growing in the Word and in Faith

Sara Snow, a Methodist from Chattanooga, Tennessee, believed that we must constantly study the Scriptures if we are ever to grow in faith and be a help to others: "I've heard it likened to a baby being born. When a person accepts Christ as Savior, as their personal Savior, if you don't continue to study the Bible and pray and worship, then you remain . . . as a baby, but to grow as a Christian and mature you must do these three things, read the Bible, learn more about God's will, and pray to let God communicate what His will is for you."[16]

Rev. Henkle Little, pastor of the Calvary Baptist Church, Taylorsville, North Carolina, believed that the Word is central, but he also believed that we must study, pray about, and act on the Bible if it is to be meaningful in our lives:

I know that just reading the Bible all the time won't do the job, but praying and applying that which the Lord has given you will do the job. There's great power in prayer. The Lord told us to ask and we shall receive, to knock and it'd be opened, to seek and we'd find. That's the rule book. That's the foundation of it all—the Word of the Lord.

Mountain people, as far as I know, they accept the Bible just for what it says. Not everybody's going to believe it, but on the other hand, everyone will not deny it. But at the end of the day, it will judge us all. We'll get an account of what's contained in its lids, not what some man thinks about it, but what the Word of the Lord says. That's what the Holy Spirit is for. He comes to lead us in all the truth. He's your life source. You may try to use other things and get in a hurry. You may mean to enlarge yourself in many ways, but if you got the Lord's way, it will work. I accept the Bible myself for what it states. It's like you were in a basement and your daddy was up on the housetop. He could see farther than you. He could say, "So-and-So's coming," and you might say, "No, I don't see them." This is the condition spiritually that you are in. The Bible's the foundation. Better build on it by faith.[17]

Preaching the Word

Traditionally the Word is there to be read, pondered, expounded, and interpreted by those who are called to preach. Every age has had preachers who were able to preach the Word in a way that swayed people into a search for salvation. Rev. John Lakin Brasher, himself a powerful preacher in the Methodist church in Northern Alabama and elsewhere, described one of his mentors: "The old master preacher in eloquence was J. L. Freeman, six feet two, handsome face, magnificent personality, with pathos enough for half a dozen men, eloquence, native eloquence; 'twasn't studied; it was native, dramatic to a wonderful degree. I've heard him preach on the Resurrection until it seemed I could see the ground tremble where the saints were getting up. I never have seen a man—bishop or whoever—that could so impressively administer the holy communion. What a preacher! What a preacher!"[18]

Brasher went on to tell a story about another courageous and effective preacher in post–Civil War northern Alabama, where pro-Union northern Methodists were despised and threatened by some who had supported slavery and the cause of the Confederacy. The story shows the power of the Word as preached by dedicated and fervent preachers in the Southern Uplands:

Brother [T. R.] Parker went to a church one day, and they had skulls and crossbones pictured on the door, and underneath it said, "Enter at your peril." He rode up, hitched his horse and took his saddlebags off his saddle, and started for the door. A man said, "Don't you see what's on the door?" "Yes, I do, but I have an appointment here at eleven o'clock. That is my business, and when I'm through, you can do as you like." He went in and preached, and before he got through, some of those fellows that'd come to murder him leaped up and grabbed him around the neck and hugged him, and they celebrated together. He'd swept them clean off their feet![19]

Brasher described Parker's preaching in this way:

When he began to soar in his eloquence, he seemed to forget the audience was present, and taking a sort of look slantingly upward, puckering up his fingers as if he were hold of a thread, he began to climb, and climb, and climb—with a great marvelous climax. Sometimes he would get up and say, "I do not feel very much like preaching this morning. I will give you a little talk." And then he'd start unfolding the Scriptures, and the first thing you know, he was preaching one of the greatest sermons that man ever listened to.[20]

Luther Gibson, author of *History of the Church of God Mountain Assembly, 1906–1970,* described another perilous time, similar to the one described by John Lakin Brasher, when Pentecostals were persecuted by members of other denominations (including my fellow Cherokee County, North Carolina, Baptists) whose hands were nevertheless stayed by the power of the preacher:

Persecution began as in the days of the Apostles, and many of the ministers and Saints were whipped, and treated cruel, by the enemies of the Church, but they had the power with God. At one of their meetings where Rev. J. H. Parks was preaching, there were men who came to the church with knives and pistols for the purpose of breaking up the service. They planned to take Brother Parks out, and were threatening to kill him. When he got up to preach, he rebuked these men in the name of the Lord, and the Spirit of God caught him up against the ceiling of the church, and these men who had planned to do him harm, fell out as dead men and left.[21]

Most of the ministers I try to describe in this book are "called" preachers who feel that God has conscripted them for the all-important mission of preaching the Word. Some are educated in theological schools and ordained by mainline denominations, but many of those I quote regard the call itself as both their authority and their qualification to preach. Many of these latter preachers are relatively well-educated, being otherwise teachers, educational administrators, businesspeople, or other professionals, although they are not necessarily educated in theology and homiletics. Others have little formal education. Some feel that they are unworthy of or unequal to the mission for which they have been chosen, and I have numerous testimonies from those who have resisted. However, the feeling is strong that God knows His purpose and that He will prepare and make adequate those whom He calls. Many are little concerned with standard grammar but are insightful, fervent, and often eloquent in expounding the Word. The eminent Appalachian scholar Cratis D. Williams once remarked to me that some of the most eloquent people he had known were unschooled mountaineers who were not hampered by fear of making a grammatical error. Their minds were on what they were saying and not on how they were to say it.

There are many dramatic stories about how the Lord dealt with those whom he called to preach and who resisted. Elder John Hinkle, of Clay County, Kentucky, who had been a fiddler and fun lover and who became first a Freewill Baptist and then a Primitive Baptist, wrote of his travail in resisting the call to preach:

> I was in trouble and sold my fiddle. I agreed within myself to let the world with its fun go. In the fall of 1884, I joined the Missionary Baptists and had a quiet mind for some time. . . . I told the preacher I had done all a man could do, and I believed if I would do my part the Lord would do his part.
>
> I went on all right till February, 1885, when the Lord called me to preach. I said nothing about it and went on for a short time. He called me again, and I said nothing about it, and made no start to preach. On the night of February 25, 1885, after I had gone to bed, the blessed Lord manifested it to me again so plainly that I said within myself I could doubt it no more. I said nothing to my wife nor to any one else. The next morning I arose and went to feed a mare which was in a field. I felt so bad, as if I were forsaken, that I knelt down by a post to pray; but I could not pray. I knew I was in great trouble. I went back to the house and my wife soon put breakfast on

the table. I sat down to breakfast, but I could not eat a bite. I sat there a short time and concluded that I would go up the branch and pray. . . . I started, got 15 or 30 yards from the house, and the wrath of the Lord struck me as lightning, the best I can compare it. . . . I took another step, and His great power came the second time. I did not fall, but came very near it. It flashed in my mind that I had fled as Jonah had. I turned back to the house and when I got in at the door I dropped on my knees and told them that the Lord had overtook me as he did Jonah. I do not know how long I was there on my knees praying. It seemed as if I were lifted up in spirit in that prayer as much as I ever was in life, but when liberty was gone from me and my prayer ceased, I was afraid to move. It seemed that all of the love and mercy of God started from the top of my head and moved slowly down my body until it went out my feet. . . . I cannot tell you how sick I was. . . .

I laid down on the bed, turned my eyes upward and said, Lord, have mercy on me. The flames of hell pierced my mouth and nose, and the neighbors gathered in; and Allen Hensley came to see me. He was a member of the Primitive Baptist Church. . . . I asked him to pray for me . . . , and he prayed a good, humble prayer. The next morning I felt better, and I said if the people would gather on Sunday, which was the next day, I would preach for them. I suppose the news spread hastily, and I remember seeing the people coming in a large crowd. My mind in this world disappeared, whether in the body or out of the body, I cannot tell; but God knows, and I was brought into judgment as though it were the last day. I was placed at the head of a large congregation and was judged by the words of my own mouth. . . . I think there has never been a man on earth that suffered more than I did. . . . I received a revelation from the Lord. It was this. If all of Adam's race were to unite against you to put you to death, they could not. You will never die until the Lord is done with you on earth.

[Later] I was out at work clearing a new ground, and I felt a desire to pray. I laid down the ax, or mattock, whichever it was, went around the side of the hill for a short distance and knelt down and began to pray. I was lifted up in the spirit past common and the earth began to shake, and the more it shook the more I was lifted up by the blessed Spirit of my blessed God. I had not fears; my fears were entirely gone from me. The earth reminded me of a right handy sifting woman with an old-time sifter. . . . When he took my feet out of the pit and put a new song in my mouth, I had something to praise Him for.[22]

I treasure my visits with Elder Ivan Amburgey, an Old Regular Baptist preacher from Pinetop, Knott County, Kentucky. He had worked in a factory in Cleveland, Ohio, by day and played music on nights and weekends before his call to preach. He told of his experience in receiving the call, also comparing himself to Jonah:

> I joined the church the first day of September 1963. . . . A feeling come over me, and only a minister could explain it, I suppose. I got to thinking about it. It got to coming to me. I'd try to push it away. I'd think I had pushed it out, but it kept coming back—I'd say about nine months of being real concerned about it. It came, as one writer said in the Bible, like fire shut up in your bones. It was to the point where I had to do something. In some way I think preachers called to preach, they do make a Jonah trip. They'll rebel against God for a while, and then they'll become willing. I rebelled for about nine months after I felt God called me.
>
> I felt like God was speaking to me, in my heart, you know. I questioned that, because I was unlearned, ignorant in so many ways. I really wondered why would God call somebody like me. I honestly questioned God on that. I would try to let that go away, but that feeling never went away. . . .
>
> I took it very seriously [then]. I put my life on the line. That's the honest truth. I asked God on the way to church that night. I knowed the brothers were going to ask me, because I felt it, that they were going to ask me to introduce the service and lead in prayer that night. I prayed to God from the depths of my heart, if I wasn't called of Him to do this, for Him to let me die on the way to church that night. From the heart, I meant, because I knew if I wasn't anointed of God, I'd be a hindrance and wouldn't be a plus. I didn't want to be a hindrance, you know. I didn't want to be a stumbling block. . . . When I got to the church and the brethren got up to make arrangements that night, he said, "Brother Ivan's going to introduce the service and hold prayer." It scared me to death, and I was scared to get up and scared to not get up, because I'd been working, wrestling with that thing for a long time.
>
> Finally I got up. Course I found out the first night, it's not as easy as it might seem. . . . I preached that Saturday night, and the next

Sunday I preached. . . . And the following Sunday I preached and the following Sunday after that, I preached Saturday and Sunday both. I preached about eighty times the first year. . . . Things just went real good for me. The people accepted me.[23]

I have found that these preachers have a strong belief that God knows all His purposes and that He is constantly looking for Christians who will do His work on earth. When He selects one to preach His Word, though there may be resistance and even flight from the folds of the faithful, He will eventually prevail. This dramatic sequence of "call," struggle, and acquiescence contrasts sharply with the more incremental progression of some mainline Christians into the vocation of the ministry through joining the church, attending college and the seminary, and receiving the call to a pulpit. Elder Squire Watts, from Red Fox, Kentucky, one of the most earnest and admirable preachers I have met, told me of his Jonah-like struggle with the call to preach after he had moved from the mountains to Louisville for a job and had joined an Old Regular Baptist Church there:

I'd been in the church for about two years, I suppose, and I started being burdened down, feeling incomplete. I thought sure I'd made a mistake by even getting in the church. I'm the kind of person you almost have to hit over the head with a hammer to get a point across. . . . I couldn't understand why God had any use for a person like me, you know, an old country boy. I worried with it a long time, and I started getting in trouble spiritually. Also, about this time it was on my mind to move back to the mountains. . . .

It was at this time this other feeling come over me. One day a young preacher got up to preach—hadn't been preaching long. For me that day, he really preached, and I enjoyed it thoroughly during his sermon. The Spirit spoke to me strongly, "There's what I want you to do for me." Right there's where I really started getting fearful. I really was in trouble. Jonah got in trouble because God called him to preach to the city of Nineveh, and he wasn't willing to do that. I wasn't willing either. . . . In my mind I was willing to do what He wanted, but you want to be sure. This is serious business. Well, the way I get along when I get in trouble, I just find a place and pour my heart out to God. I said, "Now, Lord, if this is what you want me to do, show me in a way that I can understand. I'm not wanting lightning flashes or hearing voices, but I really want something that I can understand. If that's what you want me to do—I don't want to bargain—but let me get up there [to the mountains] and get settled and find myself. Just let me alone for a little while, and then if that's what you want me to do, then when I get settled and straightened out, then you can pour it on."

So help me, that's how it happened. It left my mind, and I was free of that—wasn't burdened. We moved [back] to the mountains, moved our membership to Cedar Grove Church, and everything was going just fine. . . .

Then all at once, I was sitting over there in the Cedar Grove Church, and here it come again, said, "Your time is up." I really got scared that time. Like I said, I'm not one to get up before a crowd, never made a speech in my life, but I knew it was time to do something. So I told Brother Elwood [Cornett, moderator of the association]. He said, "Whenever you're ready, we'll help you any way we can."

It was in my mind . . . , if a brother feels he's called to preach, he should tell his home church. I thought, Saturday's the time to do that [at the Saturday evening business meeting]. "I'll get up on Saturday when they're doing their church work, and I'll tell them what I feel." Well, I'd get so scared and uptight when church was winding up, I'd still be setting there. Of course I'd already told Brother Elwood, and he wasn't putting any pressure on me. I'd made up my mind, "This is it. The next time the church meets, I'm going to tell them." Well, I didn't. There I'd set, and the church was over again.

They were having church at Little Dove on the fourth Saturday night. I was in a pretty bad way. Brother Fess Blair and Brother Elwood Cornett noticed, I guess, that something was wrong. So after church, they asked me what the problem was. I told them. Elwood said, "Well, it's not too late." They talked with me and helped me.

So the next morning, we were going to Cedar Grove Church. That night I made up my mind that I was going to have to do something. I got to church the next morning. Sometimes the moderators make arrangements. They'll get up and welcome people. If we have visiting preachers, they try to use them. They ask, "What's your mind today? Would you like to open the service? Would you like to hold prayer?" and so on.

He asked me, "How do you feel?" I said, "Well, I feel terrible, but today's the day. It's today or nothing." He got up to welcome the people, and he told the church, "We've got a brother here today, and he feels he's called to preach. We want to give him the right to express his gift." So he called on me to open the service. I'll never forget, when I was setting there on the seat I knew that this was the time. I was running through my mind what I was going to say, and that's the first lesson I learned, that you don't make up anything when it comes to preaching. That's not preaching to us. I remember as I walked across to the stand, I was shaking all over. I put my hands on the podium, and everything left me [he laughed]—this little talk I'd prepared. I probably couldn't have told you my name. I don't remember exactly what I said but something to the effect that Jesus had called the apostles and made them fishers of men. That's what I thought He wanted me to do. I probably didn't say fifteen words. Then I sat down, but that really set me free. The burden was gone. I just felt free spiritually. I didn't preach any that day—probably didn't preach any the next few times, but the way had been opened for me. I went to work [studying the Bible]. . . . I started preaching.[24]

Finally, Elder Milford Hall Sr., a Floyd County, Kentucky, Primitive Baptist, who was a violent and dangerous sinner before he was saved, told of his struggle with God after the call to preach:

I was gladly received and baptized by an old school Baptist minister into "the church of God." They greeted me as a long lost angel from heaven. Now I was happy again and felt as though I was free forever. . . .

But ere long the burden to preach the gospel began to put in its appearance every now and then. This was very obnoxious and terrifying to me. I sought to stifle these thoughts. . . .

I fought against this with all my power for about five years. . . . I fought a losing battle all the time; but fight I would, and did. I had excuses galore. But none eased my mind or suffering conscience. The more I resisted His will the more I suffered. . . .

Finally the "revelation and appeal" of God was made so plain to me that I was afraid to dillydally with His grace and put Him off any longer. I was now born again; I could not doubt that. Perfect love has cast out all fear. God, by His spirit, had descended into the grave of "original pollution" and had brought up my soul from the "lowest hell." I knew that I had passed from death unto life because I loved the brethren. I could find not a single excuse for any further delay in the matter. It was preach or die.[25]

Richard Floyd, a Southern Baptist from Chattanooga, believed all Christians, not just preachers, are called to do God's work: "I think every Christian has a purpose in life and that God has him fitted into His pattern and He will eventually find his purpose in life. Maybe it's not to be a preacher or teacher, but maybe it is just to win someone to Christ who will become a great preacher."[26]

Elder Elwood Cornett, an Old Regular Baptist associational moderator, also touched on a belief that some in addition to ministers are called by God to serve, and he then stated his conviction about his own call to preach: "I'm a member of the Mt. Olivet Church, [and] I'm thinking of a brother there. Another person that I'm thinking of is a sister in the church, a member of that church. I've got a job to do that happens to include being a minister, a calling from God. This brother's call may be to sing, or to help sing. This sister's calling . . . is to sing praises to God. Mine is to get in the pulpit and do my best to offer myself to God in such a way that He would bless me to preach His Gospel."[27]

A member of the Green River Pentecostal Church in Kentucky contradicted the Calvinist belief that God will always prevail if He calls you to do something and gives you the gifts to do it. This person believed that those who fail to use the special gifts they have been given will have them taken away:

> Brother Willie Brown was preaching the other night, and he said, "Every child of God has a gift of some sort or other." I think in talents and abilities, God does give everybody something that they can do. . . . If you don't exercise it, do you know what happens? It's taken away from you. It's handed over to people who're trying to do something. That ability, that talent and that usefulness we could be using for God, is took away from us and given to somebody else. So let's not let ourselves get rusty in the Lord.[28]

Some preachers were called to preach but then became dissatisfied by the doctrines of their denominations and felt the call to preach other doctrines. For many years, since before America was formed, there has been honest disagreement on such subjects as limited versus universal atonement, as well as the nature of the human condition, whether we can rise above the sins of the flesh in an earthly existence, or whether we can backslide once we have been saved. The question of sanctification is still one of the hottest items in debate between the Calvinist Baptists and the perfectionist Methodists and Pentecostal-Holiness people. Rev. J. H. Bryant, a Church of God preacher, told how his father, a Baptist pastor, was won over to the Church of God:

> Dad came in home one evening from the old Patterson Creek Baptist Church where he was pastoring and I saw something was wrong with him. He had nothing to say and looked very sad, so when bed time came he called us all around to pray. . . . Dad prayed so long I thought he would never get through, but he finally closed his prayer and went to bed, but along in the night dad awakened us crying out, "Glory Hallelujah." About that time, grandma cried out, "Stephen, what in the world is the matter with you, all the neighbors will think you are Sanctified." Dad said, "Thank God that is what is the matter and I wish that the whole world knew it right now."
>
> The next morning dad told us how it all happened. Brother Anderson Alder was over at Patterson Creek, Sunday and while dad was preaching Brother Alder would cry out, "Glory Hallelujah." After a while dad called him down and told him to be quiet until he got through, that he was disturbing him, so Brother Alder obeyed him. . . . Brother Alder was waiting for dad and grabbed him by the hand and said, "God Bless you Brother Bryant, I love you." Dad said, there was something got hold of him then and when they got on the outside, Brother Alder got on his little mule and started off. As he went over the hill out of sight all but his head, he looked up and cried out at the top of his voice, "Glory Hallelujah," Dad said something like lightening went to his heart, and something spoke to him and said, "He has something that you haven't got, or he couldn't be feeling so good after the way you treated him." Dad began to seek that blessing, and after he received the blessing, he started preaching Sanctification, telling his experience wherever he went.[29]

Even within specific groups such as Baptists, Methodists, Holiness-Pentecostals, and Christian, there are differences in belief that cause members, or preachers, to depart for another group. Elder John Sparks, one of the most learned and articulate of the preachers I interviewed, had difficulty with doctrine and practice within the Freewill Baptist Church and told why he moved to the United Baptists:

> I joined the United Baptist Church in November 1987. I had been before that an ordained minister for some years in the Freewill Baptist Church. My parents belonged to the Freewill Baptist Church.

My grandparents were United Baptists—three of my four grand-parents. . . . I had some doctrinal disappointments with the Freewill Church that had built up for a number of years. . . .

When I started preaching in the Freewill Baptists, I was seventeen years old. I was probably immature and green—had a lot to learn, I suppose. There were a couple of old preachers who took me under their wing, and they were an older type of preacher—came from the older school. When I got out to preaching in the Freewill Baptists, I was told that I needed to learn the precepts that were in a document called *A Treatise of the Faith and Practice of Free Will Baptists,* which is pretty much their confession of faith . . . , and so I began to study the treatise and found that some of their articles were not in line with my own beliefs.

Then there was another matter—a practical matter. I began to go out and work with preachers in the Freewill Baptists. I had to be un-der the watch and care of the church for a year, and then I had to be licensed by the Conference, the next highest organization of the local churches. Then I had to be ordained. There were some methods of evangelism that I had been used to among the older preachers. The methods being advocated by some of the younger preachers I dis-agreed with very much. Generally when we have services, we give the invitation to the lost, if they want to come up, or come give their hand for prayer.

Along about the time I started preaching, it began to be intro-duced as a concept around here that praying at the altar was not as important as confessing with the mouth. The tenth chapter of Ro-mans was very important to Freewill Baptists: "The word is nigh thee, even in thy mouth, and in thy heart: that is, the word of faith, which we preach; That if thou shalt confess with thy mouth the Lord Jesus, and shalt believe in thine heart that God hath raised him from the dead, then thou shalt be saved. For with the heart man believeth unto righteousness; and with the mouth confession is made unto sal-vation" [verses 8–10].

They were trying to put a whole lot of emphasis on confession with the mouth. If you believed it with the heart, all you had to do was confess it with the mouth, and that would complete the thing. It led to a cycle of—a word we coined—"overpersuasion": very long al-tar calls, the preacher getting right out and almost trying to drag people up to pray or make a confession of faith, and then when one would come, they'd begin to grill them with questions like, "Do you believe Jesus is the Son of God? Well, you've got to confess it with your mouth. Now, do you believe?" It led to a whole lot of things where people would end up making a profession of faith and being baptized and go to church for a few weeks and then, they'd call it, backsliding.

Although I disagreed with it, I tried to work with it for some years. I was very dissatisfied with it. Then I felt like the Lord gave me an impression to go with the United Baptists, and I went. The United Baptists, by and large, they put more emphasis on the grace of God, that it is salvation by grace of God, that it is salvation through faith. The emphasis is on preaching the Word. It is completely acceptable to give an invitation for anyone who wants to come up, but I don't know of a United Baptist church where anybody would be rushed into making a profession of faith. It is an idea—a cherished thing—to let people alone to pray. Let the Spirit do the work.

I'd like to say I'm not trying to condemn the Freewill Baptists. My wife is a Freewill Baptist, and she takes our kids to Sunday School every Sunday, and I like that.[30]

Most of the mainline denominations split in the nineteenth century over the question of who was to be saved—just those predestined by God or anyone who might hear the Word and repent. Hinging on this all-important question were other problems: denominational authority over individual congregations, missions and evangelism, Sunday Schools, musical instruments, and the kind of music that was acceptable in worship. To some extent debate on these topics continues today, and people sort themselves according to beliefs about such matters. The more Calvinistic hang onto such churches as Primitive, Old Regular, and United Baptist. The more Arminian move to Freewill Baptist, Methodist, Pentecostal-Holiness, and Churches of Christ. The Word is preached in these differing churches and interpreted according to basic beliefs.

Ordination of Preachers

Most ministers have been approved or ordained to preach by a local church, by an association of churches, or more formally by a denomination. Some, however, have simply begun preaching after receiving the call and have drawn believers to form a church that may or may not be associated with other churches. Mainly, preachers are examined by a body known among the Old-Time Baptists and some Pentecostals as a presbytery, which includes preachers or deacons from an association or other body larger than the local church. The neophyte preacher's doctrine and preaching ability are monitored, and he may be counseled, corrected, or even enjoined from preaching if he strays from the accepted doctrine or exhibits traits or behavior that call into question his suitability for his high calling. If he meets with approval, there comes a time when he is considered for ordination.

Elder Ivan Amburgey told of his ordination and explained the process in the Old Regular Baptist Church:

I had been preaching about eighteen months when they ordained me. The pastor of the church mentioned it to me, and I really begged him not to do that. I had no desire whatsoever to be ordained. I just wanted to preach. After I'd begun preaching for about a couple of months, they did give me a motion and a second, in a business meeting on Saturday, to give me the right to preach, hold services and all. Then when they ordained me . . . in 1967, there were eighteen ordained authorities to examine me that night. . . . I'd never seen over one ordination before, and I was scared to death. . . .

Everybody would study [for ordination] to a certain extent, but I really didn't do that much. I read some and studied, but you know they're going to ask you questions that you never read. You have to have a good understanding about a lot of things. They asked me some pretty tough questions concerning double marriage [being divorced and remarried]. I knew the moderator felt one way and some of them had a different view. So I had to answer to satisfy both sides, ones to the left and ones to the right. It scares you half to death, but with the help of the Lord, I made it. They'll ask you some pretty tough questions, the old timers will, but sometimes the old timers will be a little easier on you than the young minister that wants to be seen and heard. He may have been ordained only a couple of months ago, and he'll jump up and ask you a real tough question.

[Then] one brother will ask for the floor and say, "We've asked this brother a lot of questions, and I feel he's answered them, and I feel at this point we ought to cease and ask for prayer and lay hands on this brother. I feel he's ready to be ordained." Somebody'll second it, and that's the way it will be. They'll sing an old song, an old-time hymn—line it—and at the end of the song, everybody will come and stand around the one being questioned, and when they come down on their knees in prayer, one brother will be chosen to hold prayer and lay hands on that brother. He'll lay his hands on his back or

head, and all the brothers that can will lay their hands upon him
somewhere, and if they can't, they'll lay their hands on a brother
that's nearby who has his hands on the brother. There is a connection
all over there. There'll be a move and a second to ordain him, and all
the deacons and elders would sign the paper—the ordained deacons
and ministers at the gathering, whether three or thirty. One of them
would make a move. It might be the moderator of the association, or
it might be the moderator of another association—he'd move that
someone stand as clerk of that work. So the clerk would start preparing the letter. . . . He'd pass it around, and all the deacons would sign
one side, and the ordained elders the other side. Everything that was
done, the clerk would write that down, every question that was asked
and every answer that was given, and who made the move and who
the second. If anything should ever come up, they would go back to
the record.

After you have got up from the prayer and the hands being laid on
you, the moderator of the presbytery that day would ask another
minister to get up and give a charge to the young brethren, however
many were being ordained, and he would get up and speak a while
concerning the charge and how to study to be approved a workman,
to rightly divine truth. . . . The brother will give the charge. Then
they have a move and second to dissolve the presbytery. Then the
moderator would ask the church to receive the brother into the
church as an ordained minister. They would get a move and a second
from the church to receive that brother back as an ordained elder.
Then the church would write out credentials that he is an ordained
minister. The brother's name would be recorded by the church and
by the association as an ordained minister. You'd have to go to the
courthouse and register yourself as an ordained minister if you'd like
to marry people.[31]

Preaching Styles

Preaching in the Uplands among the churches reflected in this work is usually impassioned. The preaching style across various bodies has some common characteristics, such as a chanted and cadenced musical tone, spiritually revealed inspiration, and an energetic delivery. Many have questioned
the origin of the chanted sermon, which is found across the spectrum from
the Calvinistic Primitive and Old Regular Baptists to the Arminian Pentecostals. No doubt it goes far back in history, at least to the First Great Awak-

ening. Erasmus W. Jones, a nineteenth-century preacher, took it back further, to Wales, the place of origin for many Americans, and the preaching style that glorified *hwyl* (pronounced in the neighborhood of "hoo-yel"), an indescribable eloquence:

> The effect often produced by the popular Welsh preacher is wonderful. . . . Their preaching . . . is usually marked by a great variety of intonations. I do not know the origin of this chanting style of preaching prevalent among the Welsh. . . . The judicious use of it is confined to the more passionate or pathetic parts of the sermon. It differs entirely from the monotonous tone that is heard in English churches . . . ; it is melody of the purest nature. . . . The minister is never at a loss how to apply the words to the melody; they appear to run together as by musical attraction. The sentence is started, for instance, on E minor. The minister has his own peculiar melody. It ranges from here and there to the fifth, often reaching the octave, and then descending and ending in sweet cadence on the keynote. I am sure that in the genuine *hwyl* the intonations are always in the minor mode.[32]

My observaton is that the preaching of some Old Regular Baptists, such as Elder Russell Jacobs, of the Left Beaver Church in Floyd County, Kentucky, closely resembles the singing tone described by Erasmus Jones. Jacobs can be heard in the Appalachian Film Workshop's film *In the Good Old Fashioned Way.* The lining chants, sermons, and prayers of these churches today are highly melodic, and praticioners are keenly aware of rhythm and poetic turns of phrase. For example, Elder I. D. Back, of the Indian Bottom Association of Old Regular Baptists, opened the service one morning with these words, "We thank thee, Lord, for lengthening out the brittle threads of our lives."

Preaching styles are varied among what some would call fundamentalist preachers, however, ranging from closely reasoned prepared sermons to those relying entirely on inspiration or revelation from above. Some preachers may skip from one subject to another with Scriptures quoted from memory, whereas others' sermons are based on carefully selected verses in support of an intellectual argument. The tone may range from a quietly spoken one to a highly emotional chant that may at times be unintelligible to one unaccustomed to the style.

Henry T. Mahan, a Grace Baptist pastor in Ashland, Kentucky, who has a forceful style but presents carefully reasoned sermons, stressed the primary purpose of preaching, which is to spread the Word of God. He was critical of some popular preaching styles, however: "No use of me pushing this pulpit back and walking up and down in front of here, ranting and raving, take my coat off and sweat and yell and holler. . . . What you need, my friends, is to hear God's Word, the truth of God about these important matters. That's what you need. Preachers are entertaining; they're acting foolish, claiming power that they don't have. They're drawing disciples after themselves. They're building great monuments to their own names."[33]

In another sermon Brother Mahan discussed salvation and the role of preaching, motivated by a Calvinist belief that God is the author of faith and will work His way with the sinner and bestow His grace:

Salvation is of the Lord. Salvation is not something a preacher does for you, or a soul-winner does for you. You know, the average revival meeting today is like a political convention, recruiting supporters. I'll tell you this, if a man can talk you into a profession of faith, another can talk you out of it.

What we need to do is preach the Word of God to sinners and wait upon the Lord to make the seed live. No pressure, no emotional coercion, no salesmanship, no begging. Just preach the Gospel. Salvation is of the Lord, and God will work in the sinner's heart, and God will bring him to faith. Faith's not coming to the front of the church. It's coming to Christ, in the heart. Faith is not believing what a preacher says; it's believing what God says. Faith is not repeating a prayer from the mouth of another. It's calling on God myself, from my heart. . . . It's to receive a new heart, a new nature, and a new spirit.[34]

Licentiate preacher Mike Mullins, a Primitive Baptist, echoed the same opinion one morning in a sermon in the Berea Primitive Church in Rockcastle County, Kentucky:

We have people who are preacher worshippers. Paul told Timothy, "Preach the Word. Be instant in season and out of season; rebuke, rebuke, exhort with all long-suffering and doctrine" (2 Timothy 4:2). That is not an easy task for a preacher. Today people want to hear what they want to hear. They don't want to hear reproof and rebuke and instruction in righteousness. We want to hear smooth things, [but] we need preachers who will stand up in the pulpit and reprove and rebuke no matter what is going on. He needs to stand up and say what is wrong, not emotional but from the Scriptures. Listen, I believe in preaching Christ, but if you don't preach the whole Word, you're not preaching Christ. We need to preach all of the Word.

Some people say, "Brother So-and-So, he's a good teacher, but he's not a preacher." Well, that person is not knowledgeable in the things of the Scripture. A good teacher is also a good preacher. If a preacher doesn't teach, then he's not giving me a thing. Not only should he teach, but he should edify in his teaching.[35]

Elder Ivan Amburgey, who worked as a musician before his call to preach, likes to use the term *entertainment* when he talks about preaching. His beliefs are at variance with the remarks of Henry Mahan just quoted, but it should be noted that many Old Regular Baptists often comment that worship services are the most enjoyable times they have. Here Brother Amburgey talks about the joy he finds in hearing another brother preach and the satisfaction he feels in being able to move an audience:

I guess I had an awkward way of saying things, but it was interesting. If you can't entertain the people, you can't preach. You got to be an entertainer. That's what preaching is, entertainment. To me, the best entertainment I ever heard in my life is good preaching, you know. . . . Well, it's pleasant to hear. It's great entertainment. If you go to a concert and listen to songs; you enjoy that. When you go to church and a fellow gets up to preach and he's boring, that's not much entertainment, is it? So, when a brother gets up and he can capture the audience, and when he can be blessed to preach, thirty, forty, forty-five minutes can go by before you know it. I've listened to brethren preaching, and get up and preach an hour, and absolutely, I couldn't believe it, because it went by, I enjoyed it so much, and it went by so fast. I've seen brethren get up for ten to fifteen minutes and it seemed like ages, because they were boring. . . . So, if you sing a good song, it's entertainment, you know. If you preach, if you hear good brethren preaching, to me that's great entertainment.[36]

Elder Claren Williams, a black Old Regular Baptist from Red Fox, Kentucky, also used the word *entertain* in regard to preaching, but he also explained the Old Regulars' beliefs about preaching: "We don't prepare a sermon. We depend upon God. When a preacher gets up, he'll entertain the people, just talk around until his mind is revelated, gets on a certain thing. Then he'll preach that out. He doesn't just get up and read it. He waits for the revelation. Maybe a certain text will come to mind. He'll quote that Scripture maybe, and he'll preach from that Scripture. That's what you call a revelation."[37]

Inspired Preaching

Claren Williams's brother, Elder Lovell Williams, added: "A man is supposed to look into the Scriptures to find what they mean, but you might do that all week. Still, when you get up to speak, your subject will be on a different thing, maybe something that you never thought of. God will lead your mind into that. It's just like the ones who wrote the Bible. They didn't know what to write until the Spirit told them."[38]

Although some television evangelists and some mountain pastors may be guilty of Brother Henry Mahan's charge that they are calling attention to themselves rather than to the Lord, most of the preachers quoted here are modest about their abilities to preach the great message of God and take care to keep the emphasis on God and His Word rather than on themselves. A Primitive Baptist preacher prefaced his sermon with the following remarks: "I don't know if I can preach a lick or not. I know one thing. I know the God of Glory is able to bless me to preach if that's His will. The thing I don't know is if it's His will or not. So the only thing I can do is that I can try, and if I can't, I can sit down."[39]

This humble tone and the belief in the need of help from above in preaching were echoed by Old Regular Baptist Chester Gibson, of Leyburn, Kentucky: "I've got something wrong with my throat this morning. I'm a sick man that preaches anyway. If God sees fit this morning to bless me, He will, and then if He don't, then I'll just have to take my seat."[40]

Elder Danny Dixon, another Old Regular Baptist, also stressed his humility and doubtfulness about his ability to preach, emphasizing the Old Baptist view that God speaks through the preacher to articulate what He wants to be heard. When Brother Dixon says, "I do knock people who study preaching," he is careful to explain that he refers to "those who attend seminaries and other religious institutions for the purpose of learning how to prepare a sermon." He is especially concerned that there are "those who have not been 'called' or sent by God and [yet] seek the ministry as an occupation."[41] He began a recent sermon with these words:

This morning, I'll just talk a little bit. I never learned how to preach. I never tried to learn how. I've never been to school to try to practice this job. I don't knock people that go to school to study the Word, but I do knock people who study preaching. I think God calls men to preach the Gospel, and I believe they cannot preach without the Spirit of God that comes from heaven and overshadows them and revelates their minds to say things that will pierce the hardest and most wicked man or woman of the world and cause them to become humble as a little child and call mightily upon the Lord. That's what I'm here for today. I hope God will bless me to speak words, not that would be poetry to satisfy the flesh, but the Word of God that it would burst somebody's heart to cause them to cry out, "Pray, God, have mercy on me, a sinner."[42]

Elder Mike Smith, a Primitive Baptist from Pike County, Kentucky, also touched on the necessity of having the blessings of the Lord in order to preach:

It is impossible to preach the Gospel without the blessing of the Lord, no matter who the preacher is, no matter how much experience he has. When I first started out introducing the service, I made a pretty bad failure one day, and one of the brothers told me, "I've had a lot more experience than you have, Mike." It wasn't long until they called on him to introduce the service, and I didn't tell him that he made a failure. He come to me and looked at me and said, "I learned a pretty good lesson from what I told you." I asked what. He said, "Experience don't make the difference."[43]

John Lakin Brasher, the eloquent Alabama Methodist preacher, had a less humble tone, although a firm conviction in the necessity of having the Holy Spirit, when he declared: "If all our Methodist preachers and members in North Alabama had this enduement of the Holy Spirit . . . , we could capture this whole North Alabama, give the devil lockjaw, and hang crepe on the doorknobs of hell in a little while."[44]

Hassell Mullins, of the Church of the Brethren in Dickenson County, Virginia, also stated his belief that God calls preachers, making them capable of the job and inspiring them with a message. He had no respect for the sermon composed and written down beforehand: "I believe that God calls a preacher. He calls him in justice, and when He calls him, He qualifies him, He equips him. He puts him out to preach, and he needn't be afraid if he don't say it as it's wrote down, but to get up and preach—preach the Word. I don't believe in writing down a text and getting up trying to remember it, like the fellow who wrote his sermon and it blowed out the car window as he went to church. He couldn't preach. I believe in calling on God."[45]

Paying the Preacher

Another Church of the Brethren member in Virginia spoke of the custom among many churches in the mountains—Primitive, United, and Regular Baptists, as well as some Brethren—of not paying the preachers a salary but expecting them to earn their basic living by working like everyone else:

> Us in the neighborhood here, we don't believe in paid preachers, a man that is hired to preach for a living. Paul said, "I preach the gospel. If I do this willingly, I have a reward. . . ." He said he must make it without charge. So we don't believe in hiring a preacher, making him a salaried man to go around and preach the Gospel. Because he [Paul] said, "A workman is worthy of his hire." I believe if a man preaches freely, from the heart, without charge, that God will furnish him both spiritually and naturally what he needs. He [Jesus] sent His disciples out, sent them with neither money or script, and even told them not to put sandals on their feet. But I believe if a man is not physically able to work, he should be provided for.[46]

This belief that giving the preacher a salary is a problem goes back to Colonial days, when people were taxed to support Anglican churches and clergy. Baptists and others objected to this collusion of church and state, but there was also a profound belief that paid ministers were not free to preach the unvarnished Word and were beholden to those who paid them. Many followed the example of Baptist pastors in Wales and elsewhere in Britain who worked at some job to support themselves and preached without salary.

Elder Lovell Williams, a black Old Regular Baptist from eastern Kentucky who earns his living in the construction business, is strong in his opposition to preachers' accepting a salary from the church. "I don't believe in it," he said. "I've never took a penny for preaching." He goes on to give an example of a problem he and other preachers had with doing what they thought was their pastoral duty and how they resolved it:

> This brings back to my mind, one time a lady over at Isom, her husband died, and her children came in here from different states. There were four of us preachers, and they wanted us to have something for our services, because we go so much. Sometimes we have two or three funerals through the week. They gave me an envelope, gave my brother and the other preachers one. I got home, I opened it up

and—I don't know how much was in it now, $20, $30, or what it was. Oh, that tore my mind! What shall I do? I hate to hurt their feelings.

The next day I got up and went back. I said, "I'll give it to the mother, tell her to use it on burial, or something that way." When I got over there, there were two of the other preachers who had done the same thing. They came out while I was going in, and none of us knew that the other was going to be over there. The Lord said He would supply our needs.[47]

Elder Elwood Cornett, who works as a professional educator, stated his belief that he should earn his own living and that he should serve the needs of people in his church or others who need him without additional pay. He is aware that many people in eastern Kentucky cannot afford to pay, although this is not the reason he serves without pay:

Last night I got home late from work. I think it's my duty to earn my living. I got home, and there was a young man that had died about twenty-five miles from my home, and they called and wanted me to be there. Barring some very serious circumstance, I think I'm compelled to go. My understanding of what God commands me to do is to go when you're called and needed . . . , and I went and did the best I could to help the family to understand that things may not be as bad as they thought they were, because after all, the eternal life is much more important than the natural life anyway. . . .

They had him dressed in his work uniform. Sometimes I've seen people dressed in overalls. Sometimes I've been where the family had almost nothing, and I think it's my responsibility to go to them just as quickly as I would go to a family that had a million dollars, and I'm not going to accept any pay from that family today. They may not have any money. I don't know. And I'm not going to accept pay from the fellow that might have a million dollars, who would want me to come to the funeral of some of his loved ones. . . . If I received pay from somebody, I've got to do sooner or later what they tell me to to. This [policy] gives the person the independence that he needs.[48]

Primitive Baptists, too, generally expect their preachers to work to support themselves, although they may contribute some money toward the preachers' needs. The late Almeda Riddle, an Ozark folksinger who was a

Primitive Baptist, told me in an interview: "We don't have a fixed salary, and we don't take up a collection publicly. Each one gives what he feels he can, and we take care of our ministers."[49]

Elder Steve Casteel said the following about preacher salaries, without being too clear as to what financial support the preacher might get:

> We frown on paying a salary, and we don't have any preachers that require a salary in the Primitive Baptists. We believe in support, because the Scriptures teach it. We believe in supporting the ministers in every way, including financially, through gifts and offerings that come into the church. We don't believe in preachers so emphatically demanding this that they won't get out and scratch around a little for themselves. A lot of our preachers receive as much in a year's time as these salaried preachers do. Normally, most of them do work to support the very ministry that they are engaged in, to help support it.[50]

Brother Henry T. Mahan raised questions about ostentatious preaching. Many criticisms have also been aimed at opulent living, especially as exemplified by several television evangelists. Some Upland preachers, especially in the towns and county seats, are paid well, and congregations may also provide comfortable parsonages and even expensive automobiles. That is almost never the case in the majority of churches with which I have been concerned in this study. Nonetheless, some of the very churches that have found their parishioners among the poor have flaunted their success in a better economic age. Some feel that if you are doing God's work, He will bless you with material goods. Dr. Donald Bowdle, professor of history and religion at Lee College, which is affiliated with the Church of God, Cleveland, and a minister in that church, felt that some Pentecostals exhibit an attitude of "I came from the wrong side of the tracks but bless God, I'll show them." He remarked: "I think that is why we overbuild our churches and parsonages. The problems identified with television evangelists, the 'overliving,' is the problem we have among many Church of God preachers."[51]

The attaining of worldly security does change one's fundamental values. A study in West Virginia by John Photiadis and B. B. Maurer shows that being rural, poor, and relatively uneducated are directly related to dependency on God and the church. As people become better educated, find security in a job, and so on, they tend to place their faith in such things as education and the right job or career, with God and the church given less emphasis.[52] I confess that this knowledge has troubled me, for I have spent much of my life involved with programs of economic and social uplift. Yet

I too have observed that some of the most sincere and devoted Christians with whom I have talked are among the economically marginal people. An obvious conclusion is that when we gain in one value, we sometimes—some would say always—lose something in another. Church leaders, all of us, should consider well the implications of the Photiadis-Maurer study.

Herbert Barker commented on economic independence versus religiosity and the added importance of preaching the Word: "We do become self-dependent, and the more of the world's goods you have, the less you depend on God. If you don't have a lot of the world's goods, you see that you have need, but if you have everything you need already, you may not even need God. It does not have to be that way, but there is a tendency in man, in his fallen and depraved nature, which we all have, to have an inclination away from God, not toward God, and that is why preaching is so important."[53]

Brother Harold Kelly, pastor of the West Bend Church of God in Powell County, Kentucky, had a clear purpose for his preaching, and in making the following comments, he had in mind "false refuges," such as wealth and property:

> I want to bring a light and a warning to those who are not saved. Our desire is to lift up the Lord Jesus Christ. We're not here to promote some denomination, not here to lift up some individual, but we want to promote the simple Gospel of Christ. . . . I was thinking while preparing for this broadcast today of the many false refuges people have. Folks are trusting in a lot of things to get them to heaven, but I'm glad there is a real refuge. Isaiah said the refuge would be a man, and I'm glad that man is Jesus Christ. . . . He not only can save us from sin, but He can keep us as long as we are in the world, and He is able to present us faultless and blameless before the Father.[54]

Most of the people people with whom I have talked in the Uplands believe that much of life's meaning can be learned from the Bible and expounded by called preachers from the pulpits. Discerning the Word is serious business. It is also a continuing process. Most believe that going to church to hear the Word preached is central, and almost all believe that we can find new truths each time we read or reread the Bible. My sister, Vertie Jones Mintz, of Marble, North Carolina, has read the Bible completely through eleven times—and the New Testament, twenty-three times—and she continues daily reading.

5   *Salvation*

The Lord is my strength and song, and he is
become my salvation: he is my God, and I will
prepare him a habitation; my father's God, and I
will exalt him.   —Exodus 15:2

Be it known unto you all, and to all the people of
Israel, that by the name of Jesus Christ of Nazareth,
whom ye crucified, whom God raised from the
dead, even by him doth this man stand here before
you whole;
  This is the stone which was set at nought of you
builders, which is become the head of the corner.
  Neither is there salvation in any other: for there is
none other name under heaven given among men,
whereby we must be saved.

—Acts 4:10–12

People I have talked with expressed anxieties about their existence
here on earth and about death and whether there is something
beyond. My interviews with them have revealed visions of heaven and hell
that are engraved on their minds from countless sermons intended to bring
them to grace. They know the Scriptures that give a plan for attaining
heaven, but they argue about the different notions they hold about the
plan. One thing I saw was that Upland Christians are concerned with
salvation—being saved, finding security in the Lord, and gaining an eternal life in heaven. They fear that through Satan's guile, our willfulness, our
lust after things of the world, and our inability to remain faithful to our
commitment, we may end up in the other place. But we need God, and

we seek Him, although not always with the persistence that the Scriptures call us to adopt.

I found that the poor, those who lack security in life because they live on the edges of existence and who often fail to get respect from other people, express more of a need for God than do those with tenure, money in the bank, and respect from others. The study cited at the end of the last chapter shows that basic values and intensity of religiosity change as a function of income, education, and economic and social security.[1] Coal miners in hard times, sharecroppers, and unemployed people have shown an absolute devotion to fundamentalist churches where they are reaffirmed as persons and are made to feel worthy.

The Faith of Upland People in Salvation

Rev. Henkle Little, pastor of the Calvary Baptist Church of Taylorsville, North Carolina, and a singer and recording artist with his family before his death in 1988, commented on the faith of the mountain people with whom he grew up and on his own salvation:

> God and man in Appalachia is the same as God and man in other areas. . . . Faith comes by hearing, and hearing by the Word of God (Romans 10:17 and Matthew 24:35). However, the more adverse the circumstances, the more you look to the Lord. The more heartaches and trouble and sorrows and having no other person to look to, you look to the Lord more. In some sense of the word, faith is handed down from one generation to another what God has done for them. It is so in the days that we live. We want to hand down what God has done for us. It works that way in the mountains of North Carolina, Kentucky, Tennessee—in Appalachia—it works that way.
>
> It's the most personal thing that's ever happened to me, this thing of salvation. Strange as it may seem to you, I know the salvation of the Lord better than I know my name. The day they named me, I was there, but I was just a kid and didn't know the day my parents named me, but I was there and old enough to know at twenty-seven years of age when the Lord saved me in 1949, January 23, and it's so simple a fool could not err therein, as Isaiah said in 35:8, "And an highway shall be there, and a way, and it shall be called the way of holiness; the unclean shall not pass over it; but it shall be for those: the wayfaring men, though fools, shall not err therein."

It's been personal to me . . . when it comes to salvation. Our part is to repent and believe. It's unique in the way the Lord sends it, and unique in the way it keeps you. It's unique in bringing love and joy and peace and long-suffering and gentleness and goodness and faith and meekness and temperance to you.

Now to me, the people in the mountains have more common sense because the environment calls for it. They live off the land, and also there are times they are called on to use nothing but faith in the Lord. Circumstances a lot of time calls on us to use our faith. One day in the lion's den old Daniel had faith in the Lord, and it worked. The Hebrew children when they were in the fiery furnace, their faith worked. . . . I find the people in the Appalachian areas, they are people who live closer to the heart of God than most. I can't say what the difference is but they seem to have a more steadfast and surer faith in the Lord. They're not involved in the hustle and bustle of life, and they look to the Lord.

You take my daddy, an uneducated fellow, but still he knew many, many things that were a blessing and a help to his family, that he saw in the Lord. Mountain folk will let you know exactly what they believe, and they'll stand on that. I appreciate it in them. They are not fools when it comes to the Scriptures and standing on what they know. . . . These people in the mountains seem to have a more burning desire to know the Lord. People are wicked everywhere and people believe God everywhere, but people in the mountains, to me, are close to the heart of God. . . . The men and women of the churches of the mountains, they look to their minister as a man of God. . . . These people in mountain churches trust their pastors, in most cases, [although] I know you'll find a rotten apple in every barrel. Church members in the mountains, they seem to love one another as people that are related, have a respect for one another that is brotherly and sisterly love. It's more a family situation than in the city churches. Mountain people, to me, seem to look to the Lord and to thank Him and trust Him, praise His name, maybe not in big outbursts, but by everyday living. That's a delight to me. . . .

I know there are some things in life that are a great benefit to us—money, education, finery, houses, and land—but that'll not do the job in that other country. A person is born to live somewhere in eternity, either in heaven or hell. Both of these are there because He says so. Just how valuable is this salvation to a person? The Lord, religion, salvation is of more value to you and than anything in this world. I want to say again that I do think that mountain folk trust the Lord in a different way, and I really don't know how to explain it. I wouldn't say that it is a different culture, and yet in another sense it may be. But to me, I think faith is the same all over. Maybe I should put it this way, that mountain folk appreciate it more. That's the best way I know to clarify it.[2]

I agree that Upland people have thought long and hard on salvation. They believe that God has laid out a plan for persons to redeem themselves from their sins and to prepare for another life beyond death, a life of eternal bliss, rather than one of condemnation and suffering in a place prepared for those who do not heed the call to salvation. Herbert Barker said: "God has not left man in the predicament that he found himself in after the Fall of Adam. God has sent His Son to reconcile man back to God, through faith in His death, burial, and resurrection. That has to be imputed to me. Before I can become a Christian, God has to see me, in Christ, crucified, buried, and risen."[3] Lydia Johnson, a Kentucky Free Pentecostal, said: "The Holy Ghost convicts the sinner of sin, and then he will repent, and we can't do that for him. He has to do that for himself. But if he will only repent . . . and pray to God earnestly enough, and is sorry enough to forsake his sin, then God will forgive him, and he'll feel that in his heart and knows that he is God's child."[4] Mrs. James Neal, a Baptist from Tennessee's Carter County, said: "We think too much about salvation and not enough about God. We want to remember where salvation comes from. It's God's wonderful love bestowed upon us, and that ties in with . . . the grace of God. Salvation is by the grace of this wonderful God, who not only is our creator, but He is our Savior, through His Son, whom He sent down on Calvary to suffer in our place."[5] Ralph Snead, a Tennessee Freewill Baptist, commented: "We believe in the sovereignty of God. We believe in salvation by grace. We believe in the atonement of Jesus Christ, and we believe that apart from Jesus Christ and His atonement, there is no salvation."[6] Charlie Cole, a Southern Baptist, added: "Salvation is a gift of God. . . . That makes an escape from hell. Without salvation we would all perish."[7] Gene Wells, another Southern Baptist, added further: "We believe that while you are here in the body, that is your chance to accept Christ, and you must come to the age of accountability before you can accept Christ. . . . You have to come to the realization where you know you are in sin. When you die you have no more chance then to accept Christ. God has given us many chances while we are here on earth—when we are living in the body."[8] Rev. C. A. Williams, pastor of a Free Pentecostal church in Laurel County, Kentucky, said: "We think that the Word is the seed, sowed by the minister, and it is conceived in your heart, and a conviction grows when you hear the Word, and it matures and you develop into a Christian. You are born of the Spirit that way."[9]

Conviction

Brother Alfred Carrier, pastor of the Green River Pentecostal Church in McKinney, Kentucky, outlined the way to salvation, beginning with the work of the Spirit on the hearts of sinners, bringing conviction that they are lost:

> In order for people to be saved, there has to be an act of the Spirit. One area we have not touched on is conviction. Conviction is an act of God's Spirit brought by reading God's Word, hearing it preached, and could possibly happen through the singing of a gospel song. We feel that to have true repentance and a true rebirth, there has to be a conviction of the Spirit, because man is a fallen creature and has to be converted. He's got to have a complete, total change within his heart if he's going to fulfill what God wants him to be in this life. So we are of the opinion, and I believe it is absolutely necessary, that a person totally confess and repent.
>
> After conviction seizes upon a person, we make an altar call. Now, we don't say that a person has to go to the altar in the church to be saved, but we do say that he must have an altar somewhere and give a total, complete repentance and confession before the Lord, and we say *definitely* a public confession must come before you can fully please the Lord. Now, we prefer and I believe that people should be bold enough to walk out publicly and bow themselves down and confess and repent, and then when that experience comes—and I'd like to add, experience of a new birth—I believe that we can and must know that our sins are forgiven. We teach that the blood of Christ is the only atonement for sin today, and when the blood is applied through the Spirit, that we are aware of the fact that we have been made free from sin and that we are now a child of God and qualify for entrance into heaven.[10]

The Need for Repentance

Most Uplanders believe that salvation begins with conviction that they are sinners, after which repentance must follow. Elder Frank Fugate, an eastern Kentucky Old Regular Baptist, describes the gospel of repentance:

The prime cause of the Baptist people is the doctrine of repentance, which many churches are leaving out. Repentance is a godly sorrow set up in the heart. You never do a wrong but what you are sorry. That's God a-making you feel condemnation. We all repent, but whether or not we repent to the extent of satisfying God's wrath and receive God as our strength is the thing about it, that we can resist doing these things that we have to repent about. The real thing that people need is that strength . . . , the need to recognize that strength when it intervenes into their hearts and minds. . . . We know when we love the pleasures of sin, and whenever we repent and lose all of the pleasures for sin. It's taken out of our hearts and minds [and] we know it. We know that we have been saved from the enjoyment of drinking, or seeking revenge, or hate. That's the reason why we can tell people we've been saved from our sins and about love and tenderness.[11]

Garfield Sloan, another eastern Kentucky Old Regular Baptist, echoed others in speaking of a person's need to be repentant in order to be saved: "You can't teach a man, you can't enlighten a man, unless he is a repentant man. 'A godly sorrow that sets up in the heart worketh repentance unto salvation to him that believeth,' one writer said. When you believe, that's when you seal with the Spirit of the holy promise. He said, 'The time will come that whosoever calls my name shall be saved.' But you have to be a-wanting salvation."[12]

Brother Vernon Harrison, pastor of the Church on the Rock, a Pentecostal church in Stanton, Kentucky, in a fervent radio sermon, preached Jesus as the way to salvation, repentance, and forgiveness:

I'm thankful that in the shadow of death there is a light the Bible talked about springing up, the Light of the World, which is Jesus Christ. He, praise the Lord, came to give us life and give it more abundantly. I'm thankful that God so loved the world that He gave His only begotten Son. I'm thankful that there was a way made on Calvary. Everybody that's listening today that's lost and undone, the most important thing that you need to know about salvation is that you need to repent and fall at the foot of the cross and receive salvation for the forgiveness of sin (Mark 1:15).

They's people listening today that don't know Jesus as your Savior. You need to know that you need to repent in order to receive the kingdom of Heaven. . . . You need to know that you have to ask forgiveness of your sins. . . . The Bible says that we all have sinned and come short of the glory of God. . . . That no longer applies when I'm washed in the blood of the Lamb. That means that until you have come to a full knowledge of God and accept Christ Jesus as your Savior, you are lost and undone. Repent ye and believe the Gospel.

Somebody listening today, God's knocking at your heart. You need to be seeking out a church somewhere. You need to be listening to the Gospel, listening to somebody give the altar call that says, "Come ye that are heavy laden, and I will give you rest. . . ." Somebody needs to tell you that [even though] you live a good moral life, that you pay all your bills, you don't beat your wife and children, that [though] you are a good man, good moral men and woman are not going to go to heaven. Praise the Lord, the world's going to be judged according to the standards of God—not mine and your standards. The Bible says that men and women will be judged for their deeds one day—whether good or bad—we'll stand in the presence of God. When Jesus died on Calvary, he took and nailed sin to the cross, showed the world that the Spirit had triumphed over the flesh. He showed the devil that it was possible that we could come into this world full of trouble, full of sorrow, and we can go out with no sin attached to us, that we could go out into the hand of God. He showed the world, praise the Lord, that it could be done! He said it's the Father's will that none should perish, but all should come to repentance. . . . You need to know that you will not go to heaven unless you repent. He said, "If ye believe in me, ye shall never die." I believe that. I believe that Jesus Christ was the Son of God. I believe that Jesus Christ's blood cleanses me from all sin. I know that I cannot stand in the presence of God except that Christ is the way.

There's somebody listening who's never bowed a knee in humbleness and said, "Have mercy on me, Jesus. I'm lost and undone. I know you died on Calvary for the sins of the world. I'll give my sins unto you. I want you to be my Lord and Savior." You need to repent. You need to ask forgiveness for your sins. Unless ye repent you'll likewise perish. . . . The kingdom of heaven is at hand. Repent! Repent! Repent![13]

Wetzel Ball, clerk of the Mount Zion Regular Baptist Church in Logan County, West Virginia, wrote the following about salvation of sinners:

If a man in his natural state is found to be a sinner, under condemnation, with the penalty of death hanging over him, an alien from

God and without hope in the world, what is the remedy? What is the cure? How can man be restored to favor or become reconciled to God? In answer to these questions, first, in brief, we will say to the man who is a sinner that the blood of Jesus Christ cleanses from all sin. That we are reconciled unto God by the death of His Son. That there is no condemnation to those who are in Christ Jesus who walk not after the flesh but after the spirit; for the law of the spirit of life in Christ Jesus has made us free from the law of sin and death. For what the law could not do in that it was weak through the flesh, God sent His only begotten Son in the likeness of sinful flesh and condemned sin in the flesh that the righteousness of the law might be fulfilled in us who walk not after flesh but after the spirit.[14]

Upland Christians, like those elsewhere, make a great distinction between the laws of man (or of the Old Testament) and the grace that was brought by the sacrifice of Jesus for our sins. The saving and cleansing qualities of Jesus' blood is also frequently mentioned in sermons and in song. There is a belief that people have to be made aware of their sins by the preaching of the Word, that they have to come under conviction, repent, and confess. A member of a Pentecostal church in DeKalb County, Alabama, put it this way: "Well, the first thing with the sinner, God has to exhort them—they have to have knowledge that they are sinners. They have to repent, be sorry of the things that they have done. Then Christ will forgive them, and then we believe that after they are justified by faith, they can have Jesus' blood applied [to] cleanse them from all the filth of the flesh, and then they are fit subjects for baptism of the Holy Ghost and the indwelling of the Spirit."[15] Lenora Neal, a Cumberland County, Tennessee, Church of God of Prophecy member, spoke of being born again in this way: "Regeneration is acceptance of the Word in full belief. It is God's Word. And then repentance brings regeneration, because when we repent of our sins and quit sinning, then we are justified before God. So regeneration and justification constitute the born-again experience which is the inner man being made anew."[16] The biblical concept of the "inner man" and the "outer man" is important in many churches, as is discussed elsewhere in this book.

Grace and the Holy Spirit

If anything is important to Upland religion, it is the concept that God can bestow his grace to us, although some believe we are never worthy of it, whereas others believe we have to make an effort to become worthy. In addition, I have found that people talk freely and often of the work of the Holy Spirit. Elder Hapner Mullins, a Virginia Old Regular Baptist, spoke of conversion, grace, and the absolute importance of the Holy Spirit in the salvation process:

> Conversion is the doorway to Christian life. No one is a Christian without it. One who has such an experience of grace has undergone a deep reaching and transforming experience. He's no longer the same man he was before. Something has happened to him that has made him different, so that, really, he is a new creature in Jesus Christ. He's a new man and such he must be before he can live a new and changed life. The Holy Spirit is the sign and seal of this new life. And every child of God possesses the Spirit of Christ. To everyone who repents and believes in Christ, the Holy Spirit comes as an abiding presence and is ever ready to accept the leadership and control of our lives. . . .
>
> God's plan for us is not bound by years and time, but stretches to the distant ages of eternity. None of us will ever know the fullness of God's plan until we stand with our feet on the shores of eternity and look with unveiled eyes on the glories of His presence. To hope for the promise of God while we do not possess the Spirit is to hope for that which we will never have. But to have the Spirit is an assurance that some day, in the love and wisdom of God, we shall inherit the promises. . . . What the heart needs is transforming experience, which we call conversion, and this alone is possible in the Spirit, might, and power of God. And, when we have this glorious experience we enter into the highest life, the richest of all lives, the life of the child of God.[17]

Brother Phillip Banks, a Kentucky Freewill Baptist pastor, added this:

> The salvation that the Bible talks about involves lost humanity, lost and condemned and damned forever and ever because of the inherited nature of our parent Adam. Christ, the only begotten Son of God, who was without sin, born in this world of a virgin, came into this world and offered Himself an atonement for sin. Now He is like the brave fireman rushing in to rescue the child. When we believe this, when a person is willing and able to acknowledge the moment, see himself for what he really is, a sinner before God, hell-deserving, damned and doomed without hope in the world, when he sees by the eye of faith the Son of God, dying for his sins, and believing in Him and trusting Him.

This is salvation, not only from the fires of hell, but for life in this world, for a new purpose, new goals to tell other people about this Christ who has rescued him. Salvation involves more than this. It involves all that happens to a man from the time he's saved on down through life, through death, through the grave, and on through eternity.[18]

Elder Mike Smith, a Pike County, Kentucky, Primitive Baptist, stressed the strong Calvinist belief that salvation depends on the grace and mercy of God through the sacrifice of His Son and not on our worthiness:

The Old Baptists have been trying to tell ever since I belonged to them that we are saved by God. We're saved by the grace and mercy of God through the shed blood of Jesus on Calvary. I don't know of anything better to tell anybody than that Jesus already paid the price. Jesus paid it all, and all to Him we owe. The Bible says that we're less than nothing without grace. Man in his best estate is nothing. We've got nothing to plead, no righteousness. The only righteousness is the imputed righteousness of Jesus.[19]

Grace versus Works

I have heard numerous arguments between Calvinists and Arminians, who are divided by the idea of unearned salvation solely through the grace of God, on the one hand, and salvation through good works along with grace, on the other. In addition to requiring good works, some believe that we need to reform our character so as to be worthy of salvation. Rev. Harold Pritt, pastor of the Bethany Independent Baptist Church in Charleston, West Virginia, spoke on this subject:

Reformation of character, that comes under the heading, in a sense, of works, is not the cause of salvation later, but is the result of salvation previously. Man is prone to want to work for himself and refuse any outside help toward his own salvation. But the Bible says not by works of righteousness that we have done but according to His mercy He saved us, and then again in Ephesians, second chapter, he says, "For by grace are ye saved through faith; and not of yourselves: it is the gift of God: Not by works, lest any man should boast."

So then, I believe salvation is not reformation of character, although this happens and generally is a very definite result of someone accepting Christ as their Savior and being born again and having a spiritual birth, but salvation is not a reformation of character, but it is the possession of a life. The Bible says, "He that hath the Son hath life, and he that hath not the Son hath not life." It is an experience—very definitely an experience.[20]

Grace is all important to Upland Christians. The Calvinists speak of it to emphasize the point that salvation comes from God and not from our innate goodness or from our works. But the Arminian Christians also emphasize it. Deborah McCauley argues that the doctrine of grace helps to define Appalachian Christianity:

> This emphasis on the centrality of grace is a major characteristic distinctive historically and today of mountain religious life. It stands in contradistinction to the fully Arminianized interpretation of [Charles G.] Finney, the "father" of modern revivalism, who by 1835 was calling revivalism a "science," something that now relied on human initiative and God's cooperation. This represented an earth-shaking shift in emphasis, one that accounts most of all for the tenacious resistance of "Old School" Baptists, a majority of whom were in the mountains of Appalachia. . . . This "Old School" viewpoint was lampooned and caricatured by a host of writers on mountain religious life. . . . This drumbeat of ridicule and misapprehension about the nature and necessity of grace in Appalachian mountain religion has yet to end in writings on mountain religious life. It's most popular label is "fatalism."[21]

Herman B. Yates, who was pastor of the Grace Baptist Church in Dingess, West Virginia, until his recent death, strongly emphasized grace in a sermon about the salvation of one of the thieves crucified along with Jesus:

> God is the God of grace, and by grace are ye saved, and it is by grace from beginning to end, grace-planned salvation, grace-provided salvation, and grace works within His elect to overcome the hardness of their hearts, the obstinacy of their wills, and the enmity of their minds. This makes them willing to receive salvation. This doesn't jibe with modern thought; I know that, but it is grace that begins, grace that continues, and grace that consummates our salvation.
>
> The dying thief . . . had no moral life before his conversion. He respected neither God's law nor man's law. After his conversion, he died with no opportunity to work for Christ's sake. . . . What is the bottom line? It is this, if he was saved, he was saved by grace alone.

He had nothing to offer. Free and sovereign grace alone saved him. . . .

Instead of attributing salvation of lost sinners to His infinite grace, many try to lay it to human influence, instrumentality, and circumstance. The preacher or the prayers are looked on as the main causes of salvation. God does often use these things to arouse, to awaken people from their slumber to their great need for salvation that God has provided, but God is not limited to these things. His grace is all powerful. . . .

Beloved, unless we see ourselves in this dying thief, we'll never be able to join him in saying, "Lord, remember me." Abasement comes before exaltation. . . . We must come to God as beggars, empty handed, before we can receive the gift of eternal life. . . . Man is slow to learn this lesson. . . . It is not until the sinner comes to the end of his resources that he will run to the Savior.[22]

Elder Milford Hall Sr., a Floyd County, Kentucky, Primitive Baptist, wrote of his travail in seeking salvation, caught between the Arminian belief in good works and keeping "the laws" and the Calvinistic belief in salvation of sinners only by the grace of God through the imputed righteousness of Christ. Hall, like others whom I have heard, told of going through anguish and despair and being near death before he encountered what was, for him, the true way to Christ and forgiveness:

Father taught me to be honest, truthful, and sober. But alas! I soon forgot much of his teaching after marrying and leaving his roof, and especially after the death of my wife. Very few months after her death had elapsed before I fell in with some wild boys and men, and I went to excess in drinking and carousing. I had wild blood in my veins. . . . I thought I had found a way to drown all my troubles. I sinned against all of the laws of God and man. . . . I soon became the worst outlaw of my riotous company. . . .

I saw that something was radically wrong but I could not tell what was the matter with me, or what to do about it. Here I stood hopeless and helpless on the brink of an awful eternity. . . .

I felt forced to believe and plead that a soul could in some way or another be saved by "good works." I had a hope—yet a very faint one—that I could somehow atone for my sins by keeping the law, thus "meriting" the grace and mercy of God. . . .

I was trying to work my passage to heaven by keeping the Ten

Commandments. . . . I gave alms to the poor hoping to atone for my sins thereby. . . . Finally, after many sad failures to act perfectly to God's holy law, it began to dawn on me that I must look elsewhere . . . for some kind of power to save. . . .

I saw that to be saved by the works of the law, we must be as holy as the angels, and be as pure and immaculate as Jesus. The law requires perfection. . . . I had tried every plan upon earth that my poor mind could conceive, and had experimentally found out by many trials that my strength was just as deficient and rotten as my righteousness was filthy and imperfect. I had been about this solemn business now about six years with no success. . . .

I saw very clearly and felt keenly that everything depended solely upon His manifesting or concealing His power; but nothing depended on me. . . . I was now thoroughly converted from my righteous self; I could no longer wear or admire my garment of self-righteousness. . . . I had proved beyond a shadow of a doubt that the poor returning prodigal need not look for mercy upon the ground of his "good works."

Yea, moreover, I saw that God had in the person of His Son finished the redemptive work on the cross, and that there was nothing left for me to do as the ground of my acceptance with God. . . .

Suddenly and very unexpectedly one day while despairing of any hope forever, a great peace came over me; now all my sins and guilt were gone, I knew not where. Now I was free and happy because of this undeserved and unexpected clemency. . . . I felt like a bird let out of a cage. I was born again!

Thanks be to God, through Jesus Christ, I could never lay hands on the old burden of sin again. . . . Now I was shining in the borrowed righteousness of my substitute and sponsor; now I was very, very happy and completely clad in His robe of perfect righteousness: I was born again into the spiritual world; I had on the best robe. Now I saw that God's mercy in Christ has no motive but His own will; now I saw that if God showed mercy for any foreseen "works" . . . mercy would then be turned into justice and would lose both its name and its nature. . . . I saw very clearly that self-righteousness is the secret bane of Christianity and the chief root of all our sins.[23]

I believe the grace theology that Mr. Hall described is the basis for the often remarked modesty of mountain people. It emphasizes our many shortcomings. Brother Vernon Harrison, a Pentecostal, suggested that we don't always open ourselves to grace until we are in trouble, that we are often too busy to bother until that time:

> Oh, we don't have time. We come into the house, and we become couch potatoes, and we bug our eyes out at the TV. The next thing we know the clocks run by, and we eat so much supper we can't bend over to pray without heartburn. We ain't got time to draw near to God.
>
> Oh, but when the wolf gets at our door, we want to draw nigh to Him then. When affliction hits your body—members of your family come down with sickness—then you want to holler, "O God, I'm drawing nigh to you! I need you to draw nigh to me. Here's your little old servant. I'm so humble, I'll do anything you ask me to do, God. Now it's time to answer my prayers."[24]

Many Arminian Christians talk about grace and the work of the Holy Spirit in transforming human behavior after salvation. But I have talked with others who are concerned primarily with the Holy Spirit in the salvation process itself, with emphasis on the emotionalism one can observe as the sinner "comes through" and praises God with shouting, dancing, or other unusual display of emotion. Harold Pritt talked about emotionalism as part of the conversion process, dealing with the belief that emotional conversion is the only real sign of the presence of the Holy Spirit:

> I think the degree of emotionalism connected with it may many times depend upon the emotional makeup of a person or the degree of sin sometimes that we have fallen into. I think you would find a difference in the emotional experience between a person who is perhaps fallen into the gutter, so to speak, and someone presents to him a plan of salvation of God's love for them and Jesus Christ dying for their sins on the cross, offering to him forgiveness and that person sees that perhaps clearly for the first time. . . .
>
> Whereas there would be a difference between a person like that than there would be if one of our own children that we have taught the ways of the Lord from when they were very small. Maybe there may not be a great transition period, not necessarily a great emotional experience in their lives when they came to learn of the Lord. They may have been taught that there may be a time when they definitely will come to a place of decision whether to receive Christ as their Savior or to reject Him, and very definitely do it [receive Christ]. But

it would not, I don't think, be necessary to have an emotional experience as some other persons have.[25]

This interview with Pastor Pritt was done by Earl D. C. Brewer in 1959 as part of the Southern Appalachian Studies (resulting in the book edited by Thomas R. Ford, *The Southern Appalachian Region: a Survey*). I called Mr. Pritt in 1994 to talk with him about his service since then. He had several interesting things to say. When I asked whether he had changed since the 1959 interview, he said, "Yes, I have changed, but I have not changed doctrinally. I am still a fundamentalist, a word I hesitate to use because of what it may mean to people today." He mentioned that he is currently attending an American Baptist church (instead of an Independent Baptist church, in which he had previously preached) while working full time for Union Carbide, as he has always done. (He has led in the building of congregations and two church buildings.) Then he said that he has come to feel that the exclusiveness of some churches, such as the Independent Baptists, is more of a hindrance than a help, adding: "Salvation is an extremely personal matter, and you can't have an edge by being a member of a particular group. Absolutism is limiting." Mr. Pritt intends to be active full time as a minister when he retires from Union Carbide.[26]

Faith of the Head or Heart?

Herman B. Yates outlined in the previously quoted sermon, "A Thief's Eye View," the path to salvation for sinners, starting with an awareness of a lost condition, repentance, and a saving faith. He examined the two thieves crucified with Jesus, one who rejected Christ and the other who accepted Him and repented. He saw this story as reflective of the people of the world, some of whom will turn to Christ and some of whom will turn away. Mr. Yates's sermon was Calvinistic, and he touched on predestination, on the intellectual and emotional part of salvation, and especially on the thief's unworthiness to receive God's grace:

> Jesus Christ came into this world to save sinners—helpless, hopeless, dying sinners. We're talking about repentance. What does repentance and faith mean? Repentance . . . takes a change of mind about sin, of course. It takes a sorrowing for sin, of course. It takes a perception of sin, of course. Yet there is more in repentance than these things. Repentance is the realization of our lost condition. It is the discovery of our ruin. It is judging ourselves. It's the owning up to the fact of our

lost estate. Repentance is not so much an intellectual process as it is the conscience acting in the presence of God. . . .

But here's the proof of genuine repentance. . . . The thief's repentance toward God was accompanied closely with faith toward the Lord Jesus Christ. In thinking about his faith, let's notice first that it was an intelligent head faith. . . . We've already talked of God's sovereignty and His irresistible and mighty grace in the thief's conversion, and now we return to another side of the truth, and this is of equal importance and it does not contradict what we have already said. In fact, it complements and supplements it. The Bible does not teach that if a man is elect that he will be saved whether he believes or not. . . . No, the Bible teaches that the God who predestinated the end also predestinated the means to that end. The God who decreed the salvation fulfilled His own decree by giving him a faith with which to believe (2 Thessalonians 2:13). We see this with the thief. He believed the truth. His faith took hold of the Word of God. Over the cross was this superscription, "This is Jesus, the King of the Jews." Now I know for a fact that Pilot didn't mean good by putting it there, but it was the truth nevertheless . . . , and the thief had read it, and divine grace and power had opened his eyes to see that it was indeed the truth. His faith grasped the kingship of Christ. . . .

Now a distinction is often made between head and heart faith, and that's the way it ought to be, for the distinction is very real, and it is very vital. Sometimes head faith is said to be of no value, but this is foolish. There must be a head faith before there can be a heart faith. We must believe intellectually before we can believe savingly in the Lord Jesus Christ. . . . I hurry to say that I know that head faith will not save unless it's accompanied by heart faith, but I must insist that there can be no heart faith unless there has first been head faith (Romans 10:14). It's true, now, and never forget it, a man may believe *about* Christ without believing *on* Christ, but a man may never believe *on* Christ without first believing *about* Christ.

That's the way it was with this dying thief. He's never seen the Lord before this day, but he had seen the superscription, identifying and testifying to His kingship, and the Holy Spirit used this as the basis for his faith. That's why we say that his was an intelligent faith—first an intellectual faith—believing the written testimony . . . and secondly a heart faith, resting confidence in Christ Himself, as Savior of sinners. A knowledge of the historic Christ isn't enough. You may believe all *about* the Savior. You may believe His perfect life,

His sacrificial death, His victorious resurrection, His glorious ascension, and His promised return, but, Beloved, this is just not enough. Gospel faith is more than a faith of conscience. Its more than a faith of correct opinion *or* a train of reasoning. Saving faith transcends all reason. Look at the thief. Was it reasonable that Christ should notice him? He was a crucified robber, a self-confessed criminal, one who a moment before had been jeering and mocking Him. . . . Would you think that the Savior would transport such a one from the brink of death into paradise? Is that reasonable? The head reasons, but the heart never does, and this man's prayer came from his heart. He didn't have the use of his hands and feet . . . , but he did have the use of his heart, and he did have the use of his tongue, and these were all he needed. They were free to believe and confess (Romans 10:10).

Then, his was an humble faith. He didn't pray, "Lord, honor me," or "Lord, exalt me,"[but] "Lord, if thou will only look on me. Lord, remember me." How full and appropriate that prayer was. . . . There was one who remembered him, the Lord Jesus Christ Himself.

Let's notice one other thing, his was a courageous faith. . . . The repenting thief stops his jeering, turns to his companion, and says, "Doth thou not fear God?" He rebukes his companion right in the hearing of everybody. I say that took courage. . . . Not only does he bear testimony to the innocence of Christ, but he also confessed His kingship, and so by those words, he cuts himself off from the favor of his companion and of the crowd.[27]

The Importance of Baptism

Upland Christians believe some form of water baptism is important to salvation. Water is necessary to life, and it is also a cleanser. In the religious context, water is the universal metaphor for cleansing, renewal, regeneration, and rebirth. The term *baptism* comes from the Greek verb *baptidzein,* meaning "to dip" or "to plunge." Ancient non-Christian people had water rituals. The Hebrews required a ritual bath for those admitted to Judaism, representing ethical purification. This was a ritual cleansing similar to the idea of preparing food in the orthodox manner. When John the Baptist preached baptism for the remission of sins, he was introducing a new idea. John preached a preparatory, provisional act to be superseded by the Messiah, who "will baptize you with the Holy Ghost and with fire."[28]

When Phillip baptized the Ethiopian eunuch, "they went down both into the water . . . [and came] up out of the water" (Acts 8:38–39). Paul says in Romans 6:3–4 that "so many of us as were baptized into Jesus Christ were baptized into his death." He went on to say, "Therefore we are buried with him by baptism into death; that like as Christ was raised up from the dead by the glory of the Father, even so we also should walk in newness of life." This is the basis for the belief among many, especially Baptists, that immersion is the only true baptism. The symbolism is twofold: first, the burial from the old life and the resurrection to the new; and second, the cleansing from sin (Acts 22:16). Of course, in the desert and many other places, there was not always adequate water for immersion, and so the practice of pouring or sprinkling became a substitute. No doubt some in later churches considered sprinkling to be a more convenient and perhaps dignified method than immersing. I have heard much controversy over methods of baptism, and some humor:

> An Old-Time Baptist preacher was obsessed with preaching total immersion as necessary for salvation. The congregation got tired of it, and eventually the deacons asked him to preach on something else. The preacher said he would preach in the old tradition of letting the Bible fall open wherever it would, and take the first passage his eye lighted on as evidence that the Lord wanted him to preach on that text.
>
> So the next Sunday, he let the Bible fall open, and he read, "And the voice of the turtle is heard in our land." He studied a minute on the text and commenced. "This morning as I was a-crossing the creek on the way to church, I saw an old mud turtle a-sunning hisself. When he saw me he went ker-plunk into the water. Now, he didn't reach down there and get a little bit of water and sprinkle it on his forehead. No! When he went in, he went all the way in, and there you have your doctrine of total immersion!"

Here are some thoughts from a variety of people on baptism. Mrs. Albert Sears, an American Baptist from Nicholas County, West Virginia, commented that baptism "sets forth His [Jesus'] death, burial and resurrection. It's a new life."[29] C. J. Queen, a Boyd County, Kentucky, Baptist, spoke in similar way: "It represents death, burial, and resurrection. Baptism is showing faith to the world that you are a new creature. You are borned again . . . from death to a new life."[30] Rev. Raymond Wallace, of the Church of God of Prophecy in Cumberland County, Tennessee, said: "Water baptism is following the Lord's example. . . . Water baptism does not save, but it does have a great part to do with our salvation.[31]

Another Baptist, from Tennessee, Rev. Charles Davis, explained the importance of baptism as a sacrament: "We want to follow the divine example of Jesus in any way we can, and one of the main features of being baptized is showing the world that we are dead to our sins, as we rise to follow a newness of life, and we want to show others that we have been born again, and to show the death to our sins and our rising to walk in a new life with Jesus Christ."[32]

An unidentified Church of the Brethren member from Dickenson County, Virginia, talked about their manner of baptism, the other sacraments, and also the holy kiss (which is also practiced by some Pentecostals):

> We believe in three dips, trine immersion in the name of the Father, the Son, and the Holy Ghost. . . . We pay honor, we pay tribute, to the Father by baptizing with the first dip and tribute to the Son, by baptizing with the second dip, and then we pay honor to the Holy Ghost, the third part of the godhead.
>
> We believe in the salutation of the holy kiss, and we believe in the Lord's Supper, eating of the flesh and drinking of His blood. We believe in the complete thing, the way He commanded.[33]

With some humor, Donna Ramsey, a West Virginia Methodist, told me of a Dunker church she remembered from her youth: "There was a religious sect lived across Dogwood Ridge. They had this little church building there in the woods, and when they baptized, they dipped them under ever so many times—not once but a lot of times. I laughed the other evening. I said, 'They've all disappeared. I don't know whether they drowned each other or what, but they're all gone. They have faded away.'"[34]

Few practices have stirred more controversy than that of infant baptism. The Anabaptists and later the Baptists preached against it, because it was such a prominent part of Catholic and Anglican ritual. These early Anabaptists and those influenced by them believed fervently in "believer baptism," meaning that only those who have come to an age of accountability, repented, and accepted Christ on their own are appropriate for baptism. Will D. Campbell, a Mississippi Baptist now living in Tennessee, told of his Baptist father being asked whether he believed in infant baptism, and his reply was, "Believe in it? I've actually seen it done!"

Of course, several churches in the Uplands do baptize, or dedicate, infants in a special service: Episcopal, Methodist, Presbyterian, and Lutheran, among others. A Presbyterian from Mingo County, West Virginia, said this about baptizing infants: "I believe that is the parents dedicating that child, that they will do the best that they can by it to bring it up in a Christian home. . . . Later on, I think that child, when it comes of age, should make up its mind on its own and receive Christ."[35] Ingerna Indy, a Lutheran from Pendleton County, West Virginia, said, "We believe in infant baptism, and we also believe it is one of the sacraments of the church." Myrtle Armstrong, a fellow member of the same church, added: "It is only through baptism that we can be saved. . . . that is necessary. A child that isn't baptized can't be saved." Irma Judy, of the same church, said, "When you sponsor a child in infant baptism, that is the responsibility for the sponsors until that child does become of confirmation age and renews their vows."[36]

As previously indicated, there is also controversy over whether baptism is necessary for salvation. Most allow for some circumstances that might prevent baptism, as in the case of the thief on the cross with Jesus, but some are dogmatic about the efficacy of baptism. The Disciples of Christ (the liberal wing of the Christian movement), Christian Churches (the moderates), and Churches of Christ (the conservatives) are all accused of being even more attached to water than are the Baptists. I asked Tom Smith, a Tennessee Church of Christ minister, about this emphasis on baptism:

> We have been accused of putting more emphasis on baptism than any other group. If you went in and listened to some sermons you would think that we believe that what you do is to get people wet and they're saved. We've been accused of that, but most teach in the context of faith and in the context of repentance. You don't just baptize somebody. There's got to be a faith response to God, but there is a strong emphasis on baptism. . . . You've got to have some standard of the church reflected in the New Testament. . . . There may be some Christian Churches and Churches of Christ that might say that if a person repents but is not baptized that they are lost, but I think there is enough leeway to say there is grace involved. . . . A lot of people talk about inward reality and outward symbol. . . . If it is a repentant believer, there is an effectual meaning to baptism, that there is a washing of sins and a reception of the Holy Spirit.[37]

Footwashing as a Sacrament

Baptism and the communion elements have already been mentioned as sacraments. Many of the Old-Time Baptist, Brethren, and some Pentecostals also wash feet as a part of the sacramental service. A description of a Dunker, or Brethren, foot-washing ceremony in Pennsylvania in 1889 serves as an accurate account of foot-washing services today even in present-day Old-Time Baptist churches, except for the holy kiss:

> The first ceremony is that of the washing of the feet, each sex performing this duty for its own. Those who are to engage in the ordinance presently enter the meeting, carrying tubs of luke warm water, and each member on the front benches removes his or her shoes and stockings. A man on the men's side and a woman on the women's then wash the feet one by one, taking the right hand of each individual as they finish the washing, and giving the kiss of peace. After the one who performs the washing follows the other with a long towel girded around the waist, who wipes the feet just washed, at the same time giving the right hand and the kiss of peace. As one benchfull has the ceremony performed, it gives place to another. While this ceremony is being conducted, the minister or teachers make a brief speech or read appropriate portions of Scripture relating to the subject.[38]

The title of the article from which the foregoing excerpt is taken is "A Peculiar People," which the Dunkers sometimes call themselves. Old Regular Baptists and some Pentecostals also call themselves "a peculiar people," as in Titus 2:14, "Who gave himself for us, that he might redeem us from all iniquity, and purify us unto himself a peculiar people, zealous of good works." Thus they keep the old ordinances. Jesus washed his disciples' feet, a job usually performed by house servants, to teach the lesson of humility. Many Upland Christians believe that the bread and wine show a vertical relationship with Christ. Foot-washing shows a horizontal relationship with one's fellow human beings.

In the Old Baptist churches, the annual sacrament meeting is also a time to question oneself and one's relationship with others. Anyone who has problems with another church member or anybody else is expected to seek reconciliation and forgiveness before partaking of the sacraments and in foot washing. It is an important time both socially and religiously in these churches.

The Holy Spirit

All Christians talk of the Holy Spirit being present on such occasions as conversion and baptism, but Pentecostal-Holiness people speak of something more dramatic, a baptism of the Holy Ghost, harking back to the time of Pentecost, when "suddenly there came a sound from heaven as of a rushing mighty wind. . . . and there appeared unto them cloven tongues like as of fire, and it sat upon each of them. And they were all filled with the Holy Ghost." (Acts 1:2–3). For many Pentecostals, this is a third act of grace, when they are baptized with the Holy Ghost and are then able to speak in other tongues, dance, or do other extraordinary things. Mrs. Burl Cooper, a member of a Cumberland County, Tennessee, Church of God of Prophecy, said: "The Holy Ghost is the greatest blessing that has ever come in my life. For thirty-two years I've had that blessing, and it's the most wonderful thing I've ever had. And to be without—I'd rather give up everything in life or in the world than to give up the Holy Ghost. It is a comforter and a leader and a guide and a blessing. . . . This is the most blessedest thing that has ever come into my life."[39]

Mrs. Cooper's pastor, Brother Raymond Wallace, added the following:

> Different Scriptures and prophecy refer to the time when Jesus would pour out His Spirit on all flesh, and John in speaking said, "I indeed baptize you with water unto repentance, but He that cometh after me, whose shoes I am not worthy to unloose, He shall baptize you with the Holy Ghost, in the name of the Father." Jesus told His disciples before He went away He would pray the Father to send another comforter, which would be the Holy Ghost. . . . On the day of Pentecost, the Holy Ghost came with the evidence of speaking in tongues. This is a definite experience separate from that of regeneration and a born-again experience and sanctification. This is the gift of God, and it brings great joy and also gives us the direct leadership of God, because He said that when the spirit of truth is come, He shall teach you all things and guide you in all truths. I'm certainly thankful that I have received the Holy Ghost as the Scripture teaches, and I feel like it is a great blessing for everybody to have.[40]

The Meaning of Salvation

As is the case with other theological matters, there is disagreement over what salvation means. The differences are part of the Calvinist-Arminian debate over whether salvation is limited to only a few, those predestined by God to be saved, or open to all who heed the Word, repent, and ask forgiveness. The Calvinists generally believe that anyone who is saved is saved for all time. The Arminians believe that one may fall away from grace—backslide—and must then repent and be saved all over again to reach heaven. Some of the latter groups believe also that salvation ought to make you a new person.

John Wesley preached a second act of grace, known as sanctification, that could literally lift the believer above sin. The Calvinists, on the other hand, believe that anyone still in the flesh is heir to the sins thereof. Will D. Campbell, the prophetic Baptist quoted previously, succinctly puts this belief about the human condition in relation to God: "We are all bastards, but God loves us anyhow." Several of the Holiness-Pentecostal groups preach a third act of grace, a visitation from the Holy Ghost that enables the individual to do extraordinary things—be healed or to heal, speak in other tongues, dance in the Spirit, etc. Such gifts are known as "signs following" the visit of the Holy Ghost.

Following are several arguments for the Calvinist beliefs related to predestination and perseverance of the saints, or as the Baptists put it, "Once saved, always saved." Elder Johnny Blackburn of the Coon Creek Primitive Baptist Church in Pike County, Kentucky, differing from some Primitive Baptists, argued against the idea of all things being predestined (known among Primitive Baptists as double-predestination, that is, that those to be saved as well as everyday happenings are predestined). He goes on to present his concept of God and salvation of those whom God has chosen. He also deals more fully with predestination and speaks of heaven and hell:

> If we were already saved before the foundation of the world, then you tell me why God sent His Son into the world to save us? We were lost. If we were not lost, Jesus would not have come to save us. . . . Jesus came into the world to save sinners. . . . Wouldn't you hate to believe that God would turn a deaf ear to a poor sinner? I'm so glad that He is a friend of sinners. He came to seek and to save that which is lost.
>
> I want to clear up a few things that the Old Baptists are accused of real bad. . . . I love to defend the doctrine of salvation by grace, and I love to tell people about the things Old Baptists have been accused of that are false. I've heard that Old Baptists have been accused of saying that God predestinated you and me to do everything that we do and there ain't a thing we can do about it. I want to tell you one thing, everything that God did predestinate will be exactly like God predestinated it, regardless of Satan and all his hosts. It will stand; it is that way. But here is the point: What did He predestinate? He never predestinated people like you and me to do anything. I love what He did predestinate, and it ought to be a great encouragement to you, a great comfort. He predestinated us, however many there are of us, to be conformed to the image of His Son. Doesn't that comfort your soul?

People will get up and say the Lord will do so and so if you will let Him. I'd hate to believe in a God like that, hate to believe in a God that has to wait and see what you and me are going to do about it—that we have to let Him before He can do what He wants to do. I tell you, that is not Israel's God. That is not the God of Abraham, Isaac, and Jacob. He's a God who does His will in heaven and on earth to save you *from* something *to* something. He didn't save you *in* your sins but *from* your sins. Yes, He did, to a home in heaven. Oh, what a joyful thought, that when this life is over, when it's all over and done, and we have made our last struggle in this world, and we lay down, we are just getting ready to really live and never die! It's once to die and twice to live![41]

An unidentified member of a Hiwassee, Georgia, Baptist Church spoke of eternal salvation:

This question of once saved, always saved has been a hard question for lots of people, but it has never been too hard for me because I believe that it is true. . . . When Christ or God forgave me of my sins, I think He saved me at that time for eternity. . . . Of course, there is sin, and we sin every day. But a true Christian, when he sins, immediately knows that he sinned, and he is not satisfied until he asks God's forgiveness, and in that way I think a person who has really been regenerated is not able to lose his salvation because of that Holy Spirit, which immediately tells him when he has done a wrong and causes him to turn again to God.[42]

Brother Lial Osborne, of the Fairview Baptist Church in Boyd County, Kentucky, made the argument for eternal salvation very personal: "I have a boy, and I'm very fond of him. . . . Should he go out here and do something that was displeasing to me, that doesn't make him *not* my son. He is still my son. If my Savior has saved my soul, I should never have to worry about it from this point of view, because once you're saved, you're saved forever."[43] Lucille Lawson, a member of the Riverview Baptist Church in Knoxville, used the same argument: "We know that once the Lord has made us His child, that we are His child forever, and that it would be just like a child that was born into a home, regardless of what the child does, it would still belong to the parent, and firmly I believe that once we are born into the kingdom of God that we are His for keeps."[44]

Rev. Charles W. Davis, a Knox County, Tennessee, Southern Baptist pastor, put emphasis on God's power to save and to keep us, thus giving us the security to be concerned about the souls of others:

> I can't understand how anyone who believed that we could be saved today and lost tomorrow could ever feel secure. I believe that our God is powerful enough to save us once and for all. . . . We could not be concerned about other lost people if we had to be concerned with our own souls, day after day, and I believe our main concern as Christians is the concern for lost souls, other lost souls, because we are saved once and for all.[45]

Brother Herman Yates argued strongly that there is eternal security for those who are saved:

> Many of God's children . . . understand how all of their past sins could be forgiven, all that they had committed before they received Christ, but . . . many folks believe that they can "sin" away the pardon that God has bestowed. Oh, but what value would it be to have a pardon if it could be taken away at any time at a moment's notice. Surely there can be no settled peace when my acceptance by God is made to depend on *my* obedience or *my* faithfulness. The forgiveness that He bestows covers *all* sins, past, present, and future. Believer, didn't He bear your sins in His own body on the tree? And weren't all of your sins future sins when He died? Surely they were. . . . You had not committed a single sin when Christ died. So Christ bore your future sins as well as your past sins. . . . I am completely forgiven, so much so that sin will never again be laid at my door. I am no longer in the place of unforgiveness. . . . That's why it's written, "There is now no condemnation to them who are in Christ." How could there be if all trespasses have been forgiven? None can lay anything to the charge of God's elect.[46]

Summing up the idea of eternal salvation, Bert Stamper, of Tennessee, said, "I think as a Baptist, we kind of believe in an eternal God doing eternal things."[47] Piper Cox, a black Union Baptist from Virginia, said: "If you are born again, you may stray away from God, but you'll come back. When God lays a hand on you, you are all right."[48] Rev. James Miller, a Southern Baptist pastor from Carter County, Tennessee, added: "One thing it means to me is that it is eternal. Salvation means being eternally saved, now, on and on, which gives me consolation."[49]

Sanctification and Backsliding

I have often heard the term "to backslide" in Arminian-type churches, such as Methodist and Pentecostal-Holiness, and it is linked to the idea of perfection, the notion that if you are truly saved, you may have a second blessing—sanctification—that can perfect your life and enable you to live above sin; conversely, if you do sin, you have backslid from what is expected of you as a Christian. It is preached further that if you should die while you are in such a lapsed state, you are in danger of going to hell. Sanctification is important to many Christians. Sybil Mallard, of the Church of God in DeKalb County, Alabama, said: "Sanctifying will take away the desires of the world and the habits. . . . It will take away the old man, so to speak, and get us ready for where we're going."[50] Katherine Smith, of the same church, added: "Jesus' blood is applied after we've been forgiven. It cleanses us from sin—all sin—and one place it [the Bible] says for us to sanctify ourselves—that means to lay aside all things that would hinder us, that would not be right to do."[51] Bonnie Garrett, member of the Church of God, Towns County, Georgia, commented: "Well, it is another step in salvation. It makes you stronger. It helps you to live better and have a closer walk with the Lord, makes you stronger in the Lord." Jameson Garrett, from the same church, said: "I believe this on the second blessing, the second definite work of Christ in the heart again, cleanses from the inbred sin because Jesus said if we would walk in the light as He was in the light, we'd have fellowship one with another and the blood of Jesus Christ would cleanse us from all sin. . . . When we get sanctified, we become a joint heir with Jesus Christ from the experience because it is a new blessing when you get sanctified . . . , a real blessing separate from getting saved."[52]

Buster Roberts, a Virginia Pentecostal, talked about what it means to be saved and then to give up the sinful life, but he also talked about backsliding. He refers to the seven wicked spirits entering a man described in Matthew 12:45:

> Well, I think that a Chrisian life is a good clean life. I mean, I believe you're supposed to be separated from sinful people. I don't believe you're supposed to partake in what they do, you know, like drinking and things like that, and go where they turn up. It's not decent.
>
> You have to be willing yourself to give up the world and ask forgiveness for the things you have done, and then He will do the rest. . . . Ask the Lord to forgive you. That's when you get saved,

but when you get saved, you can't go on doing the things you did before. That's the way I think about it. . . . When you're saved, the Lord cleans you up, and you don't ever want to do the things you did. The Bible says, "Come ye out of the world and be ye a separated people."

Oh yeah, you can backslide. . . . The Bible says you get seven more devils worse than the one that come out of you first, if you backslide. . . . They [backsliders] go back to sin. . . . Yeah, they are seven times worse than before. . . . Once an individual gets saved, the demon spirit leaves out, and then it goes seeking for a place to rest. If it don't find no place, it'll come back trying to get in the house, which is the heart of man—[now] clean, garnished, and swept. Well, there's no place in there for it then because he's put away everything . . . . He's got the Spirit of God in him which cleans him up.

And then, when after this man backslides, the demon spirit will come and bring seven other demons with him and makes the individual seven times worse than what they were to start with; and if you've ever had the experience of noticing sinners when they backslide, you can see that they are worse than they were when they were in their natural sinful lives.

Yeah, they can be resaved. They can get forgiveness of all sins, all except blasphemy against the Holy Ghost, and that is denying God and calling Him an unclean spirit.[53]

Rev. Raymond Wallace, pastor of the Lawrence Chapel Church of God of Prophecy, Cumberland County, Tennessee, stressed the difference between being born again and sanctification:

We also believe that this regeneration, being born again, does not add us to the church. This born-again experience adds us to the family of God, but not to the church. After we have become children of God, then if we feel it [sanctification], we are to unite with the church.

Sanctification is brought about by actively applying the blood to our souls. This is the connection with Hebrews 12:13–14, "And make straight paths for your feet, lest that which is lame be turned out of the way; but let it rather be healed. Follow peace with all men, and holiness, without which no man shall see the Lord." A number of other Scriptures also teach sanctification. . . . Jesus prayed definitely that His disciples would be sanctified.[54]

Rev. L. O. Johnson, an evangelist in the same Church of God of Prophecy, talked of the difference between the flesh and the spirit or soul of a person, of salvation, and of sanctification:

Jesus said, "That which is born of flesh is flesh; that which is born of spirit is spirit." Man himself is spirit clothed in the flesh of the body. The body shall be destroyed or otherwise returned to dust from which it came, but the spirit lives forever. When we refer to the soul, we are thinking of the man that dwells in the tabernacle of the flesh, not the body. . . . We believe that the eternal part of man lives forever and that man, though he may be lost, will live forever in torture, in a hell that he never leaves. When we speak of saving the soul, we are thinking of that person being delivered from the bondage of sin and being set free from it so he will not have to go to hell forever. That's what we refer to as the saving of the soul. . . .

Sanctification is the moving out of the depraved nature that came into the human family through the Fall of Adam. Adam, the father of the human race, fell from grace in the Garden of Eden, and there was a depraved nature that has taken place in the life of man, and sanctification has removed that depraved nature and places within him a divine nature. It makes him prone to righteousness equally as great as he would be prone to sin without it. We are born into the world with a sinful disposition, a depraved nature that makes us prone to sin, but when sanctification has done its perfect work . . . , we become more godly because we have a godly nature. Sanctification brings that.[55]

I asked Dr. Donald Bowdle, professor of history and religion at Lee College, a Church of God school in Cleveland, Tennessee, and an ordained minister in the church, what he thought about the ability of those in the Pentecostal-Holiness churches to live above sin in the world. He said that he felt that southeastern Pentecostals make too much of their Wesleyan origins and of sanctification, pointing out that the Assemblies of God, also Pentecostal, have non-Wesleyan origins from Keswick, England. When I ask him how Pentecostals can truly live a sinless life, Bowdle said, "The danger is in redefining sin."[56]

Rev. Donald D. Damerow, a Lutheran pastor from Chattanooga, Tennessee, spoke of backsliding:

I feel that there certainly were individuals in the Bible who were fine Christian people at one time, but who fell away from the faith and certainly were damned and went to hell, but from the life they led, they certainly were disciples of Christ at one time. Some denominations say they [who] fell away never were saved to begin with. I don't think you can say that. We have no basis. . . . There certainly are some fine Christians that . . . have fallen away from the faith and as a result are living a life of sin, and according to God's Word, they cannot inherit eternal salvation.[57]

Rev. Tom Smith, a Church of Christ pastor from Tennessee, commented on grace and the belief that one can slide away from it and be in need of rededication:

Most people in the Christian movement make allowance for grace. They don't believe in "once saved, always saved," but they would say that there is some security, mainly on the basis of First John, the faith in Jesus, the way you love your brethren and the way you obey the Commandments. If you are doing that, the best that you can, with grace, and making allowances for mistakes, you are okay. There is the old practice of rededication in a lot of our churches, where if you've been a backslider, you go forward and renew your commitment.

One thing that our churches do in their emphasis on the Lord's Supper—we have the Lord's Supper every week—that is made a time of recommitment. Some would say that the effectual power of baptism is repeated in the Lord's Supper, that there is some sort of spiritual nourishment there.[58]

Here is a final thought on sanctification from the somewhat Calvinist perspective of the late Herbert Barker, a Presbyterian freethinker from Point Pleasant, West Virginia: "Sanctification in Bible terminology simply means that you are set apart from the world, positionally, not conditionally. We have a position with God, which is perfect because we have been put into the family of God by the new birth. That is our standing, but our state, our condition, is another thing, and that is far from perfect. Our standing in the family of God is as if we had never sinned because our standing and our state is in Jesus Christ. The Christian has the imputed righteousness of Christ. That's perfect."[59]

Heaven or Hell?

Elder Johnny Blackburn, the Primitive Baptist quoted earlier in this chapter, said that Jesus came into the world to save sinners, and then asked,

"What did He save us from? Now, He was bound to save us *from* something *to* something. . . . He saved us from a burning lake to a place of peace and joy and love and happiness." Most Upland Christians talk of the choices we make as resulting in the two polarities—heaven or hell. Heaven is a place of beauty and peace with none of the world's trials, sickness, or troubles. It is often described as a place of golden streets, mansions, choirs, harps, and balmy weather. Hell, on the other hand, is a place of torment, raging fires, and unremitting pain.

Yet there are some who refuse to accept hell as a place of eternal punishment for those who have not sought salvation. The late Warren Wright, a nondenominational minister and social activist from Letcher County, Kentucky, in his book *The Law of Redemptive Love,* argued that hell came out of paganism into Christianity. He called this "the torture dogma," which has been quite prominent in Christianity, at times more so than its antithesis, the idea of heaven. "The gospel has never been preached by the historic denominations without the adjunct of overhanging lurid threat, which means a subverted gospel," he wrote, and added:

> There is a caring God; let Him be eternally praised. This is a pardoning, redeeming God. . . . Would [Jonathan] Edwards have us believe an angry God looking in disgusted surprise upon His loathsome creation [referring to Edwards's "Sinners in the Hand of an Angry God"]? . . . God was not surprised, having all foreknowledge. If not surprised, He always knew of the degeneration to which we would come, must come, without Him. Was He therefore an eternal sadist, merely waiting for the human inevitable, the fullness of the cup He had created, in order to enjoy us in the fire? Did He create nerves to shrink and scream eternal protest? . . . Was pain a protection for the organism, or a source of pleasure for the Creator?
>
> The God and Father of our Lord Jesus Christ was, of course, never surprised, nor will He ever enjoy His creatures' pain. . . .
>
> Let us receive the simplicity. His human creation is truly loathsome—*but never loathed.* If Jonathan Edwards never saw this, his prodigious labors were in vain and detrimental. . . . Mature Christian hearts come to realize that there would never have been sin and suffering had God not had a Remedy prepared.—and His remedy was not *more sin and suffering* as the hell advocates blindly advise. . . . "For as in Adam all die, even so in Christ shall all be made alive" [Corinthians 15:22].[60]

Howard Dorgan reports on research he did on twenty-eight "No-Heller"

Primitive Baptist churches in three associations, published as *In the Hands of a Happy God: The "No-Hellers" of Central Appalachia:*

> Succinctly, this doctrine is a variation of "universalism," holding first (as in traditional Primitive theology) that only a limited body of people, known from the beginning of time, become God's elect; second, that only these elect can experience the in-this-life joys of redemption from Adam's sin; but, third, that hell exists only in the temporal world, as an absent-from-God's-blessing condition; and, finally, that "resurrection" will treat all men the same, uniting them in heaven as a fulfillment of the promise that Christ "tasted death for all men. . . ."
>
> In a very real sense, this is a wonderfully liberating theology, freeing these happy Christians to celebrate the ultimate rapture of all of Adam's seed. "Some Baptists take delight in assigning sinners to an eternity in hell," says Elder Farley Beavers of Tazewell, Virginia, "but that's not us. We're happy that everybody escapes that kind of eternity." "That's the reason Christ died," argues Elder Reece Maggard of Mayking, Kentucky, "so all mankind can benefit." "That death on the cross was for us all," declares Roy McGlothlin of Blountville, Tennessee, "and we can't escape its blessing no matter how sinful we are. . . ."
>
> "No Heller" universalism fosters a religious lifestyle filled with immense joy—joy arising primarily from the belief that the deity has planned an eternity equally rewarding to all, a heaven of inexpressible glory guaranteed to "all" mankind. That is the "kinder, gentler" nature of this theology.[61]

Adda Leah Davis quotes Elder Landon Colley on the hell beliefs of the Primitive Baptist Universalists. He touches on the "natural" and spiritual" parts of the human condition:

> If the natural man does the sinning here on earth then the spiritual man shouldn't have to pay in another life. . . . God prepared the lake of fire and brimstone for the devil and his angels and anything prepared is not eternal. I wouldn't tell nobody that there is not a lake of fire but the transgressors of the law are the only ones who get in it and it is here in time. Primitive Baptist Universalists believe we have to pay for every sin we commit but we believe we pay for them right where we did the deed. Young Elder Aaron Williams once said "God didn't issue credit cards. It's pay as you go."[62]

Death and Eternity

Most Upland Christians do believe in a hell for those who have sinned and have not sought salvation, but in the materials I have collected here, there is much more about a loving God and about heaven as a place of reward than there is about an angry God and hell as a place of punishment.

Central on Christians' minds is the question of eternity, of what lies beyond their death and where and in what form they will be. Brother Darrell Mullins affirmed how he and others can escape the fear of death and eternity:

> God's love will feed you and take care of you. He takes care of the sparrows of the air. He takes care of the animals in the woods, and He'll take care of us because we are made in His image. A lot of people do not believe because they are concerned about what's going to happen tomorrow, but why don't you ask the Man who's got tomorrow in His hand?
>
> My friend, when you serve God, there's peace of mind and hope that passes all understanding, and joy! God gave me that desire in my heart. He took away my fear. No more do I fear dying, but I look death in the face and say, "O death, you have no grip on me no more. O grave, you don't have no sting for me no more. One of these days I'll fly off to be with Jesus forever."[63]

Susanna Jacobs Combs, an eastern Kentucky woman, was definite in her beliefs about eternity and heaven and hell:

> When you die, your soul goes back to the one who give it to you—to the Lord. And when He gets ready to come back, at the end of time, He takes the righteous first. . . . I believe the wicked are left here on earth to burn. You know, they never burn up—the wicked. Their souls, they burn forever and ever, according to the Scriptures. . . . Hit's an eternal thing . . . , and so hit's a really serious thing, if you dwell on it enough and think on it. . . . You don't have no promise of tomorrow, and a person oughtn't, shouldn't, put it off to save their soul, because you might die before you're saved.[64]

Elder Squire Watts, a Knott County, Kentucky, Old Regular Baptist, was more hesitant to talk about who might go to heaven or to hell and stressed the need to comfort the bereaved ones at funerals regardless of the spiritual condition of the departed:

Death is a scary subject. That's final. Our funerals, I'm really pleased by the way they're conducted. Leadership is so important. There are those that people look to for leadership and guidance. . . . You don't want to be in a big hurry or cut God short or anything, but there is a right way to do anything. . . . Families, when they have a death, it's up to them what preachers they want in that funeral. . . .

I don't like to see anybody preached into heaven or hell. I've heard preachers say pretty strongly that this person is in heaven. That's all right, I guess, but we don't know that. The best thing I know is to depend on God, and He'll come to the rescue. And stick with the Scriptures. A person that's been in church, lived a good life and walked close to God, makes it so much easier on a preacher that has to stand up there than a person who's never made a confession and up to the point of death, maybe, has been a wicked person.

A woman called the other day. Her mother had died, and I didn't know this lady. I went to the funeral home. I got the obituary they'd written out, and I talked with the daughter. I like to know as much about that person as I can. I don't want to make the hurt any worse.[65]

Anna Mae Cook, a black Pentecostal preacher, spoke of the death of her church's white assistant pastor, Charles Hollon, and how the funeral turned into a celebration of his life:

Oh, you should have been here that day! That was a glorious time— no mourning, no nothing—the Spirit of God falling. Yeah, we had a glorious time—church full—had a big bunch of them.

Oh, yeah, it was a celebration. He [Mr. Hollon] went out talking to the Lord, telling Him he loved Him and everything—went out praising the Lord! It wasn't sad at all. Well, you know, that's what you live right for. If you don't live right, you liable to go out any kind of way, fighting and scratching, cussing, and all that, but he didn't do that because he didn't live that kind of life.[66]

I have heard many questions asked about what happens after death. Does the soul go directly to heaven or hell, or does it sleep with the body until the Resurrection? Are the body and soul reunited on Resurrection Day? Do we have our earthly bodies or take some other form? When will the end of time come? The Bible has many answers, but some seem contradictory. It speaks of Jesus' Second Coming and His reign on earth for a thousand years and finally the Rapture of the saved up to heaven. Rev. John Pritt, West Virginia Baptist, spoke of the doctrine of the Last Things:

The doctrine of the Last Things centers around the Second Coming of Christ. All who believe in Him will be taken up to meet the Lord in the air. Following is the period of tribulation, roughly about seven years, during which the Bible says God will pour out his wrath upon those who believe not His Son and receive not His Son as their Savior.

After that is the period of the revelation of the Antichrist, which can be thought of as the personification of evil—the devil. He reveals himself at the end of seven years. Then begins—after God destroys the Antichrist—what the Bible calls a thousand-year reign, or the millennium, a thousand years of perfect government, of which Christ will be the head and His saints will be the administrators.

After which, Satan will be loosed; he has been bound for a thousand years, and he shall be loosed for reasons God has chosen to keep to Himself. The nations will gather and God will destroy them with fire out of heaven. Then, in the Book of Revelation, John the Revelator says, "I saw a new heaven and a new earth descend of God out of heaven."

The doctrine of the Second Coming is what sustained the early Christians. That's what gave them courage to live lives which were clean and which gave them the grace to die.[67]

Emily Phillips, a member of Pastor Pritt's Independent Baptist Church in Charleston, West Virginia, had done considerable thinking about the end of the world:

This doctrine of the Last Things is very real to us Christians. It isn't something vague and just something that we talk about but something that is going to happen, and a lot of people don't realize that. Scripture is literal. It is going to happen, and nothing can prevent it.

I have talked to a lot of people who didn't know what the Rapture is all about. . . . You have heard Christians talking about the end of the world, and it is such a vague term to them. . . . They have no idea of all what is to take place—the tribulation, the millennium, the Rapture, the judgment seat of Christ and the great white throne. These things don't mean anything to them because they don't know anything about them.

Scripture tells us that we shall know as we are known, and I'm sure I wouldn't recognize any of you by your spirit. I mean, if I were floating around in space, I'm sure my spirit wouldn't recognize yours, but since we will know even as we are known, I think it indicates we are going to have a body. We are not going to be dismembered spirits floating around.[68]

Many people believe in a literal resurrection and have no patience with the notion that at death the soul flies off to heaven and that the body is no longer important. Elder Steve Casteel, Primitive Baptist, said that he would hate to miss the Resurrection, explaining that "some of God's people will not experience that because they will be changed right here, when the Lord comes down 'in the twinkling of an eye' to be caught up with those others who have come out of the grave."[69] Pastor Henry Mahan, a Grace Baptist, believes that the Resurrection is fundamental to the Gospel:

> Without the Resurrection, you have no Gospel. . . . It is foolishness to doubt the Resurrection of the Dead. Paul said if there is no Resurrection, then Christ has not risen. If Christ has not risen, our preaching is in vain. . . .
>
> But the truth is that Christ is risen. He has risen as our representative. He has become the first fruits of them that slept. . . . Since by man came death—from that representative man Adam from whom we all came—even so, in Christ—all who are in Christ shall be made alive.
>
> How are the dead raised? Is anything too hard for God? Is God not able to raise the dead, who created Adam out of the dust . . . breathed the breath of life into him and made him a living soul? What's to prevent Him from raising someone who's dead and gone back to the dust?
>
> This flesh and blood cannot survive in the kingdom of God—in the glory of it, in the beauty of it. So this flesh, the dwelling place of evil, has got to be changed. We bury this old flesh, buried in corruption, raised in incorruption; buried in shame, raised in honor; buried in weakness, raised in power; buried a fleshly, natural body, and raised with the moisture of holiness, of everlasting life, of righteousness and the life of God that can never die.[70]

Woodrow Runyan, a Presbyterian from Mingo County, West Virginia, dealt with the question of body and soul as two entities: "I believe that our bodies will be resurrected after death, and our souls will reenter the body. I think our body goes down now to the grave as a mortal body. It goes to the grave as a corrupt body and will be raised as an incorruptible body and will receive the soul that belongs to that body. Our bodies will receive our souls the day of judgment, on the last great day."[71]

These quotations from people with a wide range of belief highlight the importance of salvation and how it may be attained and made secure. Salvation is at the core of religious belief in the Uplands. It is yearned for and brings relief from the chilling questions about our purpose on earth, our fear of death, and what lies beyond.

Baptism at Little Dove Church,
Indian Bottom Association of
Old Regular Baptists, in the waters
of Carr Creek, Knott County,
Kentucky, October 14, 1979

Then Peter saith unto them, Repent, and be baptized every one of you in the name of Jesus Christ for the remission of sins, and ye shall receive the gift of the Holy Ghost. (Acts 2:38)

Elder I. D. Back, Moderator of Little Dove Church, preaches the meaning of baptism.

One Lord, one faith, one baptism.   (Eph. 4:5)

Elder I. D. Back embraces convert Lona Faye Bentley.

This is he that came by water and blood, even Jesus Christ; not by water only, but by water and blood. And it is the Spirit that beareth witness, because the Spirit is truth. (1 John 5:6)

Elders Back and Ivan Amburgey pray before baptizing Mrs. Bentley.

. . . he that sent me to baptize with water, the same said unto me, Upon whom thou shalt see the Spirit descending, and remaining on him, the same is he which baptizeth with the Holy Ghost. (John 1:33)

Elders Back and Amburgey raise Mrs. Bentley from the water.

Mrs. Bentley rushes to embrace her husband.

And as the people were in expectation, and all men mused in their hearts of John, whether he were the Christ, or not.   (Luke 3:15)

Members of the congregation and friends witness.

And there went out unto him all the land of Judea, and they of Jerusalem, and were all baptized of him in the river of Jordan, confessing their sins. (Mark 1:5)

Brother John Preece and Elder I. D. Back lead Cooley Bashears into Carr Creek for baptism . . .

*Are ye able to drink of the cup that I shall drink of, and to
be baptized with the baptism that I am baptized with?
They say unto him, We are able.*   (Matt. 20:22)

. . . and return rejoicing.

And now why tarriest thou? arise, and be baptized, and wash away thy sins, calling on the name of the Lord. (Acts 22:16)

Brother John Preece reaches a hand to Sheila Rose Collins, assisted by Elders Ivan Amburgey and I. D. Back . . .

Therefore we are buried with him by baptism into death: that like as Christ was raised up from the dead by the glory of the Father, even so we also should walk in newness of life. (Romans 6:4)

. . . and she is brought up out of the waters by Elder Back and Brother Preece.

Denver Melton (*left*) weeps after being baptized by his uncle, Elder Henry Melton.

Go ye therefore, and teach all nations, baptizing them in the name of the Father, and of the Son, and of the Holy Ghost: Teaching them to observe all things whatsoever I have commanded you: and, lo, I am with you alway, even unto the end of the world. Amen. (Matt. 28:19–20)

Elder Ivan Amburgey brings the benediction.

6 *Praise in Zion*

Confess your faults one to another, and pray one
for another, that ye may be healed. The effectual
fervent prayer of a righteous man availeth much.

—James 5:16

If any man speak, let him speak as the oracles of
God; if any man minister, let him do it as of the
ability which God giveth; that God in all things
may be glorified through Jesus Christ: to whom be
praise and dominion for ever and ever. Amen

—1 Peter 4:11

By the rivers of Babylon, there we sat down, yea, we
wept, when we remembered Zion. We hanged our
harps upon the willows in the midst thereof. For
they that carried us away captive required of us a
song . . . saying, Sing us one of the songs of Zion.
How shall we sing the Lord's song in a strange land?

—Psalm 137

I have heard Upland people praise God in numerous ways, but they
do so primarily through preaching, prayer, testimony, and song. I
have already dealt with preaching in chapter 5, and so here we will listen to
Upland voices on prayer and testimony and on a subject dear to me, the
songs of Zion.

Prayer

Most Christians believe that prayer is essential to the spiritual life, some finding it easy to talk with God, and others feeling that it is something that they must be disciplined to do. Still others feel that they cannot speak directly to God but must go through their mediator, Jesus. In Matthew (chapter 6) Jesus gives instructions for praying, warning against doing it publicly so that you might be heard by those you want to impress but rather saying, "when thou prayest, enter into thy closet, and when thou hast shut thy door, pray to thy Father which is in secret; and thy Father which seeth in secret shall reward thee openly." He goes on to say that you don't need to repeat yourself, for God knows what we need even before we ask, and then he gives the Lord's Prayer as the example of how it should be done, with reverence and appreciation of God's majesty, a simple request for our basic requirements for life, a statement of our need for forgiveness of our sins, and a pledge to forgive others for theirs.

Later (Matthew 26:41) the writer reports that Jesus said to His disciples, "Watch and pray, that ye enter not into temptation; the spirit indeed is willing, but the flesh is weak." This verse is often quoted to show the necessity of prayer in leading a Christian life. Rev. Dennis M. Moore, pastor of the Isoline Baptist Church in Cumberland County, Tennessee, spoke of prayer in this way: "Prayer is the sincere desire of our hearts, praying to Jesus because He is our high priest, our interceder to God. And we are to pray with the sincerity of our hearts, to Christ Jesus, in order that we might receive the things He is ready and willing to bless us with."[1]

I present here excerpts from a sermon by the late Herman B. Yates, then pastor of the Grace Baptist Church of Dingess, West Virginia, entitled "The Throne of Grace." His text was Hebrews 4:14–16: "Seeing then that we have a great high priest, that is passed into the heavens, Jesus the Son of God, let us hold fast our profession. For we have not a high priest which cannot be touched with the feeling of our infirmities; but was in all points tempted like as we are, yet without sin. Let us therefore come boldly unto the throne of grace, that we may obtain mercy, and find grace to help in time of need." His sermon is about prayer and what it can do for us. It is also about the different roles of God, Jesus, and the Holy Spirit, especially about the majesty of God and the belief that Christ must be the intercessor between us and God:

> True prayer is the actual approach of the soul through the Spirit of
> God to the throne of God. It's not words; it's not just feelings and

desires. . . . It's the spiritual approach of our nature towards the Lord our God. True prayer is communing with our Creator. . . . Our spirit within us, begotten by the Holy Ghost at our regeneration, sees the great Spirit, communes with it, presents to Him our request, and actually receives from Him answers of peace.

Now, true prayer, then, is a spiritual business from beginning to end, and its object is not man at all, but God. We must have the Holy Spirit's help for true prayer. If all we needed were words, we have that, and if all we needed were desires and wants, we have these too. Every natural man has needs and wants, but when it's a spiritual desire, and when that desire is for fellowship with the Great Spirit, then the Holy Ghost must be present all through it to help our infirmities, and to get life and power, or else it is just impossible. . . .

Just as prayer will not be true prayer without the Holy Spirit, it cannot be effectual prayer without the Son of God Himself. He, the Great High Priest, must go within the veil for us. By His crucified person, that veil must be entirely taken away, removed, for until then we are shut out from the presence of God. The man who tries to pray without the Savior insults the deity. . . . God will not accept anything for a sacrifice except through the blood of His Son. Wrought in us by the Holy Spirit, presented to God for us by the Christ, prayer becomes power before the Most High God. . . .

In prayer God is to be looked upon as our Father. What a great and high privilege that is, so very dear to us, but still we must always remember we are not to regard Him as though He were such a one as ourselves. . . . He is to be regarded as king! Absolute monarch and king, and in prayer we come to the great throne of the king of the universe! The mercy seat is a throne, and we must never forget that. If prayer is to be regarded as an entrance into the royal court of heaven, and if we are to behave in a manner befitting one who is in the presence of the illustrious King of Kings, then we won't be at a loss to know the right spirit in which to pray. If in prayer we come to the throne, then it's clear that our spirit and attitude should be one of lowly reverence. A subject of a king should pay him homage and honor, shouldn't he? In our case, the king before whom we come is the highest of all kings. Emperors and earthly kings are but shadows of his imperial power. . . . The Lord alone has divine right, and to Him alone does the kingdom belong. He is the blessed and only potentate. Be sure you prostrate yourself before such a one as this. . . . His throne has sway in all worlds. Heaven obeys Him cheerfully.

Hell trembles at His frown, and earth is constrained to pay Him homage, either willingly or unwillingly. His power can make, and His power can destroy. So be sure that when you approach the omnipotent, who is a consuming fire, put thy shoes from off thy feet and worship Him with the lowest humility.[2]

Fannie Hunter, of the African Methodist Episcopal Church in Transylvania County, North Carolina, spoke of prayer's centrality in her life:

Well, I would say that I wouldn't think of rising in the morning without giving thanks to the Lord that He has watched over me. I make a practice of doing that every morning when I open my eyes and before I get out of bed. I thank the Lord that He has brought me through the night, and I am always thankful for one more day, and I will try to practice that in my home with my children, the whole family, to give thanks for this day, because we don't know what the next day will bring. If we teach our children [this] at home, they will grow into it.[3]

Walter McAlister, a Methodist from Allegheny County, Virginia, told a moving story about his little daughter on a life-support system in a hospital: "The little girl we lost, she was in [the hospital] bed down in Richmond, and she told me, she said, 'Daddy, you know, I'm going to forget to know how to say thank you'—for her meals, you know. She always gave thanks. . . . So after that, I told the nurse, so she let her say thanks before they gave food to her through the tube. I've often thought about that."[4]

Following are four statements from Upland Christians who I thought had something important to say about prayer:

Rev. Marvin A. Kincheloe, a Chattanooga Methodist: I believe prayer is all these things . . . , petition, thanksgiving, and adoration, but prayer not so much changes God's will as releases it. We're not asking God to change His mind about us, thank Heaven, but we're asking God to change us so we will fit His will, and that the things God wants to say to us, and to do for us, the things He wants to give us after we qualify through prayer, after we've prayed. That's why I say prayer opens the gate for God.[5]

Elder Johnny Blackburn, Pike County, Kentucky, Primitive Baptist: Would you believe that the very intent and desire of your heart is prayer—the very sincere desire of your heart is prayer to God? If that is not right, and you have to holler to get God to hear you, I want to tell you that there are some people in this world in bad shape, if that's what it takes. But it don't, and they ought to be glad and thank God for it. The little deaf and dumb child that never spoke in this world can pray just as sweetly to God as me and you can.[6]

Mrs. John Coles, a Methodist in Roanoke County, Virginia: Prayer should be a part of our daily lives. That is the thing that keeps us in touch with God, that keeps our beliefs alive for us. And certainly if we remember others in our prayers, that would keep us in touch with our fellow men. It's right hard to pray for someone and not be kind to them. You can't dislike a person you pray for.[7]

Bishop Pentz, a Presbyterian layman from Allegheny County, Virginia: I think prayer is the heart of the Christian life and one of the most important parts of life. It's a way that a man can have spiritual communication with God. And I don't think that prayers have to be spoken in words always. . . . Prayer is a thought process that connects man with God, and it doesn't have to be expressed in words necessarily. . . . Prayer is the link that brings man to God, and as such, it is a part of the Christian, the same as belief in God.[8]

Here are two examples of Upland prayers that I collected, the first in a radio broadcast from an unidentified preacher in North Carolina during the southeastern summer drought of 1986:

Lord, we thank you that the supreme sacrifice of your only begotten Son, Jesus Christ, was given, for we were all dead in trespasses of sin, and we've all been quickened, made alive through His death, burial, and resurrection, and we thank you for this, Lord. If there was ever a generation that needs mercy, it's the one we live in today, for we see the destructiveness of sin in our society, and we see many areas where we as a church have become complacent. We need you to revive us again. Move our hearts to motivate us so that we can become involved in the things that are wrong with society. We pray, Lord, that our country will not continue to fall, as it is doing. We pray that your judgment would not continue to fall on different areas as we're afraid that it has already begun to do.

We think about the situations without rain and the extreme heat in different areas of the country. We wonder if this is not part of your judgment. We pray, Lord, that you would indeed have mercy upon us, and that you would motivate us to get involved. We pray for motivation, for boldness. We pray for the powers to witness for you.[9]

The next prayer was by Elder Teddy Ball, in the Coon Creek Primitive Baptist Church, Pike County, Kentucky:

Most holy, righteous, all-wise, adored Father, in whose presence, O Lord, again a few of thy children have been permitted by Thy love and Thy tender mercy, dear Heavenly Father, to come again to this grand old church, O Lord, where we have gathered from time to time to worship you in spirit and in truth. O Father, this morning, as we bow on these our bended knees and our fast-decaying bodies, O Lord, again if it could be your will, Father, to enable us, as you did Old Jonah, to look forward to the Holy City, dear Heavenly Father.

Then, Father, teach us to pray. We realize that every time one of your children was blessed to pray, you had to teach him. O Father, this morning, if it's your will, throw your loving arms of mercy around us, dear God, and raise us up, Heavenly Father, that we may be permitted to sit together in a heavenly place again. O Father, we feel so unworthy, great God, to bow before a holy God that we ask grace for help in time of need. O Lord, if it is your will, bless every one that has come out here today.

Dear Father, bless the sick and afflicted wherever they are. O Heavenly Father, as much as it is your will to do so, supply their every need. O Jesus, if it's your will to help Sister ————. She's so afflicted, Lord. If it's your will to lay your healing hand on her, Dear God. O Father, bless old Brother ————, Lord, in his affliction, and Sister ————, and many others.

O great eternal God, if it's your will, remember our children as they gather with our brothers and sisters, and our neighbors' children. Oh, there's many of them on the highways, and one place and another, and O Father, we know that Thy long arm of mercy can reach them, God, if it's your will to turn them from the wayward paths of sin, O Lord, and bless us all, amen.[10]

Testimonies

Testifying about what God has done in your life is an old tradition in Upland churches, and I believe such personal testimonies are an important part of the religious oral tradition. McKenzie Ison, testifying in an Old Regular Baptist church, illustrated both humility and the belief that any worthwhile thing he might say comes from God and not from his own mind:

I hope you'll be patient with me. Get your mind on the Lord and above my head—on heaven—for I am very weak. It does my heart good to see people that are humble inside. I feel unworthy to be here. I sure do, but I believe the Lord changed my life. I have to work at it. I do things I'm not proud of, for sure, but I believe the Lord changed me a few years ago. I'm no longer my own keeper. The Lord sought me out and told me a few things, and finally I saw. He taught me so many wonderful things. . . .

I'm ashamed of myself at times. I'm slothful. I don't do all the things I could be doing. God showed me how weak I am. I'm just a man who was born again inside, and I have available to me a power that can bring everlasting life. . . .

If you don't know Him, you'd better be getting acquainted with Him, because I'm telling you that if I hadn't, I'd a been gone. I was heading down the road to destruction. . . .

I guess I'm a quare fellow, peculiar, whatever you want to call it [at this point a preacher said, "We all are peculiar people," meaning all Regular Baptists]. I feel unworthy. I'm glad God's given me something to look forward to in a world that's getting darker every day.[11]

Brother Vernon Harrison, a Pentecostal, offered this testimony: "Now I have repented of my sins. I've repented of my wickedness, asked for the mercy of God to overflow me, asked for the blood that flowed down from Calvary to hit me from the top of my head to the bottom of my feet and cleanse me of my unrighteousness. I have repented my wicked ways."[12]

Rev. Alfred Carrier, of Lincoln County, Kentucky, testified about his salvation, why he became a Pentecostal, and his quest for the baptism in the Holy Spirit, which he referred to as a "third act of grace," building on Wesley's "second act of grace":

When I was a young man (I was reared in the community where I'm pastoring right now), I was aware of this movement. I was rocked, as I often say, in a Pentecostal cradle. My mother was one of the charter original members of the movement in this community. When I was away from the community, my work for the Lord brought me right back to the place where I was born.

I began to get concerned soon after I married, attending revivals, and the Lord began to work in my heart, and I went to an altar of prayer, repented and confessed my sins, and was born again—truly saved. I was taught by the people that there was an experience beyond that—a great experience that would empower me to witness, to work for God, to do greater things for the Lord. They called it baptism in the Holy Ghost.

I sought the Lord in prayer and in praise for this great baptism, and I recall the night that I received the baptism in the Holy Ghost. I had been to the altar and had been praying and praising the Lord, and I'd returned to my seat, and the church stood for dismissal— stood in prayer. Then I lifted my hands to the Lord and began to pray and to give praise to Him again, and suddenly beginning to move over me was the mighty presence of God in such a baptism that it is beyond description, impossible to relate on this tape. But as the Spirit of the Lord began to move over my body, I began to shake and tremble, to move under the Spirit. Suddenly my tongue and my mouth began to be used—not I using it but the Spirit that moved over me and to use me—and I began to speak in other tongues. The Spirit gave utterance. Since that time on very numerous occasions, as often as I go before God in prayer and in praise, the Holy Ghost moves within my life, and I begin to speak in the heavenly language that gives me a sense of fulfillment within my life that is beyond description and blesses us tremendously. I find an empowering in this, an anointing that gives me courage, gives me boldness, that helps me to go on and witness for Jesus and declare the full Gospel of Jesus Christ.[13]

I have heard many riveting testimonies from Upland Christians about how salvation has changed them or those dear to them, made them different and better in this world, and given them assurance about a future life. John Lakin Brasher, the powerful North Alabama preacher who led the Methodist Holiness movement in the early years of this century, believed that the Lord will completely change a person: "When you turn your case over to Him, He will so shine inside of you that it will shine out through you until your face will have a different look from a sinner. A sinner looks down and up through his eyebrows. A converted man looks level, like that. A sanctified man lifts his head up, like that."[14]

Following are several other testimonies I have collected or discovered or that have been sent to me over many years. Some testify to the power of salvation to make them better persons here in the world. We begin with William Addison, a West Virginia coal miner, on a recording sent to me by sociologist Mike Yarrow. Addison talked about how salvation made a man of him and a better United Mine Workers of America leader:

> I used to be a man that felt these great inferior feelings. . . . If you came to my house you couldn't have a bit more got me to come in here and sit down and talk to you. . . . The most wonderful thing that ever happened to me—I committed myself to Christ. I'm a Christian man. That's what happened to me. He said, "If the Son shall set you free, you shall be free indeed." I was the sort of man that felt very inferior—like that all my life. I didn't have any educa-tion, still don't, but she's [his wife] pretty well educated. She's got a good mind. I felt inferior to her, and I depended completely on her. Her family didn't have these inferior feelings. They were fighters, but to me, a loud voice would push me backward, make me feel inferior. I couldn't take it. It would just close me right up.
>
> But after I committed my life to Christ thirty years ago, He's done these things for me. He's set me free, and He has showed me what a man really is—what God thinks about a man. It's like John L. Lewis came along and told the miners what they really were, and they be-gan to lose their inferior feelings. My testimony as a Christian is that man can get in touch with God, and God can do wonderful things for him and through him. But first, He's got to make a man out of him. The greatest thing that happens to a Christian is that He makes a person out of you. Of course, you can't do anything until you real-ize that you are a person. It doesn't make an overbearing person, or a person that's going to hurt somebody, but it makes a person who will stand.
>
> Down through the nation, the world, we've seen people who've stood up and given their lives for a purpose and cause—and contrib-uted to the world. To contribute, it will cost you. There is a cost you have to pay.
>
> When I look at death, I'm not concerned, but what I'm concerned with is what I can do in the world before I die. We think being a Christian, that we're going to heaven, but that's not the reward. That ain't what Christ came to do. He came, He said time after time, to give you life, new life. He's done that for me. It doesn't matter to me whether heaven is a race or a mansion. A great thing has already hap-pened to me. The life I had years ago is gone—is no more—and I

have a new life. My values are changed, my mind is changed, my thinking is changed.

In my work, it affects me. I work with union men, and union men will take care of it [trouble] like this. If you have a hard section boss, they'll get together and say, "We're going to cut production." They tell me, "Slow 'er down." I say, "I agree with you that the man is wrong, but slowing it down is not the way. What we'll do is, we'll call him up here and talk to him—give him a chance."

Christ doesn't dismiss nobody unless He confronts him. He tells me to live like He does. I did confront bosses, time and time again. I told them where they were wrong. I tried to help them. I wouldn't treat them wrong behind their backs. . . . If the union would adopt the Christian attitude, it'd make a better union. Your production would always be good, and that would help the men. It would [also] enrich the company. . . . The [union] brotherhood is limited to their people. Many will lay down their lives for a union brother. Anything outside their brotherhood is their enemy. It is a limited love. God's love is an unlimited love. It is love that knows no bounds.[15]

Maxine Waller is a Christian woman from Ivanhoe, Virginia, who diligently reads her Bible and tries to discern what the Lord's will is for her. Through involvement with activist women, such as sociologist Helen Lewis and liberation theologian Mary Ann Hinsdale, she has become more and more interested in improving life here on earth. She is a leader in the Ivanhoe Civic League, which works to create new opportunity for the community after the major industries moved away. She refuses to believe that salvation is just for rewards in heaven. The following quotation is from a book coauthored by Hinsdale, Lewis, and Waller, *It Comes from the People: Community Development and Local Theology:*

One of these days the Lord will call down my number, and I'll have to pull out all my practice stuff and do the real job. . . . God is a heavy taskmaster. He's really hard on you, and when he gives you something to do, he don't give you no pie jobs. He gives you a big burden to carry, but you have to stand up and take that burden 'cause you don't have no choice. He won't put more burdens on us than we can bear. God don't come down and say, "I want you to do this" and "I want you to do that." It comes about in little ways that's just laid there. Like you wake up one morning and it's laid there that you do this.[16]

Sue Cox Cole, a Pentecostal evangelist and singer, has a strong belief that those who are saved are better people in the world: "I feel honored to work for God. . . . You know, when you are a Christian, you hear that you are a special creation of God, and that you are important, that you are somebody, and that God has a place for your life. It's certainly going to make a difference in your behavior."[17] Katharine Smith, Church of God member from DeKalb County, Alabama, added, "Our Christian experience makes us better men and women, and in the community we're better neighbors . . . and the nation, the United States, it'd make us a stronger nation, if more of us was Christian."[18] Patricia Pritt, a Baptist pastor's wife in Charleston, West Virginia, said: "It's a reformation of character, because we know personally men right here in Charleston who have been drunks, but now they are really soul winners. They are just not the same. They are lifted up socially, economically, and every other way. . . . I think it is such a transforming thing. Your life isn't ever the same ever after . . . like your eyes are opened—eyes of understanding."[19] Earl Tanner, a Nicholas County, West Virginia, Methodist, had no doubt that salvation made a difference in his life: "Well, to me, if I hadn't been converted, I could have been in jail."[20]

Rev. Phillip Banks said with assurance: "My life is a whole lot better today than it was when I was lost. I used to drink, gamble and curse, and do everything else a man can do, and I thought I was happy, but I wasn't. When I realized that there was something better for me in another world and trusted the Lord Jesus and accepted Him, I automatically became better in this world. I had new goals, ambitions, new desires. I have a new purpose."[21]

Dianne Harrison, the wife of a Pentecostal pastor in Powell County, Kentucky, offered this testimony in a radio broadcast in which she dealt with answers to prayers in this life and the loss of the fear of death:

> I praise God today that I am alive. I thank God today most of all that my name's on the Lamb's Book of Life, and if death comes, it'll just make me pass out of this life and go where I've been longing to be. Children, today, if your name's in the Lamb's Book of Life and you've got everything prepared to meet Jesus, death is just a doorway.
>
> I thank God today that my name's there. I praise Him that He came by my way in the back of that old Pizza Hut, and He let me be His child. I consider it a privilege and an honor that Jesus would take time out and come by my way—somebody that wasn't worth anything in the eyes of the world—that the man who went up Calvary, He loved me enough to do that and come by my way. I can't hardly

think about him without crying, because it is a privilege, and it is an honor to me to be His child. I don't feel that He owes me anything. I owe Him everything, and I thank Him today for it.

I thank God today that Brother Vernon [her husband], that He's blessed with a better job. I praise Him and honor Him for it, 'cause we've been praying that God would help him get a better job, and God has done that. I thank God for that. He's there to answer our prayers at all times. We just have to wait upon Him and be patient, because He'll move in His time.

I'm glad that He did what He did for me—all He's ever done—and I praise Him and honor Him.[22]

Finally, here is the long but enlightening and inspiring testimony of an evangelist from Harlan County, Kentucky, whom I recorded from a radio broadcast in 1986 and whom I have been unable to identify. The testimony involves three generations of a mountain family moving from Virginia to Kentucky to Oregon, with vivid descriptions of their strivings to be better people with the Lord's help:

My daddy never spoke a word until he was thirteen years old. He lived so far back in the hills they didn't have an outhouse until the boys got grown. His daddy would come in on Friday nights drunk on moonshine and shoot out all the lights in the old log house down in the hills of Virginia, and all of the kids would have to run to the mountains to hide and wouldn't come home until their daddy had passed out.

Daddy said he went out there to pray; he was just a little fellow. He said he couldn't talk but he would pray: "If I ever have a family, it won't be like this one. If I ever have a wife and children, Lord, help me to raise them a whole lot different from what my daddy's doing."

My granddaddy died with a bullet in his back. He got the man that got him, but he died on a trail in the mountains. Through the years my daddy gave his heart to the Lord. He started serving the Lord when he was thirteen or fourteen years old. He wasn't even raised in the church, but he was determined not to be like *his* daddy.

Anyway, down through the years, he wasn't always serving God. When he was about nineteen years old, he said he was sitting in the middle of the road, and they had their moonshine, their dice, and their cards, said an old preacher came walking down the road. Dad had forgot what he had asked God. The old preacher said, "Boys, don't you want to come to church with me tonight?" He said tears started to come out of his eyes, and he remembered what he had told God. He said he went to church that night and gave his heart to Jesus.

You know what, he was able to write his name, but he never did get to go to school because he couldn't talk. His daddy had said: "Boy, you can't talk. You go to school and they'll make fun of you. You're going to work the farm." He was running a big farm by himself when he was thirteen years old. That's all that he knew. Then he started working in the coal mines when he was fifteen years old. But the Lord led him out of those old hills. He went to the doctor when he was thirty-two years old, and the doctor said, "If you don't get out of the coal mines, you're going to die in two years.

We were like the Beverly Hillbillies. We loaded up, took another family with us—fourteen or fifteen of us—and we went to Portland, Oregon. When we got out there, the Lord put Daddy under some of the great men of God—like Brother A. A. Allen—and they began to work with him, and God began to teach him and to show him . . . , and the Lord began to develop his ministry, because somewhere down the road, he had said, "Lord, I don't want this old kind of life. I want something different."

I had a brother, Arnold. He got into that big movement of the Rolling Stones there in Portland, Oregon. . . . He'd take me to the teenage festivals to watch the Rolling Stones and the Beatles, when they first came over. He even got in a band himself, playing drums. I thought, "Arnold, he's it."

One night Mama came in and said, "Arnold got saved, came into the Liberty Temple and gave his heart to the Lord." I ran as hard as I could. I wanted to see what he looked like. You know what he did next day? I went outside, and he had a stack of Rolling Stones and Beatles records, and he began to fly them records out through them fields, this way and that way. The Lord had turned his life around!

You know where I went with him then? We went downtown in Portland, Oregon. There was a Hell's Angels motorcycle gang. That was back in hippy times. These big old fellers, big old vests on, big old hairy chests, big arms and tattoos and chains around their necks. These big old fellers gathered around him, said he was chicken, poking him in the chest, and he said, "Jesus loves you, and He made a way that you can have life." This the feller that liked rock and roll, now he was down there witnessing for Christ!

I thought, "Boy, you've had it now." Arnold loved to fight. He'd fight anybody. You know how a short feller is a lot of the time. He'll fight the biggest feller around. But he was still witnessing. Over come this big six-foot feller, says, "Boys, leave him alone. Listen to him." He was the head macho man. The Lord had to use a devil.

He went to another place testifying. The buddy he had with him was a Golden Gloves boxer that had just been saved too. This whole gang of boys started wanting to fight. That was something, because I used to watch him fight big old boys, mop up the ground with them. They was scared of people from Harlan, Kentucky. Anywhere you went up North, if you was from Harlan, they was scared. They tried to get them to fight, but they kept telling them about the Lord. Arnold wouldn't fight. I knew then that his life had changed.

I got saved when I had just turned fifteen. I gave my heart to Jesus outside an old tent revival over in Harlan, Kentucky, in a coal camp. And you know what? I've never been the same. It's been like the fire of God. . . . The night I got saved, I felt like I was walking on a cloud! I knew that my life had been changed. And the Lord began to show me that very night I got saved that I was going to be one that was going to carry the Word of God.

You know what He done? He took me in this dream or vision, whatever it was. It was the only vision I ever had in my whole life that I could really say was from God. The Lord that night took me out to a big old gulf, like the Gulf of Mexico, took me to a high place, and I saw a multitude of people lined around the gulf. And coming out of that big gulf I saw lion heads and fire, and do you know what the Lord said? The Lord said, "Run" (there was a big old yellow bus, and there was fire flying everywhere). "Run, get them into the bus. That's the only safety there's gonna be." You know, the Lord was telling me right there, "Son, you're going to preach the Word over in the last days!"

We've got five preachers in the family. Only one person is not saved in our family of nine kids. We've got musicians, singers. God's blessed us. Why? Because somebody dared to say, "Devil, your curse is not going to be on my family." And I want you to know, if you have children, you can withhold the power of hell from them. I wonder what would have happened if Daddy had said, "That's what I want" [the way his father lived]. He said his brothers would come in with a big old forty-five [pistol] strapped on, down in the sticks, down where Virginia and Kentucky border is.

Anyway, he was determined in his heart not to have that. I've got uncles who are nothing but alcoholics, whose kids are alcoholics, prostitutes, and drug addicts. But you know the Lord has blessed our family. God has blessed us because a little old man about fifty years ago said, "I don't want this." If my daddy had went on and been an alcoholic and lived a life of hell, where would I be tonight?

You've got a choice. You can change your family, change everything! Neighbor, I'm glad tonight that Jesus abides within. Salvation makes a difference."[23]

This story is unique, but it reminds me of other stories I have heard from Upland people who fled poverty, joblessness, and poor schools to improve the lives of their families in other parts of the country. Yet they took their culture with them, in terms of religion, values, music, and folkways. They and their children picked up mainstream ways, but at the core, they were Uplanders still, and their values sustained them in a sometimes alien world.

The Songs of Zion

The most intriguing and expressive part of Upland worship to me is the hymnody. The tunes are both ancient and recently composed. The words of songs always tell us the basic theology of the people. For forty years I have sought out the traditional musicians of Appalachia, both secular and religious, and they have delighted me endlessly. I hold a great admiration for these people, who may be limited in educational attainment and the world's goods and opportunities but through raw talent have made some of the most beautiful and heartfelt music that I have heard.

Few places elsewhere in the county have as strong a tradition in both sacred and secular music as the Southern Uplands does. Cecil Sharp, the English musicologist, when he visited in 1916–18, marveled that people of all ages knew and sang the old songs, whereas in England only the old people sang such songs. Sharp and his associate, Maude Karpeles, published two volumes of songs of English origin with some 1,600 tunes and variants, collected on their several journeys through the highlands.[24]

These songs and others composed in America tell the history and myths of the people, their tragedies and joys. The old ballads of love both fulfilled and unrequited, of betrayal and murder, and of natural and man-made disasters were a part of the literature of the early settlers, along with Old World folktales, riddles, and other lore. Among the great legacy of song were always the songs of praise.

In the Appalachian Film Workshop's film about the Old Regular Baptists, *In the Good Old Fashioned Way,* Elder Ermil Ison expresses his feelings for the old hymns and how they tie in with his culture and religion: "We were borned and raised back in the mountains here, and we always look forward to association time to come back with our families and see old faces that we haven't seen in a long time, and hear the wonderful Gospel of our Lord Jesus Christ preached in the good old-fashioned and old-time way. And to hear the good old-fashioned songs of Zion sung in a way that's everly sounded throughout these hills, a way we don't think will ever die, a way that we feel will be practiced when our Lord Jesus Christ comes after us."[25]

The religious songs were and are neat capsules of theological beliefs, and the tunes carry additional aesthetic meaning, evoking deep feelings that cannot otherwise be expressed. Rev. Walter McNeal, a Methodist pastor in Towns County, Georgia, commented, "I think that if we sing these old songs and really sing from the heart, we can get more message out of these songs than we can get otherwise."[26] Mrs. John Coles, another Methodist, from Roanoke County, Virginia, spoke of hymns:

> Loving music the way I do, the words of the hymns are just about the grandest way to praise God. At home we sing about ten minutes before we go to bed. This is the final thing. We sing someone's favorite hymn, and it is the only time we think about the words. When we sing in church, we are thinking about getting the tune or the words right. We forget to think about the meaning of the words. [In] some of the hymns . . . the words are better than anything we could ever express. I think hymns are some of the grandest ways of showing praise—praise to God—prayer itself.[27]

Mike Mullins, a licentiate preacher in the Primitive Baptist Church, described similar feelings about religious music, with an aside about rock music, after reading Colossians 3:16 ("Let the word of Christ dwell in you richly in all wisdom; teaching and admonishing one another in psalms, and hymns and spiritual songs, singing with grace in your hearts to the Lord"):

> We need to sing "with grace in our hearts." That's a very important part of the worship service, just as important as the preaching part. You know, in some of the old constitutions, it was an article of faith. This was something you were supposed to do. . . .
>
> I remember working and singing "Amazing Grace," or something like that, and tears rolling out of my eyes. Or singing "It is Well with

My Soul," or "Peace Like a River," or "Sorrows Like Sea Billows Roll," and tears would start streaming down my face. Things would get hard, and we'd ask the Lord to help us out, and singing became an important part of life. Some of this stuff you hear on the radio, like rock and roll, I believe it is of the devil. We need to encourage our young people to sing spiritual songs and not be involved in that sort of thing. If you don't sing though the week, it's going to be harder for you to sing when you come to church. We need to sing with grace in our hearts, as children of God. It is an important part of the service.[28]

Brother Ernest Martin, a Winchester, Kentucky, Pentecostal radio preacher and singer, after rendering "The Unclouded Day," spoke of the place of the old hymns in the religious lives of people in the region. He also described his deep emotional reaction to the hymns: "They've sung the old songs, folks have, for many, many years, and yet today they still bring the hope and joy to your soul just like they used to. They never change. That's a good thing about the old songs that tell us about heaven, songs that tell us about the ways that God has made for us. It just brings something to your soul each day."[29]

I was entranced by Brother Martin's life story, as well as his devotion to God and to his ministry. He had worked as a professional musician before he developed health problems from alcohol, was rededicated to Christ, was healed of his affliction, and called to an evangelical ministry that has included both music and preaching:

I've been preaching fifty-eight years. I was born near Clay City, Kentucky, on a farm. My mother died when I was about three years old, and I didn't get to go to school very much. We had about thirty-five acres of corn and twenty-five acres of tobacco, had a hundred or so sheep and cattle to take care of. I was pulled out of school so much I couldn't make grades. I quit at the fifth grade.

When I was fifteen years old, I got saved, but then I got into music, playing all kinds of songs, went on to Knoxville and played on "The Midday Merry-Go-Round" on WNOX. I got poisoned on liquor. They [the doctors] told me they couldn't help me—thought I had TB. They gave me six months to live.

I went to praying. I don't believe a person that goes back on God—on religion and their faith—is hopeless. I believe the Spirit of God still deals with their hearts. I believe God forgives, if you come to Him. He said, "Return unto Me and I will return unto you."

God didn't call me to pastor. I felt my work was more evangelistic. I do believe that music is as much a calling as the call to preach. I was blessed with it before I was called to preach. I used it for my work, but you're not begotten by a gospel song; you're begotten by the Word. Music gets people's minds off everything through the joy of song. You go back in Bible days, David, he wrote psalms. When the Israelites came out of the Red Sea, when the Egyptian hordes were all destroyed, they sang a hymn there. . . . They used tambourines, and they used harps.

When the children of Israel were captured down by the Babylon River, they hung their harps on the willows. They thought they were through singing. They said they wept when they remembered Zion, meeting around the prophets, prophesying. . . . They'd bring in singers and pay them. They'd sing, and the prophets would prophesy. The people would gather together, and they were united in the wilderness, as a church.

But in captivity, they hung their harps on the willows and said, "How can we sing the songs of Zion in a strange land?" A fellow said to me, because they hung their harps on the willows, we should quit singing, that it was a sin to sing. It wasn't a sin for them to sing. That wasn't why they hung their harps. The other night I thought, we're in a strange land now, and if we can't sing because we're in a strange land, we might as well fold up and quit. We're in a strange land, and we'll be in it till we're gathered home.

A fellow told me one time—he used to play the fiddle at dances, and he played the five-string banjo, he said, "like you do, Brother Martin. I like the way you're playing it. I used to play it, but after I got saved, I quit." I said, "Why did you quit?" He said, "I just thought it was wrong to play it in church." I said, "Peter said at Pentecost, 'Repent ye and be converted.'" I said, "What you do is convert everything over to what you're doing." I said, "I can't play 'Turkey in the Straw' and 'Goin' up Cripple Creek' [in church] because it has no meaning to it at all." I said, "I just take my banjo and play good old gospel hymns. I just converted my banjo that I played when I was a boy over to God. We rejoice by it. He tells us to sing. He said to praise Him with a spiritual song. There's nothing wrong with music if it's used right."

But I'm not a person who worships music. I worship God. I've helped a lot of drunks—alcoholics—get saved. They heard me sing "When the Pale Horse and His Rider" and all those Roy Acuff and Carter Family songs. They'd set there in revivals and say, "I'm going." There was one man who got drunk every night. . . . He got saved, hugged his family, and I baptized him. He lived for God until tons of rock came down on him in the quarry where he was working, and he died. He was attracted by my music.

They are also attracted to my music on the air. I've been altogether on thirty radio stations in Kentucky, Indiana, West Virginia, and Tennessee. I love music. I can be down and out sometimes. I go out to my studio and get my guitar out, and I lay a song out in front of me, like "Peace, Peace, Wonderful Peace." I like songs like "The Unclouded Day." First thing you know, tears are streaming down my face. I get a good blessing. It's the hymns, the meaning put into a song, the spirit, that puts life in it. It's like the Bible. Every time you read it you're going to find something enlightening, and the songs are the same way.[30]

Mr. Martin is a product of the folk musical tradition in the Uplands, which has shaped the way he plays the guitar and banjo, his singing style, and his choice of religious songs, and he is as reverent and serious about his religion and his music as anyone I know.

Singing was an important part of the revivals that spread throughout the region during the Second Great Awakening, beginning at the start of the nineteenth century. Many of the hymns, simple and repetitive, were out of the folk tradition in an age of few books and many people who read poorly if at all. The well-known "Old-Time Religion" is typical with its verses such as, "It was good for Paul and Silas, and it's good enough for me." Then other verses were sung affirming that it was "good for" a range of other people from "the Hebrew children" to "father," "mother," "sister," and "brother." Such songs brought people together and created religious fervor, but it did other things as well. J. Wayne Flynt, in *Dixie's Forgotten People,* wrote about camp-meeting songs:

> Even the songs and structure of the camp meeting service represented one way that a frontiersman could achieve a coherent view of himself and his place in the world. . . .
>
> Important to the poor was a sense of eternal community that gave each person a way of looking at himself and the world. They drew strength from each other in order to confront their calamities.

O come and join our pilgrim band,
Our toils and triumph share;
We soon shall reach the promised land,
And rest forever there.[31]

Jo Lee Fleming, writing of a later age when singing conventions were popular, utilizing shape-note gospel songbooks published by such companies as Stamps Baxter and James D. Vaughan, showed the continuing complex needs that singing met:

The Sunday afternoon singings provide inspiration to those in attendance, and serve to supplement their other religious experiences. However, these events are also largely social, giving the people a chance to get together with old friends, to meet new ones, and to share common interests. . . .

Many of the texts dealt with the themes of the brevity of life, the rescue from sin, the virtues of right living, the companionship of Christ (the Lord, Pilot, Friend, Guide, etc.), the march to heaven, and heaven itself, with an emphasis both on the quality of life on earth and the life beyond. . . . Rural they are in attitude, but worthless they are not. They are meeting their spiritual, intellectual, and social needs in a way which is vital to them, and which has served generation upon generation of southern rural people.[32]

Bill C. Malone, in his definitive country music history, *Country Music, U.S.A.,* discussed the nature and content of southern religious music and how industrialization and urbanization affected it:

The music that flowed into the southern country churches in the middle and last years of the nineteenth century, then, flowered from many roots: from traditional British hymnody, from American revivalism, from anonymous folk composers, from Negro sources, and most important, from the gospel composers of post–Civil War America. . . . The music was often gentle, bucolic, nostalgic, and sentimental, just as the popular music of the late nineteenth century was. The Savior was perceived as a shepherd tending his flock, or as a loving father watching over his sometimes-erring family. Heaven was sometimes described as a city of gold, but more often as an abundant Beulah Land traversed by flowing rivers, and fragrant with the aromas of eternally blooming flowers. In keeping with an urbanizing society that was becoming more prosperous and secure, the songs tended to be more optimistic and complacent than the older songs. Nevertheless, blood still stained the "Old Rugged Cross" and the vision of a suffering Jesus remained the central image. And as rural American society slowly gave way to an urban society of fragile family and human relationships, songs equating rural life with Christian virtue proliferated, as did the number of songs evoking the memory of mother and the old home place or bewailing the fate of the son or daughter who had ventured into the big city. . . .

As in the case of earlier camp meeting song theology, southern gospel songs perceived heaven as a land devoid of earth's limitations (a land "Where We'll Never Grow Old" and "Where the Roses Never Fade"). Song after song described the Christian as a pilgrim in an unfriendly world, and the world as a dying, unchangeable, but temporary abode.[33]

Most of the Upland hymns are variants of British, German, and American hymns, a good many from the late nineteenth century. Many have been handed down in the oral tradition, although both music and words have also been transmitted in printed form. Some, however, are in small hymnbooks without notated tunes, in the manner used by early Baptists in the British Isles and by Charles Wesley. These texts show the meter as S.M. (short meter), C.M. (common meter), L.M. (long meter) or P.M. (particular meter, meaning no regular meter). Since the tunes are not notated, they are in the oral tradition, and may vary from one group to another and from place to place (see Beverly Bush Patterson, *The Sound of the Dove,* for more information on this style of singing).

Of course, as religion has changed and new groups have been organized, new hymns have been composed. Yet many of the old hymns are still sung on occasion in most churches, and so there are hymns that are known to most American groups, although sometimes with variant tunes and meter. Singing is an important part of worship in all Upland churches.

Listen to sentiments about the importance of religious music from several mountain Christians, starting with Elder Johnny Blackburn, a Pike County, Kentucky, Primitive Baptist:

This song, "The Day Is Past and Gone," was the last song my grandfather, on my mother's side, ever heard sung on his dying bed. It was our association time, the Mates Creek Association. I was a very small boy, about twelve or thirteen years of age. We were down there at his home, and my father had gone to the association. My grandfather had sent out to get somebody to come in that evening to sing and to pray for him and have a little service for him. That was the song that he asked them to sing, "The Day Is Past and Gone." Two or three of them tried to start it, and I was a little fellow sitting there in the corner with my mother, and they couldn't get it started in the right tune. My grandfather looked over at me and said, "Son, come over here," and I walked over to his bedside, and he said, "I never knew a Blackburn in my life but what could do something, and I want you to start that song for your grandfather."

If the Lord ever blessed me in this world, he blessed me to start that song and to sing that song, and that was the last song my grandfather heard before he died.[34]

Lizzie Combs made the following comments in *The Good Old Fashioned Way:* "I like the old-time songs the best, the ones our forefathers sang, and my daddy used to sing. We don't have musical instruments. We never had them. Well, now God gave us music. This is the sweetest music on earth, this voice He give us. That's what we use."[35]

Jesse Comer, a Virginia Baptist featured in Jeff Titon's book *Powerhouse for God,* said: "Singing . . . lifts you up in the Spirit, gets you in a good frame of mind and spirit to enjoy the Word, when it's preached. Singing'll lift you up. When the Word comes along it might cut you down."[36]

An unidentified Primitive Baptist tells this interesting story in the notes to Brett Sutton and Pete Hartman's phonograph album *Primitive Baptist Hymns of the Blue Ridge:*

I'd been out somewhere and was way in the night coming back. I was coming, and the moon was shining so bright, it was mighty nigh, you could pick up a pin almost. I was coming along ridge and wood, leaves and things all off. I was walking and singing. I never will forget, the song was "Blue Moon of Kentucky." The moon was shining so bright, that just struck me, you know, in my mind. And don't you know, as clear as it was, something got over the moon. A dark cloud just overshadowed it, and I could see nowhere. And a voice spoke to me out of that cloud. You know what it said? Called me by name and said, "You quit singing that song. The song for you to sing . . . is "The time is swiftly rolling on, when you must faint and die." And that scared me. That frightened me. I didn't sing no more of that other song. But I'm glad he took it away from me. I ain't got no more charm for them kind of songs.[37]

Elder I. D. Back, a well-known Old Regular Baptist preacher and singer from eastern Kentucky, added this: "[Singing is] just as important as the other for us. We've got a saying: if we have good singing, we're going to have good preaching. . . . You got some folks, maybe, that don't have a voice to sing, you might say, solo at all. But they enjoy the way we sing. They enjoy it so much that the whole congregation will fit right in, you see, and that's one of the advantages we've got for people that maybe they don't sound too good by theirself."[38]

Elder Elwood Cornett, moderator of the Indian Bottom Association of Old Regular Baptists, to which I. D. Back belongs, also commented on the importance of singing and brought up another important point, that people ought to be encouraged to sing whether or not they have a good singing voice:

> I really believe that God wants us to make a joyful noise. . . . I don't think He cares one bit whether we've got a pretty voice or an ugly voice, just so it's singing praises to the Lord. Sometimes I think we pay too much attention to whether or not a person has a pretty voice. . . .
>
> But I maintain that it doesn't matter if this brother over here has a pretty voice. If he wants to sing, let him sing. . . . I think God gets glory out of that, and that's what it's all about. We're not there to put on a show of singing pretty for somebody. That's not what it's about. . . . I think it's pretty hard to say it's an ugly voice if God made the voice. And mind you, I love to hear pretty singing, and I love to hear people with pretty voices sing. I think we get too carried away with those things that feed the natural person as opposed to those things that feed the spiritual person.[39]

Jesse Comer also gave his opinion about democratic singing in church:

> We give everybody a chance to sing that wants to. As you know . . . , some people maybe wouldn't even stop to listen to us, but we would give that person a chance to do what they can for the Lord. We know that we have no great singers in our church altogether. . . . But we give everybody a chance to sing that wants to. . . . We believe in giving everybody the same equal chance to sing, pray, or whatever that's done in church. . . . It doesn't make any difference how well you do it; it's how much effort you put forth that really counts.[40]

Rev. John Sherfey, Jesse Comer's pastor and the main subject of Titon's *Powerhouse for God,* also affirmed the importance of encouraging all those who wish to sing:

Now I believe you ought to keep harmony if possible, but like the brother said here this morning, that somebody because he can't carry a tune just exactly like some others, they wanted to throw him out of the choir, and all like that. And you can't do that. Lots of people can't carry the tune just like maybe I will, but yet you got to let 'em do their parts, you know. So that's the way they sung back in them days: they'd pick up a hymnbook and sing it. Bless the Lord, if somebody was out of tune, he *stayed* out of tune. But they'd sing![41]

Three black members of the Town Mountain Baptist Church, Hazard, Kentucky, talked about the importance of music in their worship, commenting on the fact that they did not have trained musicians but relied on their own natural talents. They also critiqued some contemporary religious music.

Lillian Olinger: We got the beat; it's in our blood. We are different from the downtown churches. I'll tell you the reason why. They have always had access to [trained] musicians, and we haven't had that. My mother could play the organ. Somebody had to give it [the tune] to her. She played by ear. She hadn't seen nobody play the organ. We don't have a trained musician to lead the choir. That could bring a difference. [But] we've got rhythm in us. It flows in our speech, it flows in our poetry, and it flows in our music. Whereas we don't have the right piano stuff, we'll put something in there to make it just right.

D. Y. Olinger: We add just a little extra when we sing a song, like "Praise the Lord," that is not actually written in the song. Hymns are inspirational, I think. They lift you up and make you have joy in your heart. You need to listen to the words and not just the music.

Mable Jones: You do need to listen to the words, especially if they are scriptorial. My favorite hymn is "Amazing Grace."

Lillian Olinger: Now, there are a lot of songs that I don't appreciate. A lot of people will just sing anything. You know, a song is not worthwhile unless it's giving praise to the Lord. I have a lot of trouble with some gospel songs. I can think of a lot I don't like, such as "If you miss me down here and can't find me nowhere, Come on up to heaven, I'll be praying up there." Now if praying time ain't over then, I don't know what could do it! I'll tell you another one they sing that I don't particularly like is "God, Save a

Place for Me." You go to the fourteenth chapter of John, and he says He's already got a place for us. He doesn't have to save a place. Another one they sing is "Lord, Build Me a Cabin in the Corner of Gloryland." We're supposed to have a mansion! I saw some of this new religious music on TV the other night, and they had it fixed up like a disco, with lights flashing!

Mable Jones: That's what I think about some of these gospel singers. They're not scriptorial. They don't know the Scriptures. They're always singing about all they're going to do when they get to heaven. They're not going to do nothing. The Lord's got everything worked out. The Lord's got to be in all of it. If I'm a pulpit singer, why, I have to belong to the Lord, and what I am doing has to be to the glory of the Lord that others might be inspired. That's the point.[42]

Sue Cox Cole, a Pentecostal singer and preacher from eastern Kentucky, thinks it is just as important to listen to good music as it is to read good literature: "It's very important the kind of music we listen to. In fact, the kind of music you listen to—what you feed yourself—that's what you're going to be. If you want good things to come forth, then you've got to feed your mind good things."

Mrs. Cole is a composer of religious music as well as a performer. She tells about her inspiration for writing a particular song:

We were getting ready to make a record album—had all the songs picked out, but one day when I was getting ready to go to have our picture made for the record album . . . , I had prayed that morning and had a good time with the Lord, and while I was pressing our clothes, the Spirit of the Lord came down in the space where I was working and began to give me the words of this song. It said,

> I can see the dawning of a brand new day
> When all my troubles are going to pass away.
> Hold on a little longer, child, don't forget to pray,
> Because I can see the dawning of a brand new day.

The words just kept coming so fast I thought, "I've got to get to the piano." I went right up the stairs to the living room and set down at the piano, and I began to sing the song He gave me, every bit of it, all at one time, and it's blessed my heart because I know that pretty soon the Lord's going to come, and if He doesn't come, I'm going to go by the way of the grave. Either way I go, I know there's going to dawn a brand new day. It's going to be a great time for the children of God![43]

Some people, particularly the younger ones, prefer newer music to the old, whereas many older church members want to hear only the old hymns. Elder Ivan Amburgey, one of my favorite Old Regular Baptist singers, told of getting complaints when he sang newer songs. He gave his opinion:

Well, I love the old songs. They must have been awful good people that has written a lot of those songs. My father sung them and his father and his father before him, from the *Thomas Hymnal* and the *Sweet Songster,* where we get most of our songs from. . . . But even "Amazing Grace," everybody in the world sings that song, it was a new song at one time. So a lot of the brethren and a lot of people will say, "Why don't you sing the old songs and leave the new songs off?" Well, if a new song praises the Lord, it's a good song as far as I'm concerned, and I'll sing it.

Amburgey went on to talk about his life with music and what it has meant in his ministry:

Golly, I think I was born singing. . . . I remember singing when I was a baby, just all the way back. And I loved to sing. . . . Got maybe ten or twelve years old, I got a guitar, started picking on that guitar, and learned to play. When I went to Cleveland I was pretty fair, you know. I'd go into some nightclubs and talk around with some of them, and they'd say "Hey, do you want to sing a song?" First thing you know, I was working in the club. I'd say most of the people, not bragging, but most of the people considered me one of the better singers in Cleveland in the clubs. I could go into any nightclub in Cleveland, whether it be a colored band or what, what type of music, whether it be rock 'n' roll, or what, they'd ask me to get up and sing because they'd recognize me. . . . I met a lot of the old timers: Hank Williams, and Ferlin Huskey . . . , Kenny Rogers before he ever made a hit. . . . Dottie West, she played there in Cleveland in the club, and we played in the same theater.

When I used to sing regular country songs, I'd sing them different. I'd change the tune, or I'd change the tempo on it. . . . One fellow said, "You sound like you got some extra voices down inside, you

hit some notes down inside your neck that you make that way."
When I'm feeling good and got a good voice, I can sing a verse out
and line that song without ever taking any more air in. And that's
helped me. . . .

There's a song called "Little Traveler." . . . That was the first
song to sing when I first started preaching. It was such a beautiful
song. . . . And I was just a young minister. I could go to Detroit, to
a big church up there, anywhere, Columbus, . . . where there's
some huge big Old Regular Baptist churches. I could get up and
sing that song, and sometimes I wouldn't get to preach, because it
would absolutely close the sevice out. People come join the church
after that song. . . .

You just give it everything you got, from the heart. You put your
voice in it, and your action in it, and your heart in it, and everything
else. Some people when they sing, they sing from the mouth. . . . I
try to get it from down below. To me, it sounds better, makes me feel
better to do it that way. I never did have no lessons. I believe I could
have been a great singer, though, if I'd have had lessons, learned to
control my voice. . . .[44]

Kelva Thomas, then a black Berea College student from Ashland, Kentucky, spoke of the importance of music in her life: "Music is just my way
of expressing to God how I really feel. Let Him use me. Some people preach,
some teach, and some play and sing. I feel it is a gift."[45]

These statements show the importance of music in life and in worship.
When Elder Johnny Blackburn led a song, he told how it tied him to his
grandfather and to traditions of the past. This is a powerful hymn in the
Old Baptist churches. It is stark and dolesome, but it is realistic, as are the
people who sing it. The text, by early Virginia Baptist John Leland, has vivid
imagery contrasting the simple act of retiring for the night with the final
sleep:

> The day is past and gone,
> The evening shades appear!
> O! may we all remember well
> The night of death is near.
>
> We lay our garments by,
> Upon our beds to rest;
> So death will soon disrobe us all,
> Of what we now possess.

And when our days are past,
And we from time remove
O! may we in thy bosom rest—
The bosom of thy love.[46]

Many of the Old Baptist churches still line out the hymns in a style that musicologist William Tallmadge traces to the Westminster Assemblies (1643–49), in which lining was seen as a convenient way to lead singing when there were few songbooks and not everyone could read.[47] Freewill and Missionary Baptists, as well as Pentecostal-Holiness worshipers, often sing from shape-note songbooks that grew out of the shape-note singing of early America. This older shape-note singing, using such books as *The Sacred Harp* (four shapes) and *Christian Harmony* (seven shapes), is still common in the Southern Uplands.

The words of chosen hymns of the Uplands are all important. They contain the theology and philosophy of the people. They do not shrink from the ultimate concerns, for death is prominent in the singing of the Old Baptists, as in "The Day Is Past and Gone." Such hymns bother visitors from more reticent and sophisticated churches, but they are a matter of course for those who sing them here. A favorite with United and Old Regular Baptists, who have annual congregational sacramental meetings, associational gatherings, and memorial meetings, is "A Twelvemonth More Has Roll'd Around:

A Twelvemonth more has roll'd around
Since we attended on this ground;
Ten thousand scenes have marked the year,
Since we met last met to worship here.

Full many a friend and many a foe
Have left this weeping world below,
And many a homeless wanderer's tear
Has fallen since we worship'd here.

Relentless death has hurl'd his dart'
And lodged it deep in many a heart;
Both small and great, of every sphere,
Have fall'n since we worship'd here.

Full many a father's lost his son,
And many a mother's daughter's gone;
The orphan's cry and widow's tear
Have mingled since we worship'd here.

> But we are spar'd, to heaven be praise,
> Our God has lengthened out our days;
> We've left our homes with hearts sincere,
> And met once more to worship here.
>
> Come sinners, come, your pard'ning God
> Waits to impart his precious blood;
> Forsake your sins, to Christ draw near,
> And seek him while we worship here.[48]

This hymn, like the previously quoted one, has good images, and it has a clear message that death comes to us all and that we have mileposts, like annual meetings, when we see the toll and are reminded that we must get our spiritual affairs in order.

"Amazing Grace" is probably the best-known hymn in the world. Many secular people appear to like it, perhaps because they are caught up in the title, which may bring a good feeling, or perhaps they are captivated by the fine old tune. In the more traditional and fundamentalist churches, however, it is no doubt sung for its theological content, which presents a Calvinistic message, and it is sung in some of the Old-Time Baptist churches to a different tune from the one most Americans know. (I was in a Methodist church where the hymn was sung, but out of deference to a good sister in attendance, the first verse was omitted because she had averred "that she is no wretch!") This hymn has perhaps more nearly than any other captured fundamental Christian, although particularly Calvinistic, beliefs. It emphasizes the fallen or weak condition of humans in relation to God and the hope for grace to lead us through a hard world with many trials and temptations and eventually to save us throughout eternity.

Several hymns speak of our role as pilgrims, wandering in some confusion, and meeting many troubles in our lives, a test for something more important beyond this world. Such beliefs fit a pioneer period of uncertainty about labors on earth but are less central now in more orderly and reliable communities. This old hymn that came out of the Second Great Awakening says it well:

> I'm just a poor way-faring stranger,
> A traveling through this world of woe;
> There is no sickness, no toil or danger,
> In that bright world to which I go.
>
> I'm going there to see my mother* (1),
> I'm going there no more to roam,

I'm just a-going over Jordon [often pronounced "Jerdon"],
I'm just a-going over home.
* (2) father, (3) Savior[49]

A prominent theme is that of the redeeming blood of Jesus. There are many scriptural references: "And he said unto them, This is my blood of the new testament, which is shed for many" (Mark 14:24); "Likewise also the cup after supper, saying, This cup is the new testament in my blood, which is shed for you" (Luke 22:20); "Take heed therefore unto yourselves, and to all the flock, over which the Holy Ghost hath made you overseers, to feed the church of God, which he hath purchased with his own blood" (Acts 20:28); "Much more then, being now justified by his blood, we shall be saved from wrath through him" (Romans 5:9); "In whom we have redemption through his blood, even the forgiveness of sins" (Colossians 1:14).

Most of these "blood" hymns are no longer sung much in mainline churches but are still popular in Upland rural churches.

What can wash away my sin?
Nothing but the blood of Jesus;
What can make me whole again?
Nothing but the blood of Jesus.

Chorus
O precious is the flow
That makes me white as snow;
No other fount I know,
Nothing but the blood of Jesus.
    (Words and music by Robert Lowry, 1876)

There is a fountain filled with blood,
Drawn from Immanuel's veins;
And sinners plunge beneath that flood
Lose all their guilty stains.
    (Words by William Cowper)

Would you be free from the burden of sin?
There's pow'r in the blood, pow'r in the blood.
Would you o'er evil a victory win?
There's wonderful pow'r in the blood.

Chorus
There is pow'r, pow'r, Wonder-working pow'r

In the blood of the Lamb;
   There is pow'r, pow'r, Wonder-working pow'r,
   In the precious blood of the Lamb.
      (by L. E. Jones, 1899; copyright Hope Pub. Co.)

Many of the hymns speak of heaven as a bright, balmy, wonderful place quite distinct from earth, which offers only a bleak existence in a world of sickness, toil, aging, storms, and other harsh realities of life. Yet the heaven described in hymns often is like favorite worldly places. One writer accused the Reverend Billy Graham of describing heaven as if it were in western North Carolina, where Graham now lives. In hymns heaven is paradise.

O they tell me of a home far beyond the skies,
O they tell me of a home far away;
O they tell me of a home where no storm clouds rise,
O they tell me of an unclouded day.

Chorus
O the land of cloudless day,
O the land of an unclouded sky;
O they tell me of home where no storm clouds rise,
O they tell me of an unclouded day.
    (by Rev. J. K. Alwood)

To Canaan's land I'm on my way,
Where the soul never dies;
My darkest night will turn to day,
Where the soul never dies.

Chorus
Dear friends there'll be no sad farewells,
There'll be no tear-dimmed eyes,
Where all is peace and joy and love,
And the soul of man never dies.
    (by Wm. M. Golden; copyright R. E.
    Winsett, Dayton, Tenn.)

Then let our songs abound, And every tear be dry;
We're marching through Immanuel's ground,
We're marching through Immanuel's ground,
To fairer worlds on high,
To fairer worlds on high.

Chorus
We're marching to Zion, beautiful, beautiful Zion;
We're marching upward to Zion, The beautiful city of God.
　　(Words by Isaac Watts, 1707, from his hymn "Come Ye
　　That Love the Lord"; music by Robert Lowry, 1867)

A related theme is that of heaven as home. Several hymns, especially more recent ones such as bluegrass gospel, may speak of heaven as if it were in the Cumberlands or the Blue Ridge Mountains, and there is often mention of heaven as a place where the family will all be together again, as it was in some remembered happy time.

There are loved ones in the glory,
Whose dear forms we often miss;
When you close your earthly story,
Will you join them in their bliss?

Chorus
Will the circle be unbroken by and by, by and by?
In a better home a-waiting, In the sky, in the sky?
One by one their seats were emptied, one by one they went away,
Now the family is parted, Will it be complete one day?
　　(Words by Ada R. Habershon; music by Charles H.
　　Gabriel; owner Homer A. Rodeheaver)

But of course, most of the hymns express love for the Lord or longing for a peace that comes with acceptance of Him. Singing the songs of Zion is an important part of religious life. People sing freely, while they work, sometimes on the porch or around the fire, to entertain as well as to praise. Traditional singers, old-time bands, and the newer bluegrass groups use religious songs as a part of their repertories. After singing secular love songs for part of their programs, the earlier country and bluegrass musicians would reverently and ceremoniously take off their hats and sing a hymn or two. Professional performers known for their worldly lifestyles were always respectful of religious themes and reverent in presenting hymns.

A tradition in some churches, particularly among the Old Regular Baptists, is for the preacher to sing a favorite hymn at the beginning of his sermon. This is done unaffectedly in the folk tradition, as a presentation of a religious message rather than as a performance. In most of the churches of the mountains, special music—solos, duets, trios, or quartets—are also common. Most of the rural churches do not have choirs as such; rather, anyone who wishes to sing is welcome to do so.

Elder Mike Mullins talked of singing with grace in your heart, with emotion, and singing often through the week so that you can sing on Sunday. Singing to him is not just a part of a service but a part of life—a gift, like grace. Lizzie Combs also talked of the old-time songs that her daddy sang and of the beauty of the human voice—the sacred harp—the best of all instruments, but Brother John Sherfey, Brother Jesse Comer, Elder I. D. Back, and Elder Elwood Cornett spoke of the need for all to sing together, whether or not their voices were pleasant or always in tune. This is perhaps a distasteful notion to people in modern churches with fine choirs, organs, and other instruments. To Cornett, Back, Comer and Sherfey, however, singing pretty is not the point of worshiping in song. Back thinks that singing together is just as important as preaching in that it gives everybody a chance to fit into the service. To Sister Sue Cole, the kind of music you listen to is as important as what you read, in terms of improving your mind and soul. Ivan Amburgey reveres the old songs but thinks that any new song that praises God is a good song.

Along with the unnamed Primitive Baptist who was admonished by God for singing Bill Monroe's bluegrass composition "Blue Moon of Kentucky," Elder Ivan Amburgey and Brother Ernest Martin changed the kind of song they sang after their spiritual lives changed. Amburgey put something extra into his singing, by his account, when he was singing secular songs, and now that he sings only religious music, he puts the same special talent into Old Baptist songs. His expression of pride in his singing is unusual, since Old Regular Baptists are careful to say that their singing is not a performance but rather just a part of their worship. Ernest Martin is also a powerful singer and instrumentalist who uses the skills he learned in secular music to enhance his religious music. Martin also, however, gives full credit to the Holy Spirit for his effectiveness. He said: "I had the burden on me to go do that work. I get up there, and the Spirit just overshadows me. I was annointed." He goes on to tell of an interesting encounter: "A disc jockey told me, said, 'Brother Martin, Why is it that I can get requests for one of these country songs for four or five weeks? It'll go over like hotcakes. I'll have to play it every day, and then it'll quit and I won't get another request for it.' He said, 'You're singing songs here that's a hundred years old, and you're getting requests for them. Why is that?' I said, 'The gospel songs have got life built in, and the worldly songs have got death built in because they have no life connected to them.'"[50]

Singing was important to all those who spoke about it. It is more than an art. It is a unique expression of sentiment and love and reverence for God, a vital part of worship.

Upland Christians are singers, and singing is an important part of worship, both in and out of the church. I believe that those who wish to understand religion in the mountains must listen carefully to the hymns for their layers of meaning and observe and talk with the singers so as to perceive their feelings and sentiments.

A Kentucky black Primitive Baptist preacher said the following after leading a song and before beginning another one by the noted eighteenth-century English composer Isaac Watts:

> Amen, we thank the Lord for another blessing. Dr. Watts, you know, practiced a gift from God. These songs were composed by individuals, with the Spirit of God given to them. As you know, sometimes you get in a place where you are so heavy-loaded, so burdened, that you can't pray, and you ask God to reach you—you want God's Spirit. You think of the toil, and the road is so narrow, and you ask God, "How long do we tarry?" Everybody wants the Spirit of the Lord. Singing helps.
>
> I want you to get your book and sing as you've got a right to sing. Now some of you can't sing. You come along with those who do sing. This song was composed by Dr. Watts. His steps were getting shorter, and he felt like he couldn't wait like he had to wait for the Lord, and he sang this song:

> Come, we that love the Lord
> And let our joys be known;
> Join in a song of sweet accord
> And thus surround the throne.

> The sorrows of the mind
> Be banished from this place
> Religion never was designed
> To make our pleasures less.

> Let those refuse to sing,
> That never knew our God;
> But children of the Heavenly King
> May speak their joys abroad.

> The men of grace have found
> Glory begun below;
> Celestial fruits on heavenly ground
> From hope and faith may grow.

> The hill of Zion yields
> A thousand sacred sweets,
> Before we reach the heavenly fields,
> Or walk on streets of gold.
>
> Then let our songs abound,
> And every tear be dry;
> We're marching through Immanuel's ground
> To fairer worlds on high.[51]

Upland people praise the Lord in prayer, testimony, and song. In some ways their expression is distinctive, but in others they are like Christians elsewhere in the country. In fervency of expression, however, I believe, there are few who stand with them.

7 Some Observations

For this is the covenant that I will make with the
house of Israel after those days, saith the Lord; I will
put my laws into their mind and write them in their
hearts: and I will be to them a God, and they shall
be to me a people:

And they shall not teach every man his neighbor,
and every man his brother, saying, Know the Lord:
for all shall know me, from the least to the greatest.

For I will be merciful to their unrighteousness,
and their sins and their iniquities will I remember
no more.   —Hebrews 8:10–12

Over the past thirty-some years, in gathering material for this book,
I have looked for evidence of positive and enduring values in the
people of the Southern Uplands. Along the way, of course, I have seen many
negative and disturbing things—poverty, violence, degradation, ignorance,
exploitation—partially a legacy of the region's industrial activity, which over
many years has pillaged both people and natural resources in pursuit of
capital gain. I have seen people corrupted or left unprepared and vulnera-
ble by bad politics and poor schools, although I have met many fine leaders, public educators, and teachers. We have had more than our share of ve-
nality in the mountains, both imported and home-grown, and some people
have suffered from it, not only economically, but morally and socially as well.
Many Upland natives have not reacted well to the problems they faced or
to the opportunities that others have taken.

Yet most people have prevailed in spite of their problems, and there are those who have been ennobled by them. Some are poor in cash and property but rich in values and faith, finding a deeper meaning in life than that which was presented to them by circumstance. These are the people I sought and whose words appear in this volume.

I grew up among such people in the mountains of western North Carolina. My grandfather, Francis Marion Morgan, and his brother William were Baptist preachers, but I must also report that my other grandfather, William Jones, was "churched" by the Baptists for an altercation with his son-in-law and was too proud ever to ask for reinstatement, although I doubt that this unpleasant affair affected his basic religious life. My father, George Alec Jones, was a Baptist deacon, and my remaining brother, Garnett Jones, is also a Baptist deacon. My three departed brothers, Troy, Elmer, and Willis, were all faithful to the Baptist church. My sisters, Vertie Mintz, Wilma Ciber, and Nina Cotton, are also devoted Baptists. My mother, Cora Morgan Jones, did better than the Baptist tithe by giving to the church the income from eggs her hens laid on Sundays. We children were brought up in a loving family, although we had very little in the way of cash and the world's goods. Most of our neighbors were poor also, but they were decent and honorable folk, supportive of their families and considerate of others. (I include here one neighbor who made a little moonshine on a kitchen-stove still to get by in the Great Depression. His wife, to keep me away from their secret when I was a boy, gave me a ceramic Noah's Ark that I played with then and still treasure.)

I saw courage, integrity, resiliency, and flinty values among alumni brothers and sisters and later my students at Berea College, an institution that seeks eighty percent of its students from Kentucky and elsewhere in Appalachia, all from relatively low-income families. Some came to Berea from meager economic backgrounds or real hardship to take advantage of Berea's offerings and to go on to do extraordinary work.

I admire the intensity of faith and the simplicity and richness of language in describing it that I found among the people whom I interviewed and observed or whose writing or statements I collected. I am impressed at how well ordinary people have dealt with the complexities of theology and with their ability to use the Scriptures and lore from their culture to find meaning in life.

I have concluded that Calvinism is still strong here in the Uplands. This does not mean that Arminianism is weak. It is just that in the early days, especially in the back country, Calvinist teaching created an outlook that persists. Several scholars have written that the main characteristic of Appalachians is fatalism. Fatalism does not mean that those it inhabits always believe in predestination. They may, however, believe in some kind of fate that influences their lives, as most of us do secretly. This can be attributed as much to economic circumstances and the number of choices available as to Calvinist teaching. Sociologist Helen Lewis has written that many mainstream Americans believe that Appalachians have created a "culture of poverty" and thus that their poverty and outlook are somehow their own fault. She suggests instead a different model, that of parts of the region being used as a colony by exploitive national or international industries. What appears to be fatalism is thus a response to absentee ownership and the limitations of a resource-extraction economy, a feeling of powerlessness.[1] Religion has been both a source of personal strength for those who were colonized and a means of resistance. However, many see this resistance as passive at best and fatalistic at worst.

This lingering Calvinism, along with social and economic circumstances, has influenced other values or characteristics, some of which have been mentioned previously:

Humility and Modesty I have already dealt with humility and modesty in chapter 2. The Apostle Paul's frequent advocacy of the modest mien has certainly taken hold in the Uplands. The normal stance is to downplay one's own talents or qualities and to defer to others. It needs to be emphasized that although this humility is a profound religious stance, it is also part of the manners system, a way to negotiate matters. Mountain people fear more than anything being called "forward," that is, egotistic or pushy, of thinking too highly of themselves and their abilities. Thus every effort is made to downplay one's ability. It is for others to judge. Church workers, teachers, and social workers from outside the region need to know about this value, for otherwise they may take mountain people at their self-deprecating word and thus undervalue them.

Independence The other side of the coin, however, is independence, which bespeaks a strong determination underneath the manners system. One story is of a country Baptist invited by a county-seat Presbyterian to preach in his church. When he got there, the Presbyterian asked, "Will you wear a robe?"

The Baptist, who never used such trappings, asked, "Do I have to wear a robe?"

"Well, no, you don't *have* to wear a robe," answered the city preacher.

"All right then," said the Baptist, "I'll wear one."

Appalachia has often been described as the "Lingering Frontier," with people capable of fending for themselves. Coming out of the religious Reformation, they also were imbued with a strong sense of spiritual independence in terms of discerning the Word and finding out about God on their own, without ecclesiastical hierarchy, clergy, seminaries, and other institutions that previously were thought to be necessary for religious life. It is not accidental that the Old Baptists call their ministers "moderators" rather than another title that might suggest authority over the flock.

Personalism Both Jesus and St. Paul dealt with others in personal ways, and Upland people talk of Jesus as a personal Savior. In relations with one another, they are more personal than abstract, and they are usually careful to be scrupulously egalitarian. As levelers, they resent any hint of condescension. Their religion has taught them to respect the sometimes fragile egos of others.

Familism The letters of St. Paul have had a strong influence on the people of Upland churches. Paul's comparison of the hierarchy of the family to the hierarchy of the church has seemed reasonable to them, although many women do not submit to Paul's scheme of things. The children generally are taught to be respectful of adults and to keep a modest demeanor. Most churches limit the role of women to teaching, church work, singing, and sometimes praying, although others allow or encourage women to take a leadership role or even to preach. Beverly Bush Patterson writes perceptively of the role of women among the patriarchal Primitive Baptists in *The Sound of the Dove*. More liberated outsiders have difficulty with these traditions, but many Baptist women have supported this hierarchy. In fact, however, I know that the women of Appalachia are far more influential in family matters than one might expect from the patriarchal system. They tend also to be more progressive than the men in education and health care, and they usually are the leaders in these matters. I have noted that young women from the traditional churches, after graduating from colleges such as Berea, tend to join more liberal churches in later life as a means of dealing with changing ideas about gender roles. Many, however, speak fondly of the churches of their childhood.

The strong sense of family values includes the extended family of grandparents, aunts, uncles, nephews, nieces, and the many denominations of cousins. However, forces that have wrought havoc with the family nationwide have also taken a toll in the Uplands. One-parent families with children in poverty are common now in Appalachia. In fact, because of family breakups and the lack of jobs, one out of four children lives below the poverty line in parts of the Uplands. Despite divorce and parental abandonment, however, familism as a value is strong, and frequently grandparents or other relatives care for children of broken homes.

Reluctance to Confront Others The sense of independence, the modesty, and the leveling tendency growing out of Calvinism encourage the toleration of the weaknesses of others. They also discourage the judging of others. The teachings of Paul are important: "But why dost thou judge thy brother? or why dost thou set at naught thy brother? for we shall all stand before the judgment seat of Christ. . . . Let us not therefore judge one another any more" (Romans 14:10, 13). Another reason for a lack of confrontation is kinship. People are reluctant publicly to criticize those who are related by blood or marriage. Yet another reason is that many Uplanders have limited skills at talking things out. They know that confrontation might lead to temper and violence. Nonetheless, we must remember the history of trade unions in Appalachia and the involvement of poor people in the 1960s War on Poverty, which show that when the issues are clear and important, mountain people will confront others.

The Calvinistic and Arminian polarities in mountain religion separate folks whose outlook suits each pole, and there are those in between who seek modification of extreme views. The region's social makeup has required many kinds of churches. Not all of us have the same outlook and temperament, and we seek the theology that best suits our personality, our needs, and our longings. But let me try to assess the consequence of religious choice and the efficacy of each of the polarities in helping believers to get along and find meaning in life. There are also some possible problems.

First the Calvinists. Their religion has made them independent but tolerant of others' independence. They usually don't proselytize or question the validity of the faith of others. They have a reputation for being good, moral people, although they may see themselves as corruptible and having many shortcomings. They are always aware of their imperfect condition in contrast to the magnificence of God. This has created a profound sense of humility but also a tolerance of others who fail. They have a degree of fatalism in regard to the human condition, but they are not daily disillusioned.

Their shortcomings may be that they tend to believe it is not possible to improve the basic human condition on earth, and thus they may not always work rigorously to modify the behavior of others and to solve social problems. They may also see church solely as a place of worship and thus reject any organization within the church to deal with social problems. Surely, too, the emphasis on limited atonement and reliance solely on God's grace for salvation leaves some with feelings of powerlessness and anxiety about their condition on earth and their fate in the hereafter.

The benefits of Arminian theology are obvious. Arminians teach that all who heed and repent may be saved. They teach also that saving grace makes a new person of us and that it is possible to rise above fleshly sin. If we can become better persons, then we can also make better institutions and a better world. Arminians believe that they need to work to bring others to salvation and that it is possible to work on social problems within the framework of the church.

On the debit side, Arminianism spawns missionaries who feel called to proselytize. By their very presence in the Uplands, missionaries seem to be saying that we are lacking in important ways, and they have at times convinced us that we are not only inadequate but somehow un-American. Arminians teach that salvation will transform our lives and that we can avoid sin. The failure of such a transformation can breed disillusionment and sometimes a heavy load of guilt. Arminians are perfectionists, and as such they look for things that may be a hindrance to attaining a state of holiness. Thus they are sometimes judgmental. They may preach against traditional ways that are dear to the people, such as singing and playing secular music, dancing, going to festivals, and the like. This may put some people in a serious bind.

Each spread of belief, then, has attracted those whose outlook fits it, and they have found comfort and hope therein. But religion has not done all things for all Upland people. Some have not chosen to become involved in religion, although studies have shown that almost all believe in some concept of God. The different denominations of the Uplands have attracted adherents, and their teachings, with responding commitments, have profoundly affected their members. The teachings of the churches, moreover, have extended far beyond church members. The philosophy and outlook of the whole population has been influenced. The Bible and the Christian faith are the main sources of meaning in life throughout the culture.

But religion is not the sole cause of the way Upland people are or of their economic and social problems. Isolation; subsistence farming; an exploitive economy, whether in mining or in the renter and sharecropping farming systems; and poor schools and government service have molded us also. Yet some writers have put heavy blame on religious fundamentalism for the region's psychological, social, and economic problems.

As conditions change in the Uplands, the churches and the people's relationship to them will also change. This is not to say that the churches will be better or that the people will be better Christians, but there will be change. The previously mentioned study by John Photiadis and B. B. Maurer, "Religion in an Appalachian State," shows us how religious belief may change if the educational, social, and economic lives of the people continue to improve in the mountains or if people continue to migrate to areas that offer better opportunities for economic security. Alas, the study concludes that as people became better educated, more financially secure, and more urban, their degree of religiosity lessens; that is, they began to seek security in things other than religion, such as education, a good job, income, and assets. The authors raise interesting questions in their conclusions:

> From the historical perspective, it has been the experience of organized Christianity that "man's extremity is God's opportunity." These data tend to confirm that observation. The hypothesis that the dispossessed, deprived, and alienated resulting from the upheaval of social and technological change in Appalachia would be those exhibiting the greatest need for the support of religion is substantiated in the data. The aged, poor, less educated, alienated and infirm all rank significantly higher in religiosity than do the socially well-adjusted. . . .
>
> The basic question appears to be: Can the Institutional church develop programs which are capable of meeting the multiple religious needs of people who want, (a) something in life to hold on to and give meaning, (b) to enhance and stabilize their social position and (c) to live a spiritual life in accord with their value orientation—under the same roof,—in the same Denomination? Or should the existing pattern of diversification be accepted, understood, and legitimized as the total ministry to the religious needs of man?[2]

Most of the people quoted in this book were by no means the "dispossessed, deprived, and alienated" people to whom Photiadis and Maurer refer. Yet most of them came from modest economic means, and some were indeed poor. Whatever their economic status, however, they rank high in religiosity. Regardless of their social status in life, they make meaning of it through religion. Assuming that the region will continue to improve but will also continue to trail the country as a whole in education, employment, income, and other social factors, let me try to answer Photiadis and Maurer's questions from the experience of doing this book.

Yes, the institutional church can develop programs to meet the needs of *some* of the people who want to find something to give their lives meaning, to improve and stabilize their social positions, and to live spiritual lives in ways consonant with their values. The mainline churches are there—and should be there—for those whose needs they meet, offering a choice to people who are overcoming poverty, lack of education, and opportunity, but these churches will not meet the needs of all. They do not promote or even condone the intensity of faith that is meaningful and necessary for a lot of people. Administrators and ministers in the mainline denominations should therefore develop and keep a proper humility in terms of their own effectiveness and that of their churches in reaching and serving the needs of all in the Uplands. Such humility will help them immeasurably in their relationship with the so-called sect churches—and they should have a relationship with those churches, but one built on respect for these fellow Christians.

The answer to the second big question posed by Photiadis and Maurer is, yes, the religious diversity of the Southern Uplands should be accepted. Before acceptance, however, we need understanding. The several new books on Appalachian religion show that there is a strong scholarly effort to understand the religious nature of the people. The bibliographic essay at the end of this book will be helpful to those who want better to understand Upland religion.

There have been several attempts by mainline churches, as well as other organizations, to relate in some way to religion in the region, beginning with the Conference of Southern Mountain Workers, which was formed in 1913 (later the Council of the Southern Mountains, now defunct, for which I worked for twelve years) mainly as an organization of mainline denominations and other agencies that were working to alleviate the many religious, social, and economic problems of the region. The Commission on Religion in Appalachia (CORA), founded in 1965 during the heyday of the War on Poverty, is perhaps the best known, continuing today with headquarters in Knoxville, Tennessee. It has energized churches of mainline denominations to look for opportunities to serve in the region and has directed denominational and foundation money to many grassroots organizations that are working on social problems. CORA was also in the forefront in securing money for a land-ownership study that has been important in such issues as fair-rate taxation of land and unmined minerals.

Other groups are the Coalition for Appalachian Ministry (CAM), made up of Reformed churches, which runs workshops and conferences to orient their ministers to Appalachian people and culture; the Appalachian People's Service Organization (APSO), representing some fifteen Episcopal dioceses, which provides funding for studies and for grassroots programs; and the Christian Appalachian Project (CAP), growing out of the Catholic Church's Covington, Kentucky, diocese, which raises a significant amount of money for schools, economic enterprises, housing programs, shelters, and counseling for the neglected and abused and also for grants to other regional organizations.

However, most of the efforts of these organizations and of their member denominations are concerned with the social gospel or, as Deborah McCauley has pointed out, promoting a liberation theology. The people of local sect churches are often seen as oppressed victims of absentee owners and ineffectual or corrupted government. I do not say that some are not, but I do say that well-educated, compassionate people from mainline churches (and other organizations, such as colleges) have trouble in seeing ordinary Upland people as legitimate in their culture and faith in their time and place, regardless of the problems they face. The organizations just mentioned have been far more effective in promoting social and cultural uplift— important to be sure—than they have been in relating in a mutually respectful way to fellow Christians in the nonmainline Upland churches.

A good sign is the Appalachian Ministries Education Resource Center (AMERC) in Berea, Kentucky. This is a consortium of seminaries and Bible schools from throughout the country that accepts seminarians for workshops, field trips, and church visitation to help any who choose to work in Appalachia or other rural areas to understand the people of Appalachia and their economic, social, and religious lives. This is important, for the needs of the rural churches get shorter shrift at the urban-oriented seminaries. AMERC now has the potential to offer workshops to a variety of people within and outside the region. However, AMERC must constantly guard against pressure from the mainline denominations and seminaries to use the consortiom as a how-to-do-successful-missions-in-Appalachia program. It needs to ensure also that it employs teachers because they truly understand Appalachia and its religious life and not just because they represent seminary, denomination, idealogical, or other balance.

Mainline Christians could learn a great deal about faith from members of Upland churches. These churches, despite what some have written, serve the needs of their members very well. Many of the people I have met are as faithful to God and as reliable and honorable as human beings as any Christian I have known. For one thing, they teach that each person must be treated with respect. Mainline Americans sometimes do not respect those who are different from themselves, and when they launch programs to change them, their efforts are wasted and are sometimes harmful. Effective programs, whether religious or secular, require mutual respect between helper and helped. Respect grows out of interaction and real knowledge and understanding, not from stereotype, hearsay, hasty impressions, and cultural bias. Unfortunately, people who are reared and educated to believe that all good people should strive for the high culture that the elite admire are at some disadvantage in understanding expressions that they feel to be uncultured.

I have long felt that schools should try to teach everyone observation and appreciation skills, such as are taught in anthropology or folklore classes. That is, we should all be helped to see that what any group of people do as worship, as art, or as work is meaningful to them and therefore should be of interest to all of us. As the late folklorist Richard Dorson pointed out years ago, one thing lacking in the revered liberal arts canon of colleges and universities is the oral tradition, the major part of human communication. General academic disinterest in the lives of ordinary people, indeed, calls into question just how "liberal" those who embrace the liberal arts really are.

I have been greatly enriched by the experience of interviewing admirable people, gathering information, and doing this book. My hope is that the reader has likewise benefited.

NOTES

Introduction

1. "Letters Written in Fraterville Mine," *Courier-News* (Clinton, Tenn.), n.d. [late May 1902], with thanks to John Ed Pearce, Louisville, Ky.

2. Robert Penn Warren, *All the King's Men* (New York: Harcourt, Brace, 1946), 145.

3. Frank Fugate, interview by Herb E. Smith, Letcher County, Ky., 1972, in Appalachian Film Workshop Archives, Whitesburg, Ky. Used by permission of Appalshop, Inc.

Chapter 1: The Human Condition

An earlier version of portions of this chapter appeared in "Interracial Harmony in Three Eastern Kentucky Churches and Communities," *Appalachian Quarterly* 2, no. 1 (Mar. 1997): 35–41.

1. Audrey Wiley, interview by Gary King, Floyd Co., Ky., summer 1975, in author's possession.

2. Herbert Barker, interview by the author, Point Pleasant, W.Va., 6/21/86.

3. Pansy McCay, interview by Garner Hargis, Mt. Vernon, Ky., 1975, in author's possession.

4. Garfield Sloan, interview by Gary King, Floyd Co., Ky., summer 1975, in author's possession.

5. Buell Kazee, interview by the author, Winchester, Ky., 7/10/74. Most of this interview was published in *Kattalegete* (Fall 1975): 4–10.

6. Ibid.

7. Mike Smith, interview by unidentified Berea College student, Pike Co., Ky., 1975, in author's possession.

8. Frank Fugate interview.

9. John Hinkle, *Autobiography and Experience of Elder John Hinkle* (N.p., n.d.). Photocopy given to the author by Jess D. Wilson.

10. Teddy Ball, recording by unidentified Berea College student, Pike Co., Ky., 1975, in author's possession.

11. Elwood Cornett, interview by Jeff Todd Titon and John Wallhausser, Blackey, Ky., 5/6/90, in Berea College Special Collections; Elwood Cornett, interview by the author, Hazard, Ky., 8/2/89.

12. Herbert Barker interview.

13. Sybil Mallard, interview by J. H. Walker, SAS, series V, box 63, folder 7, 6/7/59. (All SAS citations follow the form "series, box, folder"; hereinafter only numbers will be provided.)

14. Delwayne Maggard, interview by Earle D. C. Brewer, SAS, V, 78, 8, April 1969.

15. Tom Smith, interview by the author, Berea, Ky., 7/31/86.

16. Fred Lunsford, interview by the author, Vengeance Creek, N.C., 6/12/76.

17. Donald Bowdle, interview by the author, Cleveland, Tenn., 8/15/86.

18. Claren Williams, interview by the author, Red Fox, Ky., 8/1/89.

19. Garfield Sloan interview.

20. Pansy McCay interview.

21. Claren Williams interview.

22. Phillip Banks, interview by Garner Hargis, Mt. Vernon, Ky., 1975, in author's possession.

23. Fred Lunsford interview.

24. Lovell Williams, interview by the author, Red Fox, Ky., 8/1/89.

25. Jeffrey Simpson, sermon recorded by the author, Parkway Church of God, Clay City, Ky., 7/26/86.

26. Josephine Martin, interview by Gary King, Floyd Co., Ky., 1975, in author's possession.

27. Herbert Barker interview.

28. Frank Fugate interview.

29. Fred Lunsford interview.

30. Garnett M. Jones, lay sermon, "What Manner of Person Ought You to Be?" Sardis Baptist Church, Indian Trail, N.C., ca. 1980, recording in author's possession.

31. Unnamed woman and Wallace McConnell, sermon recorded by the author, Fifty-Six Baptist Church, Fifty-Six, Ark., 6/13/76.

32. W. J. Berry, "God's Order for Human Society," *Old Faith Contender* 53 (Oct.–Dec. 1975): 175–82.

33. R. H. Pittman, ed., *Biographical History of Primitive or Old School Baptist Ministers of the United States* (Anderson, Ind.: Herald, 1909), 323.

34. Lillian Olinger, interview by the author, Hazard, Ky., 7/12/95.

35. Mable Jones, interview by the author, Hazard, Ky. 7/12/95.

36. Ruby Dotson, interview by William Ashdown, SAS, V, 76, 5, 6/25/59.

37. Anna Mae Cook, telephone interview by the author, McRoberts, Ky., 8/29/95.

38. Willie Lamb, telephone interview by the author, McRoberts, Ky., 8/28/95.

39. Lois Thompson, interview by the author, McRoberts, Ky., 8/5/95.

40. Mable Jones interview; Lillian Olinger interview; Pansy McCay interview; Phillip Banks interview.

41. Howard Dorgan, "The Art of Deference and the Science of Humility," paper presented at the Appalachian Studies Conference, 1990, 5.

42. Arthel "Doc" Watson quoted in Jock Lauterer, *Runnin' on Rims: Appalachian Profiles* (Chapel Hill, N.C.: Algonquin, 1986), 101–2. Used by permission of Algonquin Books.

43. See Carl Henry Smith, "The Lined Hymn Tradition in Selected Black Churches of Eastern Kentucky," Ph.D. diss., University of Pittsburgh, 1988; Howard Dorgan, "The Little Home Church and the Question of Racial Harmony within Old Regularism," paper presented at the Appalachian Studies Conference, 1989. See also Howard Dorgan, *The Old Regular Baptists of Central Appalachia: Brothers and Sisters in Hope* (Knoxville: University of Tennessee Press, 1989), 189–94. For a discussion of black-white relations among Old Regular Baptists and a description of a service at the Little Home Church, see Rufus Perrigan, *History of Regular Baptist and Their Ancestors and Accessors* (Haysi, Va.: by the author, 1961).

44. Claren Williams interview.

45. Lovell Williams interview.

46. Elizabeth Ashley, interview by the author, Red Fox, Ky., 8/1/89.

47. Jesse Hagans, interview by the author, Red Fox, Ky., 8/1/89.

48. Vance Blair, interview by the author, Red Fox, Ky., 8/2/89.

49. Alonzo Watts, interview by the author, Carr Creek, Ky., 8/2/89.

50. Ron Short, "We Believed in the Family and the Old Regular Baptist Church," *Southern Exposure* 4, no. 3 (1976): 60–65.

51. Dorgan, "Little Home Church," 10–11.

52. D. Y. Olinger, interview by the author, Hazard, Ky., 7/12/95; Lillian Olinger interview; Mable Jones interview; Rev. John Pray, telephone interview by the author, Hazard, Ky., 8/11/95; Bill Morton, telephone interview by the author, Hazard, Ky., 8/10/95.

53. D. Y. Olinger interview; Lillian Olinger interview; Mable Jones interview.

54. Bill Morton telephone interview.

55. David Olinger, telephone interview by the author, Berea, Ky., 8/16/95.

56. Roy Moore, telephone interview by the author, Lexington, Ky., 12/18/95.

57. John Pray telephone interview.

58. Willie Lamb, interview by the author, McRoberts, Ky., 8/5/95.

59. Anna Mae Cook telephone interview.

60. William Turner, telephone interview by the author, Winston-Salem, N.C., 11/2/95. See also William Turner and Edward Cabbell, *Blacks in Appalachia* (Lexington: University Press of Kentucky, 1985).

61. From *Evelyn Williams,* video recording by Ann Lewis, Appalachian Film Workshop, Whitesburg, Ky., 1997. Used by permission of Appalshop, Inc.

62. James K. Crissman, *Death and Dying in Central Appalachia: Changing Attitudes and Practices* (Urbana: University of Illinois Press, 1994), 1, 7.

63. John Ferry Moore, *Happiness Is from the Blind Side* (Toccoa, Ga.: Commercial

Printing, 1973), 42–44. I am grateful to Rev. Fred Lunsford, Vengeance Creek, N.C., a friend of Mr. Moore, for giving me this book.

64. Charlie Cole, interview by Garland Hendricks, SAS, V, 74, 15, 5/27/59.

Chapter 2: God

1. Moore, *Happiness,* 111–12.

2. Frank Fugate interview.

3. T. G. Bates, tape recording, ca. 1973, sent to the author by Minnie Bates Yancey, Mr. Bates's daughter.

4. Henry T. Mahan, "The Throne of Grace," sermon, Thirteenth Street Baptist Church, Ashland, Ky., n.d., recording in author's possession.

5. Steve Casteel, interview by the author, Berea, Ky., 7/31/81.

6. Debbie Isaacs, interview by Joyce Ann Hancock, 4/7/79, Appalachian Museum Collection, AM-M-41A, in Berea College Special Collections.

7. Virgil Combs, sermon recorded by the author, Cedar Grove Old Regular Baptist Church, Letcher Co., Ky., 10/23/93.

8. Frank Fugate interview.

9. John Sparks, interview by the author, Offutt, Ky., 3/23/93.

10. Johnny Blackburn, sermon recorded by an unidentified Berea College student, Pike County, Ky., 1975, in author's possession.

11. Unidentified Pentecostal minister, sermon recorded by Garner Hargis, Green River Pentecostal Church, Lincoln, Co., Ky., 1975, in author's possession.

12. Squire Watts, sermon recorded by the author, Cedar Grove Old Regular Baptist Church, Letcher Co., Ky., 10/23/93.

13. Coy Miser, interview by Deborah V. McCauley, Cranks Creek, Ky., 10/16/89, quoted in Deborah V. McCauley, *Appalachian Mountain Religion: A History* (Urbana: University of Illinois Press, 1995), 335–36.

14. D. Douglas Jessee, "Unlikely Choices," sermon, Church of Christ, Union, Berea, Ky., 6/29/97, notes in author's possession. Mr. Jessee is a native of Tazewell, Va.

15. Lizzie Combs, interview by Herb E. Smith, Letcher Co., Ky., summer 1972, Appalachian Film Workshop Archives, Whitesburg, Ky. Used by permission of Appalshop, Inc.

16. Edgar Miller, interview by Meredith Henderson, SAS, V, 73, 8, 6/23/59.

17. Millard Scott, interview by John Flint, SAS, V, 67, 2, 7/26/59.

18. Ibid.

19. Claren Williams, "Circular Letter," *Minutes of the Old Indian Bottom Association of Old Regular Baptists of Jesus Christ,* Ninety-fifth Annual Session, Aug. 31–Sep. 2, 1990, pp. 16–17.

20. Teddy Ball recording.

21. Banner Manns, interview by Joey Elswick, Hueysville, Ky., 7/21/75, in the Oral History Archives, Alice Lloyd College, Pippa Passes, Ky. Used by permission of Alice Lloyd College.

22. Unidentified Pentecostal minister, sermon recorded by Garner Hargis, Lincoln County, Ky., 1975, in author's possession.

23. Unidentified individual (Methodist), interview by Thor Hall, SAS, V, 69, 1, 1959.

24. Rev. L. O. Johnson, interview by Meredith Henderson, SAS, V, 73, 8, 6/29/59.

25. G. A. Perry, interview by Meredith Henderson, SAS, V, 73, 8, 6/28/59.

26. Bishop Pentz, interview by E. Benjamin Sanders, SAS, V, 77, 7, 7/16/59.

27. Dianne Harrison, radio broadcast recorded by the author, WSKV-FM, Stanton, Ky., 8/16/92.

28. Elwood Cornett, sermon recorded by the author, Cedar Grove Old Regular Baptist Church, Letcher Co., Ky., 8/23/92.

29. John Sparks interview.

30. N. T. Hopkins, "Circular Letter of 1922," *Minutes of the Hundred and Fifty-Fourth Annual Session of New Salem Association of Old Regular Baptists of Jesus Christ,* September 21–23, 1979, Minnie, Ky., 15–22.

31. Grace Jimson, interview by Neal McGlamery, SAS, V, 70, 9, 6/24/59.

32. Brother Turner, sermon recorded by Garner Hargis, 1975, in author's possession.

33. Calvin C. Wyatt, interview by Meredith Henderson, SAS, V, 73, 7, 6/7/59.

34. T. G. Bates recording.

35. Edward Hicks, interview by Earl D. C. Brewer, SAS, V, 78, 7, 6/7/59.

36. C. A. Williams, interview by John Flint, SAS, V, 67, 7, 7/26/59 .

37. John Sparks interview.

38. Bonnie Garrett, interview, location and date unknown, in author's possession.

39. Victor Williams, interview by John Flint, SAS, V, 71, 5, June 1959.

40. Rev. Charles W. Davis, interview by Meredith Henderson and Garland Hendricks, SAS, V, 71, 5, 6/11/59.

41. Will Igon, interview by J. H. Walker, SAS, V, 63, 8, 6/17/59.

42. Mrs. Charles Davis, interview by John Flint, SAS, V, 66, 5, 1959.

43. Rev. Bailey Sadler, sermon recorded by Ralph Lamar, SAS, V, 66, 2, 1959.

44. Unidentified Berea students, interview by Bill Richards, 1974, Berea, Ky., in author's possession.

45. Members of an American Baptist church in Preston County, West Virginia, group interview by Earl D. C. Brewer, SAS, V, 79, 16, 6/21/59.

46. Henry T. Mahan sermon, "The Throne of Grace."

Chapter 3: The World and the Devil

1. Squire Watts, sermon recorded by the author, Cedar Grove Old Regular Baptist Church, Letcher Co., Ky., 8/23/94.

2. Unidentified preacher, radio sermon recorded by the author, summer 1986.

3. Ozell Bunch, radio sermon recorded by the author, unidentified radio station, 1975.

4. Unidentified individuals, testimony recorded by Garner Hargis, Lincoln Co., Ky., 1975, in author's possession.

5. Wayne Gillespie, radio sermon recorded by the author, unidentified West Virginia radio station, summer 1992.

6. Unidentified person, testimony recorded by Garner Hargis, Green River Pentecostal Church, Lincoln Co., Ky., 1975, in author's possession.

7. Sue Cox Cole, sermon recorded by Stephen Burgess, Berea, Ky., 1/23/87, in author's possession.

8. Buell Kazee interview.

9. Mable Jones interview; D. Y. Olinger interview; Lillian Olinger interview.

10. Squire Watts, interview by the author, Red Fox, Ky., 7/11/86.

11. Phillip Banks, interview by Garner Hargis, Rockcastle County, Ky., 1975, in author's possession.

12. Moore, *Happiness*, 26.

13. Ibid., 54–55.

14. Elaine J. Lawless, *God's Peculiar People: Women's Voices and Folk Tradition in a Pentecostal Church* (Lexington: University Press of Kentucky, 1988), 14.

15. Sue Cox Cole sermon.

16. John Leo, "On Society: Let the Selling Begin," *U.S. News and World Report*, July 29, 1996, p. 18. See also Robert J. Higgs, *God in the Stadium: Sports and Religion in America* (Lexington: University Press of Kentucky, 1995).

17. Buell Kazee interview.

18. Sue Cox Cole sermon.

19. Elwood Cornett, interview by the author, Hazard, Ky., 8/2/89.

20. Frank Fugate interview.

21. Herman B. Yates, "The Elect of God," sermon, Grace Baptist Church, Dingess, W.Va., n.d., recording in author's possession.

22. Harry Yeager and Lloyd Wiles, SAS, V, 79, 16, 7/21/59.

23. Mrs. John Thomas, interview by N. Woodward Finley, SAS, V, 79, 6, 6/29/59.

24. Mike Smith, interview by an unidentified Berea College student, Coon Creek Primitive Baptist Church, Pike Co., Ky., 1975, in author's possession.

25. Mrs. J. A. Ledbetter, interview by Allen Jackson and Raoul Anderson, SAS, V, 78, 9, 6/6/59.

26. Earl Tanner, interview by N. Woodward Finley, SAS, V, 79, 6, 7/8/59.

27. Mrs. Bill Hamlin, interview by J. H. Walker, SAS, V, 63, 8, 6/7/59.

28. Mary O'Dell, interview by N. Woodward Finley, SAS, V, 79, 5, 7/8/59.

29. Elder Fon Bowling, "Circular Letter," *Minutes of the Union Association of Old Regular Baptists of Jesus Christ, One Hundred Sixteenth Annual Session with the Little Hope Church, Clintwood, Virginia,* September 19–21, 1975, pp. 12–13.

30. Elder Clifton Hampton, "Circular Letter of 1985," *Minutes of the Ninetieth Annual Session of the Indian Bottom Association of Old Regular Baptist Chruches of Jesus Christ,* Sassafras, Ky., September 6–8, 1985, p. 13.

31. Paul Jacobs, "Circular Letter," *Minutes of the Thornton Union Association of Old Regular Baptists of Jesus Christ, Thirty-fifth Annual Session,* Mayking, Ky., August 15–17, 1980, p. 8.

32. Darrell Mullins, radio sermon recorded by the author, WSKV-FM, Stanton, Ky., 1993.

33. Darell Elam, radio sermon recorded by the author, WSKV-FM, Stanton, Ky., 7/11/93.

34. Pearl Spence, interview by N. Woodward Finley, SAS, V, 79, 7 6/15/59.

35. Vernon Harrison, radio sermon recorded by the author, WSKV-FM, 8/16/92. Mr. Harrison is pastor of the Church on the Rock in Clay City, Ky.

36. Harold Kelly, radio sermon recorded by the author, WSKV-FM, Stanton, Ky., 4/17/93. Mr. Kelly is pastor of the West Bend Church of God near Clay City, Ky.

37. Author version from memory.

38. Wilse Reynolds, interview by the author and Gary English, Stone Coal Creek, Whitley Co., Ky., 8/30/72, in author's possession.

39. David L. Kimbrough, *Taking up Serpents: Snake Handlers of Eastern Kentucky* (Chapel Hill: University of North Carolina Press, 1995), 162–63.

40. Lawless, *God's Peculiar People,* 14–15.

41. Ethel Owens, "Witchcraft in the Cumberlands," *Kentucky Folklore Record* 4, no. 4 (Oct.–Dec. 1959): 127–29.

42. Donald Wallace, "Beliefs and Belief Tales from McCreary County," *Kentucky Folklore Record* 3, no. 4 (Oct.–Dec. 1957): 133–37.

43. William Lynwood Montell, *Ghosts along the Cumberland: Deathlore in the Kentucky Foothills* (Knoxville: University of Tennessee Press, 1975), 90, 93–94. Used by permission of the publisher.

44. See W. K. McNeil, *Ghost Stories from the American South,* and Montell, *Ghosts along the Cumberland,* in the bibliographic essay.

Chapter 4: The Word

1. Sylvester Hassell, "The Full and Divine Inspiration of the Old and New Testament Scriptures," *Biographical History of Primitive or Old School Baptist Ministers of the United States* (Anderson, Ind.: Herald, 1909), 344, 346.

2. Darrell Mullins, radio sermon recorded by the author, WSKV-FM, Stanton, Ky., 1993.

3. Rev. Henkle Little, interview by Layna Cheeseman, Taylorsville, N.C., 1975, in author's possession.

4. Harold Kelly radio sermon.

5. Herbert Barker interview.

6. James Tanner, interview by N. Woodward Finley, SAS, V, 79, 5, 7/8/59.

7. Hassel Mullins, interview by William Ashdown, SAS, V, 76, 6, 7/7/59.

8. Ozell Bunch, radio sermon recorded by the author, unidentified radio station, summer 1980.

9. Unidentified individual (Church of the Brethren), interview by William Ashdown, Dickenson County, Va., SAS, V, 76, 6, 7/5/59.

10. Rev. Dennis M. Moore, interview by Meredith Henderson, SAS, V, 73, 8, 6/22/59.

11. Unidentified man, testimony recorded by Garner Hargis, Green River Pentecostal Church, Lincoln County, Ky., 1975, in author's possession.

12. Rev. Marvin Kincheloe, interview by Garland Hendricks, SAS, V, 71, 6, 6/5/59.

13. Danny Dixon, sermon recorded by the author, Cedar Grove Old Regular Baptist Church, Letcher County, Ky., 8/23/92.

14. Mary O'Dell interview.

15. Dianne Harrison radio braodcast.

16. Sara Snow, interview by Garland Hendricks, SAS, V, 71, 6, 6/14/59.

17. Henkle Little interview.

18. John Lakin Brasher on a recording accompanying J. Lawrence Brasher, *The Sanctified South: John Lakin Brasher and the Holiness Movement* (Urbana: University of Illinois Press, 1994).

19. Ibid.

20. Ibid.

21. Luther Gibson, *History of the Church of God Mountain Assembly, 1906–1970* (Jellico, Tenn.: Church of God Mountain Assembly, 1954), 6.

22. Hinkle, *Autobiography and Experience,* 3–4, 54.

23. Ivan Amburgey, interview by the author, Pine Top, Ky., 7/10/86; Ivan Amburgey, interview by Jeff Todd Titon, Pine Top, Ky., 5/1/90.

24. Squire Watts interview.

25. Milford Hall Sr., *Two Worlds* (New York: Hobson, 1946), 37–39.

26. Richard Floyd, interview by Garland Hendricks and Meredith Henderson, SAS, V, 71, 5, 6/11/59.

27. Elwood Cornett, interview by Joyce Ann Hancock, 11/29/79, Appalachian Museum Collection, AM-M-79-98, Berea College Special Collections.

28. Unidentified man, testimony recorded by Garner Hargis, Green River Pentecostal Church, Lincoln County, Ky., 1975, in author's possession.

29. J. H. Bryant, "The Building of God," in Gibson, *Church of God Mountain Assembly,* 51–52.

30. John Sparks interview.

31. Ivan Amburgey interview, 7/10/86.

32. Erasmus W. Jones, "The Welsh in America," *Atlantic Monthly,* Mar. 1876, pp. 305–13.

33. Henry T. Mahan, "Lessons Learned in Trouble," sermon, Thirteenth Street Baptist Church, Ashland, Ky., n.d., recording in author's possession.

34. Henry T. Mahan, "Believing in His Name," sermon, Thirteenth Street Baptist Church, Ashland, Ky., n.d, recording in author's possession.

35. Mike Mullins, sermon recorded by the author, Berea Primitive Baptist Church, Wildie, Ky., 8/17/86.

36. Ivan Amburgey interview, 5/1/90.

37. Claren Williams interview.

38. Lovell Williams interview.

39. Unidentified preacher, sermon recorded by unidentified Berea College student, Coon Creek Primitive Baptist Church, Pike Co., Ky., 1975, in author's possession.

40. Chester Gibson, sermon recorded by the author, Cedar Grove Old Regular Baptist Church, Letcher County, Ky., 10/23/93.

41. Danny Dixon, correspondence with the author, 10/23/95.

42. Danny Dixon sermon.

43. Mike Smith interview.

44. J. Lawrence Brasher, *The Sanctified South,* 87.

45. Hassell Mullins, interview by William Ashdown, SAS, V, 76, 6, 6/7/59.

46. Unidentified individual (Church of the Brethren) interview.

47. Lovell Williams interview.

48. Elwood Cornett interview, 11/29/79.

49. Almeda Riddle, interview by the author, Heber Springs, Ark., 6/14/76.

50. Steve Casteel interview.

51. Donald Bowdle interview.

52. John Photiadis and B. B. Maurer, "Religion in an Appalachian State," in *Religion in Appalachia: Theological, Social, and Psychological Dimensions and Correlates*, ed. John Photiadis (Morgantown: Center for Extension and Continuing Education, West Virginia University, 1978), 171–228.

53. Herbert Barker interview.

54. Harold Kelley radio sermon.

Chapter 5: Salvation

1. Photiadis and Maurer, "Religion in an Appalachian State," *Religion in Appalachia*, 171–228.

2. Henkle Little interview.

3. Herbert Barker interview.

4. Lydia Johnson, interview by John Flint, SAS, V, 67, 7, 7/26/59.

5. Mrs. James Neal, interview by Garland Hendricks, SAS, V, 74, 15, 5/27/59.

6. Ralph Snead, interview by G. Milton Bettini, SAS, V, 74, 13, 5/27/59.

7. Charlie Cole interview.

8. Gene Wells, interview by Meredith Henderson, SAS, V, 72, 7, 6/19/59.

9. C. A. Williams interview.

10. Alfred Carrier, interview by Garner Hargis, McKinney, Ky., 1975, in author's possession.

11. Frank Fugate interview.

12. Garfield Sloan interview.

13. Vernon Harrison, radio sermon recorded by the author, WSKV-FM, Stanton, Ky. 8/8/93.

14. Wetzel Ball, "Circular Letter," *Minutes of the 66th Annual Session of the Mud River Association of Regular Baptists of Jesus Christ,* Little Laurel Church, Myra, W.Va., August 21–23, 1953.

15. Unidentified individual, interview by J. H. Walker, SAS, V, 63, 7, 6/7/59.

16. Lenora Neal, interview by Meredith Henderson, SAS, V, 73–7, 6/28/59.

17. Hapner Mullins, circular letter quoted by Elder W. T. Swindall in a recorded sermon given to William Ashdown, an interviewer for the Southern Appalachian Studies, SAS, V, 76, 3, 1959.

18. Phillip Banks interview.

19. Mike Smith interview.

20. Rev. Harold Pritt, interview by Earl D. C. Brewer, SAS, V, 78, 8, April 1959.

21. Deborah V. McCauley, "Grace and the Heart of Appalachian Mountain Religion," in *Appalachia: Social Context Past and Present*, 3d ed., ed. Bruce Ergood and Bruce E. Kuhre (Dubuque, Iowa: Kendall/Hunt, 1991), 357.

22. Herman B. Yates, "A Thief's Eye View," sermon, Grace Baptist Church, Dingess, W.Va., n.d., recording in author's possession.

23. Hall, *Two Worlds,* 2–27.

24. Vernon Harrison, radio sermon, 8/8/93.

25. Harold Pritt interview.

26. Harold Pritt, telephone interview by the author, 5/9/94.

27. Herman B. Yates sermon, "A Thief's Eye View."

28. Robert Suder, associate professor of philosophy and religion, Berea College, personal communication, 12/21/95.

29. Mrs. Albert Sears, interview by N. Woodward Finley, SAS, V, 79, 7, 6/15/59.

30. C. J. Queen, interview by John Flint, SAS, V, 66, 8, 1959.

31. Rev. Raymond Wallace, interview by Meredith Henderson, SAS, V, 73, 7, 6/25/59.

32. Rev. Charles Davis interview.

33. Unidentified individual (Church of the Brethren) interview.

34. Donna Ramsey and Fannie Mink, interview by the author, Kathie Kiser, and Stan Kiser, Ansted, W.Va., 7/10/76.

35. Unidentified individual (Presbyterian), interview by Lois Philippi, SAS, V, 80, 2, 6/21/59.

36. Ingerna Indy, Myrtle Armstrong, and Irma Judy, interview by Lois Philippi, SAS, V, 80, 9, 7/14/59.

37. Tom Smith interview.

38. Howard Pyle, "A Peculiar People," *Harper's New Monthly Magazine,* August 1889, p. 777.

39. Mrs. Burl Cooper and Raymond Wallace, interview by Meredith Henderson, SAS, V, 73, 7, 6/25/59.

40. Ibid.

41. Johnny Blackburn sermon.

42. Unidentified individual, interview by Ben Steele, SAS, V, 65, 6, 1959.

43. Lial Osborne, interview by John Flint, SAS, V, 66, 8, 1959.

44. Lucille Lawson, interview by Meredith Henderson, SAS, V, 72, 7, 6/19/59.

45. Rev. Charles W. Davis, interview by Meredith Henderson, SAS, V, 72, 6, 6/9/59.

46. Herman B. Yates, "Sin after Redemption," sermon, Grace Baptist Church, Dingess, W.Va., n.d., recording in author's possession.

47. Bert Stamper, interview by Garland Hendricks, SAS, V, 74, 15, 5/27/59.

48. Piper Cox, interview by David Graybeal, SAS, V, 76, 7, 7/9/59.

49. Rev. James Miller, interview by Garland Hendricks, SAS, V, 74, 15, 5/27/59.

50. Sybil Mallard and Katherine Smith, interview by J. H. Walker, SAS, V, 63, 7, 1959.

51. Ibid.

52. Bonnie Garrett and Jameson Garrett, interview, SAS, V, 65, 8, 4/7/59.

53. Buster Roberts, interview, Glenmary Religious Survey, box 4, tape III, no. 5107, Berea College Special Collections.

54. Rev. Raymond Wallace and Rev. L. O. Johnson, interview by Meredith Henderson, SAS, V, 73, 7, 5/25/59.

55. Ibid.

56. Donald Bowdle interview.

57. Rev. Donald D. Damerow, interview by Meredith Henderson and Garland Hendricks, SAS, V, 71, 7, 6/14/59.

58. Tom Smith interview.

59. Herbert Barker interview.

60. Warren Wright, *The Law of Redemptive Love* (author, n.d. [ca. 1990]), 111–12.

61. Howard Dorgan, "The 'No Heller' Baptists of Central Appalachia: Primitives Adapt to Universalism," *Journal of the Appalachian Studies Association: Appalachian Adaptations to a Changing World* 6 (1994): 81–88.

62. Adda Leah Davis, *Here I Am Again, Lord: Landon Colley, an Old Time Primitive Baptist Universalist Preacher* (Johnson City, Tenn.: Sabre, 1997), 62–63.

63. Darrell Mullins, radio sermon recorded by the author, WSKV-FM, Stanton, Ky., ca. 1993.

64. Susanna Jacobs Combs, interview by Joyce Ann Hancock, 4/23/80, Appalachian Museum Collection, AM-M-80-117B, Berea College Special Collections.

65. Squire Watts interview.

66. Anna Mae Cook telephone interview.

67. Rev. John Pritt and Emily Phillips, interview by Earl D. C. Brewer, SAS, V, 78, 8, April 1959.

68. Ibid.

69. Steve Casteel interview.

70. Henry T. Mahan, "The Resurrection of the Dead," sermon, Thirteenth Street Baptist Church, Ashland, Ky., n.d., recording in author's possession.

71. Woodrow Runyan, interview by A. Ruschman, SAS, V, 80, 2, 6/21/59.

Chapter 6: Praise in Zion

1. Rev. Dennie M. Moore, interview by Meredith Henderson, SAS, V, 73, 8, 6/22/59.

2. Herman B. Yates, "The Throne of Grace," sermon, Grace Baptist Church, Dingess, W.Va., n.d., recording in author's possession.

3. Fannie Hunter, interview by Neal McGlamery, SAS, V, 70, 8, 6/29/59.

4. Walter McAlister, interview by E. Benjamin Sanders, SAS, V, 77, 8, 7/20/59.

5. Rev. Marvin A. Kincheloe, interview by Garland Hendricks and Meredith Henderson, SAS, V, 77, 8, 6/14/59.

6. Johnny Blackburn sermon.

7. Mrs. John Coles, interview by James P. Veatch Jr., SAS, V, 75, 7, 6/12/59.

8. Bishop Pentz interview.

9. Unidentified preacher, radio sermon recorded by author while driving through the Piedmont section of North Carolina, unidentified station, summer 1986.

10. Teddy Ball recording.

11. McKinzie Ison, testimony recorded by the author, Cedar Grove Old Regular Baptist Church, Letcher Co., Ky., 8/23/92.

12. Vernon Harrison, radio sermon, 8/8/93.

13. Alfred Carrier interview.

14. Quoted in J. Lawrence Brasher, *The Sanctified South*, 96.

15. William Addington, interview by Mike Yarrow, Beckley, W.Va., 10/8/86, in author's possession.

16. Mary Ann Hinsdale, Helen H. Lewis, and S. Maxine Waller, *It Comes from the People: Community Development and Local Theology* (Philadelphia: Temple University Press, 1995), 181.

17. Sue Cox Cole sermon.

18. Katharine Smith and Sybil Mallard interview.

19. Patricia Pritt, interview by Earl D. C. Brewer, SAS, V, 79, 5, 7/8/59.

20. Earl Tanner interview.

21. Phillip Banks interview.

22. Dianne Harrison, radio broadcast recorded by the author, WSKV-FM, Stanton, Ky., 8/8/93.

23. Unidentified evangelist, radio sermon recorded by the author, WYWY-AM, Barbourville, Ky., summer 1986. If anyone can identify this preacher, the author would like to hear from you.

24. Cecil Sharp and Maude Karpeles, *English Folk Songs from the Southern Appalachians,* 2 vols. (London: Oxford University Press, 1932; repr., 1952, 1960).

25. Ermil Ison, in *The Good Old Fashioned Way,* film, Appalachian Film Workshop, Whitesburg, Ky. 1973.

26. Rev. Walter McNeal, interview by Ben Steele, SAS, V, 65, 2, 4/19/59.

27. Mrs. John Cole interview.

28. Mike Mullins sermon.

29. Ernest Martin, radio broadcast recorded by the author, WSKV-FM, Stanton, Ky., 7/11/93.

30. Ernest Martin, interview by the author, Winchester, Ky., 7/1/95.

31. J. Wayne Flynt, *Dixie's Forgotten People* (Bloomington: Indiana University Press, 1980), 28–29.

32. Jo Lee Fleming, "James D. Vaughan, Music Publisher, Lawrenceburg, Tennessee, 1912–1972," S.M.D. diss., Union Theological Seminary, New York, 1972, pp. 2, 29, 47.

33. Bill C. Malone, *Country Music, U.S.A.* (Austin: University of Texas Press, 1968; rev. ed., 1985), 11–13.

34. Johnny Blackburn interview.

35. Lizzie Combs interview.

36. Jesse Comer, interview by Jeff Todd Titon, Stanley, Va., 7/23/77, quoted in Jeff Todd Titon, *Powerhouse for God: Speech, Chant, and Song in an Appalachian Baptist Church* (Austin: University of Texas Press, 1988), 254.

37. Brett Sutton and Pete Hartman, *Primitive Baptist Hymns of the Blue Ridge,* sound recording (Chapel Hill: University of North Carolina Press, 1982), 6–7 of liner notes.

38. I. D. Back, interview by Jeff Todd Titon and John Wallhaussser, Blackey, Ky., 5/6/90, in author's possession.

39. Elwood Cornett, interview by Jeff Todd Titon and John Wallhausser, Blackey, Ky., 4/1/90, in Berea College Special Collections.

40. Jesse Comer interview and Titon, *Powerhouse for God,* 255.

41. John Sherfey, interview by Jeff Todd Titon, Stanley, Va., 7/17/77, quoted in Titon, *Powerhouse for God,* 255–56.

42. Lillian Olinger interview; D. Y. Olinger interview; Mable Jones interview.

43. Sue Cox Cole sermon.

44. Ivan Amburgey interview, 5/1/90.

45. Kelva Thomas, interview by Bill Richards, Berea, Ky., 1974, in author's possession.

46. *Sweet Songster: A Collection of the Most Popular and Approved Songs, Hymns, and Ballads,* compiled by E. W. Billups (Wayne, W.Va.: Arrowood Brothers; first published, Ohio, 1854), 273.

47. See William Tallmadge, "Baptist Monophonic and Heterophonic Hymnody in Southern Appalachia," *Yearbook of Inter-American Musical Research* 2 (1952): 106–36. Lining is a method in which the song leader chants out line that is then sung by the congregation. He then gives the next line to be sung and so proceeds through the hymn.

48. *Sweet Songster,* 7.

49. *Hymns of the Living Church* (Carol Stream, Ill.: Hope, 1982), 540.

50. Ernest Martin radio broadcast.

51. Unidentified preacher, sermon recorded by John Fetterman, Sweet Loaf Primitive Baptist Church, Louisville, Ky., ca. 1971, in author's possession.

Chapter 7: Some Observations

1. Helen Lewis, "Fatalism or the Coal Industry?" *Appalachia: Social Context Past and Present* (Dubuque, Iowa: Kendall/Hunt, 1991), 221–29.

2. Photiadis and Maurer, "Religion in an Appalachian State," 221, 223.

INTERVIEWS
AND RECORDINGS

Interviews

Note: All interviews and recordings in the author's possession will be deposited in Special Collections, Hutchins Library, Berea College.

Addington, William, by Mike Yarrow, Beckley, W.Va., 10/8/86, in author's possession.

Amburgey, Ivan, by the author, Pine Top, Ky., 7/10/86; by Jeff Todd Titon, Pine Top, Ky., 5/1/90, in author's possession.

Ashley, Elizabeth, by the author, Red Fox, Ky., 8/1/89.

Back, I. D., by Jeff Todd Titon and John Wallhausser, Blackey, Ky., 5/6/90, in Berea College Special Collections.

Ball, Teddy, by an unidentified Berea College student, Pike Co., Ky., 1975, in author's possession.

Banks, Phillip, by Garner Hargis, Mt. Vernon, Ky., 1975, in author's possession.

Barker, Herbert, by the author, Point Pleasant, W.Va., 6/21/86.

Berea College students, by fellow student Bill Richards on behalf of the author, Berea, Ky., ca. 1975.

Blackburn, Johnny, by an unidentified Berea College student, Pike Co., Ky., 1975, in author's possession.

Blair, Vance, by the author, Red Fox, Ky., 8/2/89.

Bowdle, Donald, by the author, Cleveland, Tenn., 8/15/86.

Casteel, Steve, by the author, Berea, Ky., 7/31/81.

Carrier, Alfred, by Garner Hargis, McKinney, Ky., 1975, in author's possession.

Combs, Lizzie, by Herb E. Smith, Letcher Co., Ky., summer 1972, in Appalachian Film Workshop Archives. Used by permission of Appalshop, Inc.

Combs, Susanna Jacobs, by Joyce Ann Hancock, 1980, Appalachian Museum Collection, AM-M-80-117B, in Berea College Special Collections. Used by permission of Archives and Special Collections, Berea College, Berea, Ky.

Comer, Jesse, by Jeff Todd Titon, Stanley, Va., 1977, quoted in Jeff Todd Titon, *Power-house for God: Speech, Chant, and Song in an Appalachian Baptist Church* (Austin: University of Texas Press, 1988), 254–55.

Cook, Anna Mae, telephone, by the author, McRoberts, Ky., 8/29/95.

Cornett, Elwood, by the author, Hazard, Ky., 8/2/89; by Jeff Todd Titon and John Wallhausser, Blackey, Ky., 5/6/90, in Berea College Special Collections; by Joyce Ann Hancock, 11/29/79, Appalachian Museum Collection, AM-M-79–98, in Berea College Special Collections (used by permission of Archives and Special Collections, Berea College, Berea, Ky.).

Fugate, Frank, by Herb E. Smith, Letcher Co. Ky., 1972, in Appalachian Film Workshop Archives. Used by permission of Appalshop, Inc.

Garrett, Bonnie, by unknown interviewer, place and date unknown, in author's possession.

Hagans, Jesse, by the author, Red Fox, Ky., 8/1/89.

Isaacs, Debbie, by Joyce Ann Hancock, 4/7/79, Appalachian Museum Collection, AM-M-079-041, in Berea College Special Collections. Used by permission of Archives and Special Collections, Berea College, Berea, Ky.

Jones, Mable, by the author, Hazard, Ky., 7/12/95.

Kazee, Buell, by the author, Winchester, Ky., 7/10/74.

Lamb, Willie, by the author, McRoberts, Ky., 8/5/95; telephone, by the author, McRoberts, Ky., 8/28/95.

Little, Hinkle, by Layna Cheeseman, Taylorsville, N.C., 1975, in author's possession.

Lunsford, Fred, by the author, Vengeance Creek, N.C., 1976.

Manns, Banner, by Joey Elswick, Hueysville, Ky., 7/21/75, in Oral History Archives, Alice Lloyd College, Pippa Passes, Ky. Used by permission of Alice Lloyd College.

Martin, Ernest, by the author, Winchester, Ky., 7/1/95.

Martin, Josephine, by Gary King, Floyd Co., Ky., 1975, in author's possession.

McCay, Pansy, by Garner Hargis, Rockcastle Co., Ky., 1975, in author's possession.

Mink, Fannie (and Donna Ramsey), by the author, Kathie Kiser, and Stan Kiser, Ansted, W.Va., 7/10/76.

Miser, Coy, by Deborah Vansau McCauley, Cranks Creek, Ky., 10/16/89, quoted in Deborah Vansau McCauley, *Appalachian Mountain Religion: A History* (Urbana: University of Illinois Press, 1995), 335–36.

Moore, Roy, telephone, by the author, Lexington, Ky., 12/18/95.

Morton, Bill, telephone, by the author, Hazard, Ky., 8/10/95.

Olinger, D. Y., by the author, Hazard, Ky., 7/12/95.

Olinger, David, telephone, by the author, Berea, Ky., 8/16/95.

Olinger, Lillian, by the author, Hazard, Ky., 7/12/95.

Pray, John, telephone, by the author, Hazard, Ky., 8/11/95.

Pritt, Harold, telephone, by the author, Charleston, W.Va., 5/9/94.

Ramsey, Donna (and Fannie Mink), by the author, Kathie Kiser, and Stan Kiser, Ansted, W.Va., 7/10/76.

Reynolds, Wilse, by the author and Gary English, Stone Coal Creek, Whitley Co., Ky., 8/30/72.

Riddle, Almeda, by the author, Heber Springs, Ark., 6/14/76.

SAS. *See* Southern Appalachian Studies Collection.

Sherfey, John, by Jeff Todd Titon, Stanley, Va., 7/17/77, quoted in Jeff Todd Titon, *Powerhouse for God: Speech, Chant, and Song in an Appalachian Baptist Church* (Austin: University of Texas Press, 1988), 255–56.

Sloan, Garfield, by Gary King, Floyd Co., Ky., 1975, in author's possession.

Smith, Mike, by unidentified Berea College student, Pike Co., Ky., 1975, in author's possession.

Smith, Tom, by the author, Berea, Ky., 7/3/86.

Southern Appalachian Studies Collection, Berea College, Berea, Ky. Interviews by Earl D. C. Brewer of Emory University and associates, summer 1959. Used by permission. See text and notes (cited as SAS, with series, box, and folder number) for names of informants and, where available, interviewers.

Sparks, John, by the author, Offutt, Ky., 3/23/93.

Thomas, Kelva, by Bill Richards, Berea, Ky., 1974, in author's possession.

Thompson, Lois, by the author, McRoberts, Ky., 8/5/95.

Turner, William H., telephone, by the author, Winston-Salem, N.C., 11/2/95.

Watts, Alonzo, by the author, Carr Creek, Ky., 8/2/89.

Watts, Squire, by the author, Red Fox, Ky., 7/11/86.

Wiley, Audrey, by Gary King, Floyd Co., Ky., summer 1975, in author's possession.

Williams, Claren, by the author, Red Fox, Ky., 8/1/89.

Williams, Lovell, by the author, Red Fox, Ky., 8/1/89.

Recordings

Bates, T. G., sermon and comments recorded by Minnie Bates Yancey, Hazard, Ky., ca. 1973, in author's possession. Courtesy of Minnie Bates Yancey.

Blackburn, Johnny, sermon recorded by an unidentified Berea College student, Pike County, Ky., 1975, in author's possession.

Brasher, John Lakin, recording of interviews by J. Lawrence Brasher accompanying J. Lawrence Brasher, *The Sanctified South: John Lakin Brasher and the Holiness Movement* (Urbana: University of Illinois Press, 1994).

Bunch, Ozell, sermon broadcast on unidentified radio station, recorded by the author, 1975.

Cole, Sue Cox, sermon recorded by Stephen Burgess, Berea, Ky., 1/23/87, in author's possession.

Combs, Virgil, sermon recorded by the author, Cedar Grove Old Regular Baptist Church, Letcher Co., Ky., 10/23/93.

Cornett, Elwood, sermon recorded by the author, Cedar Grove Old Regular Baptist Church, Letcher Co., Ky., 8/23/92.

Dixon, Danny, sermon recorded by the author, Cedar Grove Old Regular Baptist Church, Letcher Co., Ky., 8/23/92.

Elam, Darrell, sermon broadcast on WSKV-FM, recorded by the author, Stanton, Ky., 7/11/93.

Gibson, Chester, sermon recorded by the author, Cedar Grove Old Regular Baptist Church, Letcher Co., Ky., 10/23/93.

Harrison, Dianne, program broadcast on WSKV-FM, recorded by the author, Stanton, Ky., 8/16/92.

Harrison, Vernon, sermon broadcast on WSKV-FM, recorded by the author, Stanton, Ky., 8/16/92.

Ison, McKinzie, testimony recorded by the author, Cedar Grove Old Regular Baptist Church, Letcher Co., Ky., 8/23/92.

Jones, Garnett, "What Manner of Person Ought You to Be?" lay sermon recorded by M. Jones, Sardis Baptist Church, Indian Trail, N.C., ca. 1980, in author's possession.

Kelly, Harold, sermon broadcast on WSKV-FM, recorded by the author, Stanton, Ky., 4/17/93.

Mahan, Henry T., "The Throne of Grace," "Lessons Learned in Trouble," "Believing in His Name," and "The Resurrection of the Dead," sermons, Thirteenth Street Baptist Church, Ashland, Ky., n.d., recordings in author's possession.

Martin, Ernest, program broadcast on WSKV-FM, recorded by the author, Stanton, Ky., 7/11/93.

McConnell, Wallace, sermon recorded by the author, Fifty-Six, Ark., 6/13/76.

Mullins, Darrell, sermon broadcast on WSKV-FM, recorded by the author, Stanton, Ky., 1993.

Mullins, Mike, sermon recorded by the author, Berea Primitive Baptist Church, Wildie, Ky., 8/17/85.

Simpson, Jeffrey, sermon recorded by the author, Parkway Church of God, Clay City, Ky., 7/26/86.

Sutton, Brett, and Pete Hartman, *Primitive Baptist Hymns of the Blue Ridge* (Chapel Hill: University of North Carolina Press, 1982), recording and liner notes.

Unidentified preacher, sermon recorded by the author while driving through eastern Kentucky, summer 1986.

Unidentified preacher, sermon recorded by an unidentified Berea College student, Coon Creek Primitive Baptist Church, Pike County, Ky., 1975, in author's possession.

Unidentified preacher and congregation, service recorded by Garner Hargis, Green River Pentecostal Church, Lincoln, Co., Ky., 1975.

Unidentified preacher, sermon broadcast on unidentified radio station, recorded by the author while driving through the Piedmont section of North Carolina, summer 1986.

Unidentified preacher, sermon broadcast on WYWY-AM, recorded by the author, Barbourville, Ky., summer 1986.

Unidentified preacher, sermon recorded by John Fetterman, Sweet Loaf Primitive Baptist Church, Louisville, Ky., ca. 1971, in author's possession.

Watts, Squire, sermon recorded by the author, Cedar Grove Old Regular Baptist Church, Letcher, Co., Ky., 10/23/93.

Williams, Evelyn, *Evelyn Williams* (video documentary by Ann Lewis), Appalachian Film Workshop, Whitesburg, Ky., 1997.

Yates, Herman B., "The Elect of God," "A Thief's Eye View," "Sin after Redemption," and "The Throne of Grace," sermons, Grace Baptist Church, Dingess, W.Va., n.d., recordings in author's possession.

BIBLIOGRAPHIC
ESSAY

How did the religion of the Upland South diverge from that of mainstream America or at least become perceived to have done so? Of the large amount written about Appalachian religion, too much has been produced by people with a bias, such as missionaries seeking converts, journalists looking for strange and peculiar ways, or scholars who viewed Appalachian religion as a response or adaptation to deprived lives. The last group has tended to see religion as a substitute for recreation, a rationalization of poverty, or an outgrowth of ignorance.

Except for Emma Bell Miles, who provided a favorable treatment of mountain religion in her book *The Spirit of the Mountains* (New York: James Potts, 1905; repr., Knoxville: University of Tennessee Press, 1975), no native had written on religion for a national audience until quite recently. John C. Campbell and his wife, Olive Dame Campbell, had sympathetic views of native religion that are evident in *The Southern Highlander and His Homeland* (New York: Russell Sage Foundation, 1921; repr., Lexington: University Press of Kentucky, 1969). Elizabeth R. Hooker also showed sympathy for mountain religion, especially in relation to the mountaineer's feelings toward outside missionaries, in her *Religion in the Highlands: Native Churches in the Southern Appalachian Area* (New York: Home Missions Council, 1933). This work is examined in detail by Deborah Vansau McCauley in her book mentioned later.

Three other earlier books discussed Appalachian religion at length. The first is *The Southern Appalachian Region: A Survey*, edited by Thomas R. Ford (Lexington: University Press of Kentucky, 1962). This book resulted from the Ford Foundation–financed Southern Appalachian Studies of 1958–60, conceived and directed by W. D. Weatherford Sr.; it includes an essay on Appalachian religion by Weatherford and Earl D. C. Brewer. Weatherford and Brewer expanded on their study in their *Life and Religion in Southern Appalachia: An Interpretation of Selected Data from the Southern Appalachian Studies* (New York: Friendship, 1962). Their conclusions about mountain religion are mostly negative and support the need for missionary work in the region. The third book is Henry Shapiro's *Appalachia on Our Mind: The Southern Mountains and Mountaineers in the American Consciousness, 1870–1920* (Chapel Hill: University of North Carolina Press, 1978). Shapiro shows how the arguments of mission-minded workers about the great needs in Appalachia helped to create the negative image of Appalachia in the minds of mainstream Americans.

One writer who has treated Appalachian and other rural people with great sensitivity and respect is Robert Coles, who worked in Appalachia for a time during the War on Poverty. Coles, a child psychiatrist, is especially good at talking with ordinary people and conveying their words in a dignified manner. One of his books is relevant here: *Children of Crisis*, vol. 2: *Migrants, Sharecroppers, Mountaineers* (Boston: Little, Brown, 1972).

Only recently have scholars begun to study Upland religious history, compare theologies, and observe worship practices in a somewhat objective way—that is, to study regional religion as religion. Richard Alan Humphrey, a former professor of religion and Methodist minister, wrote several influential articles on mountain religious groups in the 1960s and 1970s. Melanie Sovine, an anthropologist, wrote a fine master's thesis, "Sweet Hope in My Breast: Belief in the Primitive Baptist Church" (University of Georgia, 1978), and several articles. She also produced an important documentary radio show, *Been a Long Time Travelin': Three Primitive Baptist Women* (WBKY-FM, University of Kentucky Public Radio, Lexington, 1982), which was also released as an audio cassette. Her informants speak of women's roles in their church. Howard Dorgan, a professor of communications at Appalachian State University, Boone, North Carolina, has written four excellent books examining several groups of Appalachian Christians: *Giving Glory to God: Worship Practices of Six Baptist Subdenominations* (1987); *The Old Regular Baptists of Central Appalachia* (1989); *The Airwaves of Zion: Radio and Religion in Appalachia,* (1993); and *In the Hands of a Happy God: The "No-Hellers" of Central Appalachia* (1997), all published by the University of Tennessee Press, Knoxville. These books are based on Dorgan's extensive fieldwork and his serious study of Appalachian theology and religious history.

Jeff Todd Titon, an ethnomusicologist from Brown University, studied the Fellowship Independent Baptist Church, both its preacher and its congregation, in Stanley, Virginia, and produced a documentary recording, *Powerhouse for God: Sacred Speech, Chant, and Song in an Appalachian Baptist Church* (Chapel Hill: University of North Carolina Press, 1982); he then published an impressive book, *Powerhouse for God: Speech, Chant, and Song in an Appalachian Baptist Church* (Austin: University of Texas Press, 1988). He has subsequently produced a film with the same title.

Bill C. Malone, a historian, has written perceptively about country and religious music and their Appalachian connections in his definitive *Country Music, U.S.A.* (Austin: University of Texas Press, 1968; rev. ed., 1985), as well as in *Southern Music, American Music* (Lexington: University Press of Kentucky, 1979) and *Singing Cowboys and Musical Mountaineers: Southern Culture and the Roots of Country Music* (Athens: University of Georgia Press, 1993). Charles K. Wolfe has also written prodigiously about rural people and their music. Two helpful books by Wolfe are *Tennessee Strings: The Story of Country Music in Tennessee* (Knoxville: University of Tennessee Press, 1977) and *Kentucky Country: Folk and Country Music of Kentucky* (Lexington: University Press of Kentucky, 1982).

Two documentary recordings should be noted here: *Children of the Heav'nly King: Religious Expression in the Central Blue Ridge,* edited and with extensive notes by Charles K. Wolfe (Washington, D.C.: Smithsonian Institution, 1981); and *Primitive Baptist Hymns of the Blue Ridge,* recorded by Brett Sutton and Pete Hartman, with excellent liner notes by Sutton (Chapel Hill: University of North Carolina Press, 1982).

For tales of the supernatural that might shed some light on the search for meaning in life, I used several volumes that contained tales I had heard through the years: Richard Chase, *The Jack Tales* (Cambridge, Mass.: Houghton Mifflin, 1943) and *The Grandfather Tales* (Boston: Houghton Mifflin, 1948); Chares L. Perdue Jr., *Outwitting the Devil: Jack Tales from Wise County Virginia* (Santa Fe, N.M.: Ancient City, 1987); W. K. McNeil, *Ghost Stories from the American South* (Little Rock, Ark.: August House, 1985); and William Lynwood Montell, *Ghosts along the Cumberland: Deathlore in the Kentucky Foothills* (Knoxville: University of Tennessee Press, 1975).

Wayne J. Flynt, a history professor at Auburn University, is one of the few people writing about the poor whites of the South. I benefited greatly from his *Dixie's Forgotten People* (Bloomington: Indiana University Press, 1980) and *Poor but Proud: Alabama's Poor Whites* (Tuscaloosa: University of Alabama Press, 1989).

Deborah Vansau McCauley, a religious history scholar, after producing a comprehensive bibliography on Appalachian religious life, won the Bancroft Prize at Columbia University for her doctoral dissertation. This work is the most comprehensive study of mountain religion to date. It was published as *Appalachian Mountain Religion: A History* (Urbana: University of Illinois Press, 1995), which presents Appalachian religion as an authentic counterpart to American mainstream religion. Anyone wishing to study the development of religion and religious groups in Appalachia will need to start with this book.

J. Lawrence Brasher's book *The Sanctified South: John Lakin Brasher and the Holiness Movement* (Urbana: University of Illinois Press, 1994), with accompanying audio tape, was helpful to me in understanding the Northern Methodists in the South and the tensions over slavery, as well as the "holiness" ideal within the Methodist church. James K. Crissman's *Death and Dying in Central Appalachia: Changing Attitudes and Practices* (Urbana: University of Illinois Press, 1994) imparts attitudes about death and studies attitudes about death and mortuary practices.

The work of Charles W. Conn was essential for study of the birth and growth of Pentecostalism in the Upland region. His *Like a Mighty Army Moves the Church of God* (Cleveland, Tenn.: Church of God Publishing, 1977) and *Cradle of Pentecost* (Cleveland, Tenn.: Pathway, 1981) tell the story of the founding of the Church of God, Cleveland, and also of the split that resulted in the Church of God of Prophecy.

Recent books on serpent handlers include Thomas Burton's *Serpent-Handling Believers* (Knoxville: University of Tennessee Press, 1993), Dennis Covington's *Salvation on Sand Mountain: Snake Handling and Redemption in Southern Appalachia* (New York: Addison-Wesley, 1995), and David L. Kimbrough's *Taking up Serpents: Serpent Handlers of Eastern Kentucky* (Chapel Hill: University of North Carolina Press, 1995). Of these three books, Burton's and Kimbrough's are the most useful. Although Covington writes well, his events seem at times contrived, and his personal agenda intrudes. Other books on Upland snake handling include Karen W. Carden and Robert W. Pelton, *Snake Handlers: God Fearers or Fanatics?* (Nashville: Thomas Nelson, 1974) and *The Persecuted Prophets: The Story of the Frenzied Serpent Handlers* (New York: A. S. Barnes, 1976). The titles of the last two show some of the problems with writings about the religious practices of these particular groups.

A book with valuable information about the variety of Appalachian religion and with interviews from many Appalachians is *Foxfire 7*, edited by Paul F. Gillespie (Garden City, N.Y.: Anchor/Doubleday, 1982). This volume, with material collected by the Foxfire students of Rabun County, Georgia, High School, has a historical overview by Baptist scholar Bill J. Leonard and covers "ministers, church members, revivals, baptisms, shape-note and gospel singing, faith healing, camp meetings, footwashing, snake handling, and other traditions of mountain religious heritage" (cover).

Beverly Bush Patterson's *Sound of the Dove: Singing in Appalachian Primitive Baptist Churches* (Urbana: University of Illinois Press, 1995), with an audio tape of the singing of these Baptists, is a fine scholarly work. In addition to providing us with excellent discourses on Primitive Baptist singing, Patterson has written a perceptive chapter on the role of women in the church. Another book on Primitive Baptists should be noted: *Pilgrims of Paradox: Calvinism and Experience among Primitive Baptists of the Blue Ridge,* edited by James L. Peacock and Ruel W. Tyson Jr. (Washington, D.C.: Smithsonian Institution Press, 1989). It discusses the history, doctrine, and polity of the Primitive Baptists.

Another useful book is *Diversities of Gifts: Field Studies in Southern Religion,* edited by Ruel W. Tyson Jr., James L, Peacock, and Daniel W. Patterson (Urbana: University of Illinois Press, 1988). Although some of the groups studied here do not live in the Uplands, others live in the Carolina Piedmont and Blue Ridge. This is a study of religious "gestures," that is, expressions, in groups of believers including Native Americans, blacks, whites, and Asians from Calvinist, Wesleyan, and Pietist theological strains.

I found much useful material in places such as the Primitive Baptist Library at Elon College, North Carolina. It has a huge collection of Baptist minute books, and the library's founder, the late Elder W. J. Berry, and his widow, Mabel Marcena Berry, have reprinted many documents of Baptist history, such as *The Black Rock Address and the Kehukee Declaration,* regarding the Baptist splits in the 1840s. I also received useful information on Pentecostalism from the Church of God, Mountain Assembly, in Jellico, Tennessee. Especially useful was Luther Gibson's *History of the Church of God Mountain Assembly.* The many minute books I collected from various Baptist groups, the Pentecostal publications, and the songbooks from many places were invaluable.

I realize that I have not mentioned all books and materials that are worthy of study, but the sources listed here will be helpful to anyone studying Upland religion, and the bibliographies included in several of them will suggest other readings.

INDEX

Loyal Jones is the author of two biographies and coeditor of four collections of Appalachian humor. He is the former director of the Berea College Appalachian Center and lives in Berea, Kentucky. His primary research interest is Appalachian culture, although he is working on a book about the comedy associated with country music.

Typeset in 11/13 Adobe Garamond
with Centaur display

Book design by Copenhaver Cumpston

Composed by Celia Shapland
for the University of Illinois Press

Manufactured by Cushing-Malloy, Inc.